GLOBAL GARDENING

Increasing the Diversity of Plants
in Your Own Garden
While Feeding a Hungry World

by Hank Bruce & Tomi Jill Folk, M. Div.

Copyright © 2001 by Hank Bruce & Tomi Jill Folk

ALL RIGHTS RESERVED
Including the Right of Reproduction
in Whole or in Part in Any Form

ISBN 0-932855-74-1

Published by Winner Enterprises
On the Web: www.winnerenterprises.com
Or send e-mail to: erv@winnerenterprises.com

Illustrations by Hank Bruce
Editorial by Erv Lampert
Photo Credits © by Tomi Jill Folk

Front cover plants (from top to bottom):
Common Daylily, Moringa Leaves, Lablab Beans,
Luffa Gourd & Bath Sponge, Andean Tubers.

Front cover globe provided by NASA.

Cover Design, Book Layout, and Typesetting by
Daniel Lampert Communications Corporation
www.daniellampert.com

Printed in the United States of America

BOOKS BY HANK BRUCE

Gardening Trivia - 1988
Yankee's Guide to Florida Gardening - 1995
Uncommon Scents:
    Growing Herbs and Spices in Florida - 1996
The Pocket Library of Florida Gardening: - 1997
    Vol. 1 Easy Plants for Your Florida Landscape
    Vol. 2 Dangerous Plants in Florida
    Vol. 3 Florida Gardening for Seniors
    Vol. 4 Growing Kids in Your Garden
Gardens for the Senses, Gardening as Therapy - 1999
Gardening Projects for Horticultural Therapy Programs - 2000
The Courage to Create: A Writer's Workbook - 2001

BOOKS BY HANK BRUCE AND TOMI JILL FOLK

The Family Caregiver's Journal:
    A Guide to Facing the Terminal Illness of a Loved One - 1998
Abundant Harvest Gardens
    Vol. 1 USDA Climate Zones 9, 10, 11 - 2000
    Vol. 2 North American Arid Regions - 2001

Dedication

This book is dedicated to the people all over the world who are daily doing the global gardening to sustain their families. This is a tribute to the African mother tending the garden, the South American farmer cultivating the hillsides, the urban gardener raising food on the rooftop, those trying to feed their families in arid lands and rainforests, on mountain sides and everywhere else in this, our global village. This book is dedicated to all the gardeners growing their crops for the survival of their families, in the hope of a better tomorrow.

Thank you,

A book is grown much like a garden. Ideas (seeds) are planted and thoughts germinate and grow. They are nourished by the bright sunshine of friendship and the encouragement of people met along the way. The technical information, the stories related, the wisdom from many peoples shared all become a part of what appears on the pages that follow.

The concept for this book came from Dr. Martin Price and Mike Sullivan at ECHO, Educational Concerns for Hunger Organization. We are most indebted to them for their encouragement and patience with us as this project began to take shape. A special thanks goes to Dr. Price for the technical editing and numerous suggestions that have made this a much more accurate and readable book.

Barry Gilmore has been a lifetime advocate for the hungry and has worked in food recovery, gleaning and distribution. His sense of vision and purpose, and his ability to organize and motivate people has been an inspiration to us. Thank you, Barry.

Thanks to Dr. Amadou Makhtar Diop of the Rodale Institute who shared his experiences and insights into the causes of hunger and poverty. Thanks also to the thousands of dedicated scientists, researchers and missionaries laboring in the villages, fields, cities, and laboratories all over the world; all have had a hand in cultivating this text as they continue the never-ending quest for a better tomorrow. The people working daily to bring humanity and the environment together as they do the hands-on work of permaculture, sustainable agriculture, urban gardening and community gardens also provided much of the background that made this possible.

The families dining on uncommon foods prepared in delightfully different ways are also a valuable part of this book. These family gardeners and small-scale farmers that tend their crops all over the globe, these people who daily cultivate the fruits and vegetables discussed in this book are an unsung global resource. They possess the wisdom of experience, tradition and custom. They also possess great gifts for future generations, if only we are wise enough to accept them.

A patient publisher can be a writer's best friend. Erv Lampert of Winner Enterprises has been exceedingly understanding as this work began to blossom into a real book. Thank you Erv. A special thanks is also due to Jeanne Ballard, who did a critical reading of the manuscript and made valuable corrections and suggestions that have made this a better book.

GLOBAL GARDENING
Table of Contents

Preface 9

Introduction 13

Chapter 1: People and Plants 16
    Mythos of Garden in the Industrialized World 18
    Peace Begins with a Full Stomach 22

Chapter 2: Different Gardens in Different Places, in Different Times 23
    The Hunter-Gatherer as a Role Model 23
    Why Farm? 24
    The Weed Theory 25
    Was the Farm a Mistake? 25
    Who was Domesticated? 26
    Where the Wild Things Are 28
    A Jug of Wine, a Loaf of Bread and Civilization 29

Chapter 3: All Peoples, All Places 32
    Plants as Shelter, a Source of Comfort and Safety 33
    Healing Plants 34
    Sacred Plants 35
    Sharing Beauty 36
    Botanical Time Keepers 38
    Plants and Flowers Define Who We Are as a Culture 38

Chapter 4: The Global Salad Bowl 39
    Popcye's Delight 39
    Beyond Lettuce 51
    Greens as a Second Crop, Multi-purpose Plants 51
    Some Thoughts on Grazing Your Way through the Garden 54
    Oriental Greens for the Global Garden 55
    The Tropical Salad Bowl 65
    Uncommon Leaf and Flower Crops for Temperate Regions 70

Chapter 5: The Treetop Garden 83

Chapter 6: The Underground Garden 103
    More than Beans 103
    Those Remarkable Andean Roots 112
    A Global List of Root & Tuber Crops 123
    Yams and Sweet Potatoes 139

Chapter 7: Beans, Beans & More Beans 143
    More than Beans, Peas and Pulses 143
    Variety on the Global Dinner Table 144

Chapter 8: Melons and More, Vegetable Fruits 153
    The Tomatoes & Their Kin 153
    Dining on Gourds, Melons & other Cucumber Kin 165
    Weeds and Wild Things 185

Chapter 9: Wetlands & Coastal Gardens 192
    Bogs, Puddles & Ponds 192
    Sea Coasts and Salt Marshes 208

Chapter 10: Hunger is the Symptom; Poverty is the Disease 220
    Part I: Poverty of the Land 220
        Water Shortages 221
        Too Much Water 223
        Soil Fertility 225
        Soil Type and Climate 229
        Weeds 231
        Pests 234
        Environmental Degradation 236

    Part II: Poverty of the People 237
        Nutrition is a Part of the Poverty Cycle 237
        Conflicts, Civil Wars, and Religious Wars Cause Poverty 240
        Misguided Governments Can Cause Poverty 241
        Gender, the Garden and the Gardener 242
        Colonial Legacy Continues the Poverty Cycle 244
        Growing the Wrong Crops; Using the Wrong Foods 245

Chapter 11: Solutions to Hunger 247
    Hunger is a Global Problem, but the Solutions are Local 247
    Urban Gardening 248
    Positive versus Depletive Practices 248
    Biodiversity in the Garden 249
    At Peace with the Land 250
    Perennial Crops 251
    Preserving Our Human Diversity by Experiencing
        Diversity in the Garden 252
    Experimental Backyard Gardens 252

Chapter 12: Everyday Solutions that Involve Real People 254
    The Abundant Harvest Garden 254
    ECHO's Global Village 256
    Gleaning, Food Recovery and Surplus 256

Addendum 259
    What We Can Do as Individuals and Families
        to Solve the Hunger Problem 259
    Organizations Working on Global Hunger and Food Security 262
    Research Agencies 263
    Seed & Plant Sources for Exotic Vegetables & Fruits 264
    The Global Garden of Tomorrow 266
    Epilogue 269

Color Section 273

Index 285

Preface to Global Gardening

The objectives of this book are:

1. To create an awareness in the mind of the gardening public that there is a world of potential beyond tomatoes and green beans, zucchini and cabbages. As gardeners we can experience some exciting plants, foods, fragrances and herbs. The world is one big, wonderful, varied and fascinating garden; and we are all tillers in this, 'the global garden.'

2. To help bring an understanding to the global public of the problems involved in feeding a hungry world. We will note what some of the hunger relief organizations are doing, what more can be done, and how we can all be a part of the solution to the problems of hunger, malnutrition and starvation.

3. To introduce the gardeners of the industrialized world to some of the unique, unusual and exotic plants that have been used by peoples from all parts of the globe. In so doing, we may be able to prevent the extinction of some species, learn more about others and expand our knowledge while enjoying the thrill of growing something new. We can literally preserve and increase the biodiversity of the backyard garden. At the same time we gain an understanding of the wonderfully diverse peoples of this our planetary home, and combine our efforts to solve our problems together.

4. To explore the people-plant connection by respecting the traditions, legends, stories and cultures of diverse peoples. There is much to learn, and little time before many of these traditions are lost, great wisdom is forgotten and cultures become extinct. For almost every question there are many right answers.

5. To discover together new, different and sometimes ancient agricultural techniques and gardening practices. We will glimpse a future abundant with hopefulness as technology and humanity work together. Hopefully this text will lead us toward a partnership with nature, and a willingness to cooperate among ourselves.

In this book we become explorers discovering uncommon plants that have been used as food sources in the past; continue to be used today and have potential for tomorrow. We discuss vegetables with exotic names and unusual flavors; plants used in ways that may not be a part of your dining tradition. We ask you to open your mind to the diversity, and your garden to the variety. Hopefully you will be curious enough to seek further, dig deeper, learn more about the plants and the people who grow, harvest, and use them.

As you progress through this book you will find summaries of various vegetables, fruits and otherwise edible plants. With each plant we have tried to provide some basic information to help you identify and do further research on it. This includes the common names, their scientific nomenclature, plant family, and sometimes the name in the language of the people where it is commonly grown. You will also find notes as to mature size, geographic region of origin and sometimes cold hardiness. There are several lines of evaluation to help you in determining its suitability for your garden or for consideration in hunger relief projects. These ratings are for this vegetable's use in the family garden where space and resources are limited, not commercial fields and agro-industry. This evaluation looks something like this:

Value as a food source	9
Value as an ornamental	2
Multi-purpose	no
Continuous harvest	no
Ease of culture	8
Overall rating	***

You may well disagree with these ratings and evaluations, but this is how the author defined the categories.

Value as a food source
The numerical ratings are based on a scale of 1 to 10, with 10 being about as efficient and nutritious a resource as you can grow in your garden. This rating takes into consideration the productivity, nutrition, usefulness, storability and ease of preparation. As an example a potato is rated at 9, even though it may not be the most efficient yield per square foot of garden space, or provide for the table in the shortest period of time from planting to harvest. It does provide an easily stored, easily used widely accepted tuber.

Value as an ornamental
Again, the rating is based on a scale of 1 to 10, ten being a plant with significant landscape potential. Our potato isn't one of the most attractive plants at any stage of its cultivation. Thus it only rated a 2. The concept of beauty is different from one

culture to another, but floral charm, distinctive fragrance, beautiful foliage, and overall attractiveness are universal considerations in this botanical beauty pageant. There is no rule that says that a vegetable plant, or as one field researcher calls them, "working plants," can't be a functional thing of beauty. Cultivating beauty is one of the things that helps to define our humanity. When we surround our existence with beauty, we ourselves become beautiful.

Multi-purpose
We are accustomed to growing plants such as potatoes, tomatoes and lettuce for a single purpose, such as the tuber, the fruit or the salad leaf. However, where productivity in a limited space is essential, the gardener can seek out plants with multiple uses. Examples would include the beet that gives us delicious leaves while the root is forming, or the nasturtium with edible leaves, flowers and seeds. Sometimes the secondary use isn't as a food resource, as with the coconut or the glasswort.

Continuous harvest
We are accustomed to planting in the spring and harvesting in the autumn, but for cultures where there isn't an Albertson's or Kroger supermarket at the corner shopping center, or a freezer in the basement, fresh produce needs to be harvested as needed. Many of our leaf crops such as leaf lettuce and kale afford this possibility. Others like green beans and snow peas provide edible leaves while we wait for the seed pods to mature. There are even trees and shrubs that produce edible foliage on a continuous basis.

Ease of culture
This is again based on a scale from 1 to 10. As any gardener knows, some plants are easier to grow than others. Some are demanding as to soil type, moisture requirements or attack from insects or disease. Some vegetables don't like the cold while others can't tolerate heat. Not only are there these basic environmental requirements, there are other demands such as the need for a trellis or other support, pruning, training, hoeing, feeding and the efficiency of harvesting that are considered in this rating. Sometimes the energy expended and risks taken aren't sufficiently rewarded.

Overall rating
We have awarded each vegetable a rating from * to ***** stars. This is based on all of the considerations above plus versatility as table fare, taste, productivity, environmental impact, efficiency in intensive gardening and adaptability to a wide range of conditions. A * vegetable may be the best vegetable you can grow in one locale but it might not be possible to grow it efficiently anywhere else. A **** vegetable provides ease of culture, high yield and will grow over a wide area.

These ratings are, we must admit, rather arbitrary. Your experience with them might not agree with ours, but that's ok. There is plenty of room for differing opinions and a variety of taste preferences in the global garden. Your comments, experiences and results are welcome.

Please be aware!

It must be noted that many of the plants discussed in this book, in fact many of the more universally familiar garden vegetables do contain toxins, or are otherwise not good for you unless properly prepared. As an example the group of adventurous entrepreneurs who founded the Virginia Bay Colony in 1607 experimented with a salad of local greens, a salad containing tomato leaves. They became critically ill, debilitated by abdominal pain and hallucinations. Some beans contain saponins that are eliminated with cooking. Some greens such as taro contain oxylates that are rendered safe only after proper cooking. Many of the plants we commonly grow, and some mentioned here are safe in small quantities but can create distress when consumed in greater amounts. There are vegetables that cause allergenic reactions in some. Many people are allergic to peanuts, yet it's considered a healthy food. Take care and use caution when dining on unfamiliar vegetables, or vegetables prepared in ways in which you aren't accustomed.

There is no way we can, in this small text, explore and discover more than a handful of the vast array of edible plants that surround all the peoples of this planet. As the premier naturalist, Edward O. Wilson states in his book, *The Diversity of Life*, "Very few of the species with potential economic importance actually reach world markets . . ." He also stresses the fact that the indigenous edible diversity often defines the cultural diversity of the people. We are in this philosophical respect what we eat, and how we eat it. When we decrease the biodiversity of an ecosystem, we also decrease our cultural dimensions and diminish the wondrous garden of human diversity. We do hope to germinate some interest in your mind and perhaps cultivate the compassion that grows within the collective heart of our humanity. Perhaps someone who reads these stories of uncommon and exotic plants will be inspired to join in the effort to replace hunger with health, or work to insure the continued diversity of our global garden.

THE GLOBAL GARDEN

Introduction

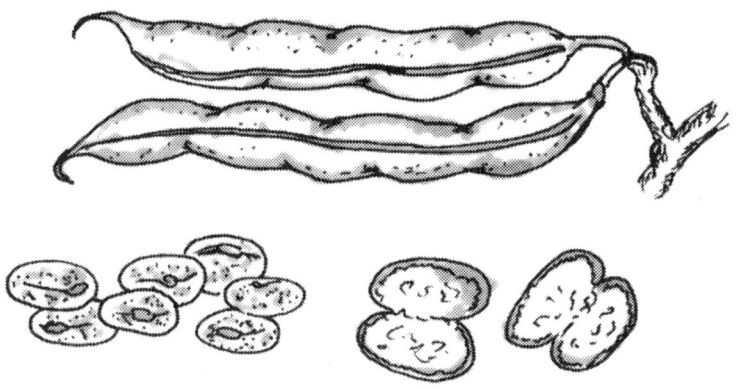

"Popping beans," he said as he handed us a small handful of what looked like ordinary dried beans. "In Peru they would heat these over an open fire until they burst, much like popcorn."

We didn't have an open fire, but we did have the electric range in our kitchen. The noble experiment began in a chef's skillet with the burner turned on high. In a few brief minutes the first of the beans made a sound somewhere between a hiss and a snap as it split open. The inside was tan colored but not puffy like we had expected. Soon all but one or two of the beans had popped. We expected something like the taste of popcorn, but it was more like a cross between peanuts and cashews. What a delight was this secret from the Andes, a food tradition that the industrialized world, with its ever dwindling list of marketable fruits, vegetables and grains, doesn't even know exists. There is so much more than the limited fare that we find on the supermarket shelves. There is a diversity in the global harvest as wonderful as the diversity of the people fed. Life is sustained all over this globe by thousands of species of plants.

We look down on the hunter-gatherers of our ancestral past. We bemoan their ignorance and give misplaced sympathy to a people whose existence was so miserable that they had to subsist on roots and tubers. We do this as we dine on potatoes, carrots and onions. In truth the wisdom and technology of the hunter-gatherer was, and still is for the few such societies still in existence, both broad and deep. The wisdom to understand the growth habits of the plant material, when to harvest, what was safe and not safe to consume, was theirs. Precious few of us could survive without the supermarket in our virtual cyber-world of technology with its avalanches of information. These so called "primitive people" possessed the appropriate technology to prepare, process and preserve foods that contained toxins. They understood how to discourage insects, how to treat illnesses, and they knew how to throw a party as they celebrated with feasts and festivals.

We, the human animal, possess an instinctive link with the soil. Within our genes is the need to be a part of the people-plant connection. Our survival is based on this. But the survival goes far beyond the dinner table or the salad bar. Our ancestors used plants for safety and security. Our homes today are little more than reconstituted trees. The music of the flute and the drum, healing medicines and intoxicating drinks, the colors and fragrances of flowers were all a part of our earliest ancestor's existence. The need to sustain the soul with beauty for the eyes and ears is nothing new. In fact it is older than time. It is through beauty that we seek our connection with the earth itself, and the Great Mystery we call God by so many different names. We wear the fibers of plants, and weave our artificial hides into things of beauty. Many of the dyes that give our garments their colors came from plants and were prepared in complex and intricate ways. Even the inviting warmth of the fire would be impossible without the fuel sources from the plant world.

This connection, this people-plant connection, was the great wisdom of our ancestors, but for those of us living in little boxes, laboring in a synthetic world of office cubicles, fearing the sight of dirt, the approach of any insect, or water that wasn't bottled in some glamourous distant country, life itself is also artificial.

The garden in the later part of the twentieth century was an interesting reflection of the way we lived. Our lives were chemically dependant, so we made our gardens and farms dependant also. In this drive to produce the perfect tomato, kill every insect, and increase production we literally poisoned ourselves, our atmosphere, our soil and our water. We grew fewer and fewer varieties of fruits, vegetables and grains, selecting only those that answered our demand for perfection and increased yield. We sacrificed diversity for efficiency, but in the diversity of food sources is the security of our own survival.

In many areas of the world, as we enter a new millennium, deserts are spreading. What was once green and productive is being destroyed by our greed and inability, or unwillingness, to engage in partnership with the land. When we farm so intensely that the soil is depleted of its nutrients, even the weeds cannot grow to hold it in place while it heals. When we use the water faster than it can be replaced in the water table, wildlife and native plants die along with our communities. When we refuse to accept the economic value of natural biomass, and instead harvest the logs to create pasture land, we alter weather patterns and change climates globally. When we destroy the protective mantle of life to expose the minerals and ores beneath, we all too often create wounds that cannot heal.

We can only halt the relentless advance of manmade deserts by working together. This isn't solely the fault of misguided industry, or greedy investors. The guilt lies with all of us who demand greater consumption, refuse to explore consequences and have no regard for our fellow residents of this, our global community. The solution lies within our grasp, but it means we must openly grasp the hand of our neighbor, and work together.

In the global community of today we must accept the simple fact that we are all neighbors, that we must learn to get beyond yesterday's differences and work together to solve today's problems. We must do this for the survival of our children and grandchildren, and their generations to come. We must do this for the survival of the planet. Let's all begin a dialogue of understanding, and let's begin it in the garden.

Chapter One
People and Plants

"When in the garden we are all one with the earth"
Anon

Humanity seeks its origins in the garden, and it is there that we can discover the essence of self. The garden is more than the source of the family's food, or the supply source for a barter economy. It is the instinctive answer to our need for a peaceful and cooperative society as a people, rather than as scattered and disconnected individuals. The garden is a source of beauty, the way most of humanity sustains life, and the way we find a sense of place and belonging. In the garden we become a part of the community we call an ecosystem. We can delude ourselves into thinking that we can control, and perhaps we can to a degree and for a short time. But in reality we are a part of a system that is ever changing, yet constant. We can, in the garden, assume our proper place in the overall scheme of things, in the grand community of life.

We don't have to limit our gardening activity to a dibble stick and hoe. There is no need to forego the gifts of progress and change to find our place in this community of life. What we do have to do is think beyond the quest for perfection, the drive for total control, and open our minds to the possibility that we are only one small part of the system. The garden is a democratic institution where the plants, weeds, bugs and people all play a part, all make a contribution, all get to vote. In the garden there is room for every member of the family, and sufficient work and inspiration to go around. It may well be that human survival in difficult neighborhoods of this global community depends on the family garden, a small plot tended by the entire family as they cultivate a variety of vegetables, fruits and herbs. The larger agro-business enterprises may well be necessary for the economic survival of a region, but the day-to-day meal on the table will depend on the women and children tending their garden plots.

There was an well-intentioned charitable organization that collected donations for tractors and sent them to certain "undeveloped" areas. They took great pride in what they were doing to help eliminate starvation. The only problem was that the villages that received these machines had no money for fuel, no place to get repair parts. Either the village became even poorer buying fuel or the tractors became piles of rust. This is one of the problems faced by some well meaning programs: the technology didn't fit. There were many other areas where the tractor was a key addition to the agriculture program and made a real difference. The technology must be appropriate for the area.

The industrialized countries have to get beyond the colonial concept of cultural superiority before the assistance can be true, genuine and useful. It is too easy for us to think that any technology, any culture that doesn't look, think or act like ours is primitive, backward, or inferior. It was the ethno-centrism of the colonial powers that upset indigenous agriculture.

It's the reluctance to try unfamiliar foods that makes some aid programs less effective than they could be. Yet the African palate embraces the chile pepper, corn and peanuts are popular in Asia, North Americans enjoy bananas and watermelons and okra, Europeans dine on potatoes and tomatoes. None of these foods originated in these areas that now consider them a staple. The culture of a people is always changing, always growing. The music, art, medicine, religion, tastes and traditions must grow, adapt, discover or become stagnant. It makes no difference whether that society hunts with a bow and arrows, a shopping cart or a computer mouse, it is the thrill of new discovery that makes us all vital and viable.

We are faced with a dichotomy here. We try to expose these "primitive" cultures to our "superior" way of life and despair at their reluctance to act like us. Then, if they do develop a taste for Coca Cola and wear Mickey Mouse tee shirts, we mourn the loss of these quaint indigenous populations, as if they should be kept in their pure ethnic state, like zoo animals, for our future enjoyment and study. This is our ethno-centrism at work again. In our zeal to replace traditional wisdom with today's technical knowledge we may well lose invaluable insights, irreplaceable arts, beautiful music, and drive to extinction valuable ecosystems. Is it so difficult to accept the obvious fact that we are all a part of the same community? Can we replace "me" and "them" with "US" as we enter a new millennium? Can we respect all people, and glory in the diversity, or must we continue to be divided by petty differences? This is the challenge we all face. For our survival we must learn to work and play together, sing each other's songs, and share the harvest with our global neighbors.

Humans have been called cruel, violent, aggressive, the most territorial of beasts, the most dangerous of animals. Yet in most cultures we find a majority ready and willing to work for the common good, express compassion, feed and care for each other. Everywhere in the world there are Mother Theresa's, Jimmy Carter's, Mahatma Ghandi's and Nelson Mandella's, all visionaries with courage, true heroes and heroines who serve as beacons lighting the way for all humanity. In the midst of all the seeming troubles and turmoil, millions are daily doing likewise. For every violent act committed in this global community, there are hundreds of acts of kindness. They are so commonplace that we don't even notice them.

We have the means at our disposal to totally eliminate hunger, but first we must stop using starvation as a military and economic weapon. As Dr Martin Price, director of ECHO, points out, "Remember, eliminating hunger has little to do with growing food. It's a matter of income. Food flows toward income." Poverty is the primary cause of hunger. We also need to view agriculture as more than an economic enterprise. In this dance with time that we call progress, we can all be a part of the solution, and that solution can start in our backyard gardens and our apartment windowsills. The garden is a safe place to experiment with the art of being human.

Mythos of Garden in the Industrialized World

In today's world of high tech agriculture the home gardeners both reap the benefits and share the sins of the adversarial posture. We plant fewer and fewer varieties of our favorite fruits, vegetables, grains and even flowers. We use genetic engineering, evolution with a profit motive, to answer market demands and produce crops that are better able to resist insects and disease. Some see great potential as an effort to play God and control the evolutionary process, while others fear the dangers that might be unleashed. Time will most likely show us that it is neither perfect solution nor total curse. The true threat is that, in the dash to cultivate the sure thing, the commercial food producers are going to lose the diversity of species that is the guarantee of survival.

The journey from rapeseed to canola

The engineering of canola oil is an example of how and why we engage in the evolutionary process and make attempts to speed up or change the direction of this most natural of changes. Selective breeding is essentially genetic engineering at a slower pace.

Rapeseed is a name applied to a number of varieties of plants which are members of the cabbage, *Brassica*, family. The seeds have been a traditional source of cooking fuel and lamp oil in India and the Orient. During World War II, when petroleum supplies were limited, it was grown and processed for use as a lubricating oil in machinery, engines, navy ships and manufacturing. It wasn't used as an edible oil because high concentrations of glucosinates and erucic acid gave it a disagreeable taste and difficult digestibility.

After the end of the war rapeseed farmers were growing a crop with a limited demand. Because of the high concentrations of sulphur compounds that acted as growth inhibitors, the crop was unsuitable as a livestock feed. The glucosinates, that's what makes mustard hot, gave it a less than agreeable taste, limiting the market as an edible oil source.

Combining selective breeding and genetic engineering using two Polish varieties of rapeseed that had tolerably low levels of these substances eventually, through planned and programmed evolution, produced a new type rapeseed. The oil produced was low in the negative compounds, making it safe for animal and human consumption. Since there was a negative connotation to the old rapeseed, in 1986 a new name was trademarked for the improved varieties that had less than 2% erucic acid and minimal amounts of glucosides. There are now over 100 varieties of this new breed of plant called Canola, and the oil is a healthy and popular part of our diet. The future for the canola farmer may become even brighter as development continues on varieties with greater suitability for drought, pest and disease resistance, use as synthetic diesel fuel and much more.

There are moral questions about genetic engineering; the ways this will affect the natural landscape are unknown, and the impact on small growers in diverse agricultural communities is also open to debate. The fact is that the future is here and it is incumbent upon us to carefully chart a course that is both environmentally friendly and humane.

Nature's garden, the fields and forests, waterways and deserts, form complex and diverse communities we call ecosystems. In these communities each species is uniquely dependent on its neighbors, and, for its own survival, cooperates to make the system work. Nature everywhere forms symbiotic alliances. The ants defend their bullhorn acacia against predators. The earthworm turns the fallen leaves into soil for the tree so that it might produce more leaves. The hemlock shades the carpet of wildflowers, ferns and mosses that keep its roots cool and moist. The insect feeds on the nectar as it carries the pollen for a new generation of plants. The grazing deer provides fertilizer for more grass. The web of life is beautifully woven and astoundingly intricate. On this colorful, living fabric appear the flowers and the fungi, the wings of butterflies and mosquitoes, the faces of pandas and people. We cannot separate ourselves from natural forces, after all nature is life itself. We may seek to control, influence, alter or redesign; but ultimately we must bow to these forces of nature and work with them.

The human community is also an ecosystem where each individual depends on his and her neighbors. We each become stronger, wiser, and happier when we cooperate rather than seek to dominate, insist on our superiority, and fear our ignorance. When we open our hearts and minds to the glorious diversity within the human community we all gain, we all survive. It is much easier, and less costly, to feed our neighbors than it is to fight them. This can begin with each of us who has a garden in the backyard, or on our patio or balcony. It can begin with a bag of surplus produce shared with a neighbor or the local food pantry or homeless shelter. It can begin with a bouquet of flowers cut from our landscape and delivered with a smile to someone elderly and alone in a nursing home. It can begin when we ask a neighbor how she grows such beautiful roses. It all begins when we share our bounty, our wisdom, our traditions and our curiosity with each other.

Our hunter-gatherer ancestors dined on over 15,000 species of plants. Today we rely on only a couple hundred commercial crops to sustain our life and life style. The earliest crop insurance was diversity. Crop failure, blight or weather patterns always left botanical survivors. Often these weren't the most delicious, easiest to harvest or most efficient to process; but they did sustain life. These were called *famine foods*, and even today in some parts of the tropics, Arctic tundra, Australian outback and Asian mountains villagers struggle to survive where some of these famine foods also cling to a tenuous existence. Unfortunately, this natural insurance policy is also being lost as we clear forest to make it field, declare every plant that isn't economically efficient a weed, and create virtual ecosystems.

It can be argued that what is actually happening as we expand global trade is that we are simply in the process of evolving a new global environment, or at least, a series of new macro-ecosystems where we expand our sphere of cooperation and increase the interdependency. Regardless of how we interpret what is happening, the simple fact is that we cannot go back, we cannot retreat from our destiny, we cannot escape tomorrow. What we can do is boldly face it with wisdom, respect and hope; not ignorance, fear and greed.

In the last century hunger was used as a military weapon, and the news media graced our dinner hour with scenes of starving children, crippled victims of land mines, and women struggling to grow their family's survival. This is nothing new. Siege warfare has been popular throughout human history, and the objective of siege is to drive the enemy into submission and surrender through starvation and disease. Warfare is no longer economically advantageous. The great ideological debates of the cold war era have been reduced to political brushfires, but the passion for war still exists in the misguided attempts to defend God, and the mythical purity of race or ethnic tradition. We continue in the tradition of Jonathan Swift. If only we could assume the role of Gulliver and visit our own backyard.

In the latter half of the twentieth century we declared war on Mother Nature as we sought to dominate and become lords of nature ourselves. Our focus was on chemical control. We produced picture perfect lawns, but nature was so controlled with pesticides that it wasn't safe for our children to walk across them. It was so easy to create chemicals that killed every bug, weed or rodent daring to invade our space. Many of these chemical killers soon proved to be a threat to the "cute" wildlife and us, and once applied some of them refused to go away. Sometimes what we did was actually breed a super bug, able to survive both our chemicals and natural controls. Ecosystems have been permanently altered by this lust to kill. But this is nothing new. When the Romans defeated Carthage in the Punic Wars 460 BC they spread salt over the fields to make them useless for life sustaining crops. Still today we use hunger as a military weapon. But, even in the cooperative network we call an ecosystem, plants and animals use chemicals to define their space and preserve their existence. The walnut tree releases a natural chemical into the soil that kills germinating seeds, thus preserving its space. The marigold produces a chemical that discourages certain nematodes. Many plants manufacture chemicals that discourage or poison insects or grazing animals. The Neem tree produces natural pest controls and has the potential to improve crop yield in developing countries.

Not only did we kill those plants we declared the enemy, we fed those we chose to embrace, and we fed with super-nutrients beyond all reason and understanding. These plant foods followed the rains into our waterways, lakes and the coasts of our seas and oceans. This affected aquatic ecosystems as drastically as the pesticides. It's easy to blame the commercial agricultural community, but those among us who lusted after the perfect lawn, biggest roses and fruit without blemish bear much of the responsibility.

We also use chemicals to control height, blooming season, encourage or delay germination, influence fruit color, prolong shelf life, and make our food look more attractive. There is nothing inherently wrong with this quest for beauty. We are all artists, we all appreciate and respect the form and color of well shaped fruit and flowers and the richness of healthy foliage. But, nature doesn't deal in perfection, she deals in survival. That celebration of life in the diverse and ever changing natural community is what makes the national parks so attractive. It is also what we instinctively seek to emulate in our gardening experience. We strive to reprise the flow of the seasons in this symphony of life.

For many of us in the industrialized, post agricultural world the cultivation and harvesting of food is little more than game playing, a senso-round virtual reality. Yet it can be through some of this 'playing with nature,' this experimenting with possibilities, that we can be a part of something bigger and grander by far. When we dabble in hydroponics, grow plants in different combinations, seek and cultivate unusual or rare species, try different fruits, preserve heirloom varieties, share by doing together, we can all be adding to the storehouse of knowledge.

Peace begins with a full stomach

"The day that hunger is eradicated from the earth, there will be the greatest spiritual explosion the world has ever known. Humanity cannot imagine the joy that will burst into the world on the day of that great revolution."
Feredico Garcia Lorca, Spanish poet, 1899-1936

During the half century after the second world war, most of this planet's conflicts were ideological. But with the end of the cold war there was less effort to control political thought. Today's wars are mostly internal conflicts finding their origin in religious intolerance or traditional ethnic animosities, often due to artificial colonial boundaries. The victims aren't military but civilians least able to withstand the horrors of war, the children and the elderly. While men are slaughtered, women are forced into the role of farmer, food producer, sole provider for the family. Hunger and starvation are again weapons of destruction.

The industrialized nations, in a generous humanitarian effort, rush tons of food into critical areas, but we are reluctant to fund programs that would promote peaceful food production and cooperative efforts. What if we all planted our gardens to celebrate the diversity of life on our planet, to increase our understanding of each other, and celebrate the possibilities for peace? What if all the gardeners in the world planted the seeds of peace in their own back yard? What a beautiful world we could together grow.

Chapter Two
Different Gardens in Different Places, in Different Times

*"The first step in the evolution of ethics
is a sense of solidarity with other human beings"*
Albert Schweitzer

The Hunter-Gatherer as a Role Model

We don't really know much about how agriculture began, or where. The anthropologists studying our origins tell us that Africa was the cradle of humanity. This means that we are all Africans, this makes us all kin. We are all one big chaotic family that has spread through river valleys, across deserts, over mountains in the never ending quest for tomorrow. We are more than a global village; we are a global family.

As Boudelaire wrote, "We are all vagabonds . . ." Perhaps this is one of the instincts inherited from our hunter-gatherer days. When humanity was young, we followed the seasons, and the crops. We wandered, free from the possession of land, free to roam and enjoy, free to discover. Could it be that we make heroes of our explorers, not so much because they claim and conquer, but because they wander freely. Our ancestral hunter-gatherer cultures wandered and thought, and created the art of the story.

Anthropologists tell us that the hunter-gatherers probably spent two to three hours laboring each day to satisfy their wants and needs. Their diet was varied and in many ways healthier than ours is today. It must not have been a difficult life for cultures that didn't gauge their success at living on the accumulation of possessions. Their groups were, for the most part, egalitarian, with equality for the sexes and cooperation among all. These small nomadic groups were in many ways a voting democracy with far more leisure time than we have today. They gathered culinary and medicinal herbs, studied the stars in the sky, not on the movie screen; they all danced and made music.

Theirs was an idyllic life long camp out where survival was achieved without cell phones, designer clothing or used car commercials. Or was it? If they were having this much fun, why did they give up the vagabond existence to be tied to fields of wheat, corn and rice? The agricultural revolution occurred around the globe almost simultaneously between 10,000 and 6,000 years ago. It began with the retreat of the last ice age. Some argue that it was a response to the decline in the herds of really big mammals like the wooly mammoth, elk, European red deer, aurochs and others. But, since it is much easier to catch a wild turnip than a cave bear that doesn't want to be the guest of honor at the dinner table, we have to question that theory.

Certain Amerinds continued to rely on the American bison as a shopping mall on the hoof; Nomads in the Arctic circle followed their herds of reindeer. They were a comfortable part of this eco-system until the herds were decimated by professional killers with an agenda that included genocide. Still, the Indian was the cowboy in a most profound sense of being a part of the herd itself.

The great tradition of the cowboy has become the stuff of heroic myth and legend in the American West, Canada, South America, the African plains and Australia. This is little more than the pastoral life style the archaeologists talk about, and it is relatively common, even today. But for most of humanity, there is more than meat on the dinner table.

We still have hunter-gatherer societies with us today, but the only ones that have survived have been pushed to the least productive places on earth. The Bushmen of the Kalahari, and a few in the Australian outback, or in the dense jungles of Africa, South America and the Pacific rim, even the tribal peoples of the Arctic circle have, for the most part, fallen victim to the mass culture of the twentieth century. For the cultures of the past we have a pale and imperfect image reflected in the mirror of time. Because bones don't as readily turn to compost as the vegetable scraps from the 10,000 year old dinner table we know what meat they ate, but little about their fruits and vegetables. However modern science is changing that. Through paleobotany studies we catch tantalizing glimpses of the plants they used and lived among. By studying ancient pollen grains, fiber remnants, the residue in discarded pots, by literally digging through the garbage dumps of our ancestors we are discovering more about their diet, their life style, shelter, clothing and art forms.

Why Farm?

Some scientists claim that humanity turned to agriculture out of necessity. Climatic change, drought, population increase, competition for food all may have been factors. For many cultures their religion and traditions tell of agriculture as a gift from the gods. Corn, chocolate, vanilla in the Americas, rice, bananas and taro in the Pacific. But in the Judao-Christian faith humanity began in the earthly paradise of a garden called Eden. In this garden there was no struggle for existence and the people were in harmony with the natural world; in fact they were very much a part of it. After a series of errors in judgement paradise was lost and agriculture became the curse, a punishment imposed on these first idyllic hunter-gatherers for committing an act of disobedience. After agriculture began we had violence and the symbolic battle of brother against brother. With the development of agriculture famine and war, disease and slavery were all possible. Perhaps Pandora's box was found in the wheat field. Why would people abandon a life style with limited labor demands, healthier diet, less disease and greater independence?

It may have been an accident. Agriculture may have simply 'happened." The hunter-gatherer knew for thousands of years all that was necessary to know to plant seeds or tubers and grow crops. There is evidence that they understood and even employed irrigation to water one area while they followed their wanderlust to the mountain or high country canyons for another season in the sun. There is even evidence that, as they harvested the roots and tubers that would become dinner, they replanted some of the smaller ones for next year's crop, and passed that way again.

The Weed Theory

I personally like the "weed" theory of the origin of agriculture. People, even those who wandered in small groups, are messy and disturb the places where they reside. They disturb the soil, create trash heaps, in general lower the value of the neighborhood. The plants that respond most vigorously to a disturbed site are what we generally refer to as weeds. These are what would have been the first to grow in such places of human habitation. Among the ruins of long abandoned Pueblo Indian sites in the American southwest are plants that must have been the invaders of the earliest disruption of the soil. In nature these plants would respond to natural events such as flood and fire, and the activities of a people are as much of a natural disturbance as the others. Many of these weeds became the herbs of culinary and medicinal value. Some yielded edible leaves, some may have been the ancestral grains. It might well be that we owe our existence today to the poor maligned weeds we so despise because they are so common, and so easy to grow. Perhaps we should pause in the reading of this little book, step outside to thank a ragweed, embrace a thistle and snack on a dandelion.

Was the Farm a Mistake?

Agriculture may have been a mistake for humanity. It may have originated out of a desire to be stationary for a while and build a better home, a bigger loom, create a more efficient pottery, and a hotter kiln. Or perhaps they simply enjoyed the view. But once we did all these things we were at the mercy of the elements, had to defend our turf, turn our plowshares into swords and our digging sticks into weapons. Because we were living, more or less permanently in one place, with ever increasing populations, disease ran rampant. Labor became specialized, status became important.

Women came to be viewed as little more than a possession that produced offspring, while men were valued only as work animals and soldiers.

As the human animal abandoned the laconic way of life to engage in self imposed slavery, the human perspective changed. Humanity became possessed by the drive to possess, ownership became a burden that we have cultivated throughout history. It was the farmer that made the multi-national corporation of today possible, made the advertising industry the driving force in our global economy. Greed replaced sharing as one group found itself competing with another. Barbarian hordes and raiding parties became the earliest form of hostile corporate takeover, and this became a perennial part of the culture of the human animal.

Who was Domesticated?

Or could it be that we under estimate the power of the little plants that we began to grow and harvest? Would corn have crossed the ocean to be grown in Africa and Asia if it had not first domesticated the nomadic tribes of Mesoamerica? Would coffee have escaped the African coast to thrive over half the globe, carefully tended by its human servants, had it not lured us with its narcotic caffeine into a global addiction? Perhaps it was the plants that domesticated us and used us to fulfill their wants and needs. Perhaps we are the ones under cultivation.

In the Americas wandering groups of paleo-Indians occupied forest and grassland, mountain and desert, coast and waterways. They thrived on a varied diet that included fruits in season, leafy vegetables, tubers, nuts, beans, but not much in the way of cereals and grains. Then they began feeding on *teosinte*, a grass that had relatively large seeds. From evidence found in caves in Mexico we know they began to eat this ancestor of today's corn almost 10,000 years ago. About 4,000 years later they had begun to plant the best seeds, developed a plant that produced more kernels on its cob and responded well to the developing symbiotic relationship between people and plant. Within a few thousand more years they had popcorn, sweet corn, field corn, literally hundreds of varieties and its cultivation spread over two continents. It was corn that made the Mayan culture possible, as well as the Aztec and Inca. The Anasazi communities of the American southwest, the ancestors of the Pueblo People of today, were able to create governments, trade and complex religions because of corn. The Iroquois and other Eastern Indian nations developed complex systems of government as they planted fields of corn, beans, squash and pumpkins.

We can grow this teosinte, *(Zea mexicana)* today and the seeds are available from Native Seeds Search, 526 N. 4th Ave., Tucson, AZ 85705. This is a valuable source for many other seeds that were of great importance to these early residents of the continent we call North America. Actually there are several varieties of teosinte and one of them is perennial. Experiments are currently underway to develop a perennial corn. Think of the environmental and agricultural implications of this. The potential benefits from perennial grains is staggering. Less fuel consumed by tilling and annual planting, new harvest seasons, less erosion, greater overall yield, and the list of possibilities could go on to fill a book.

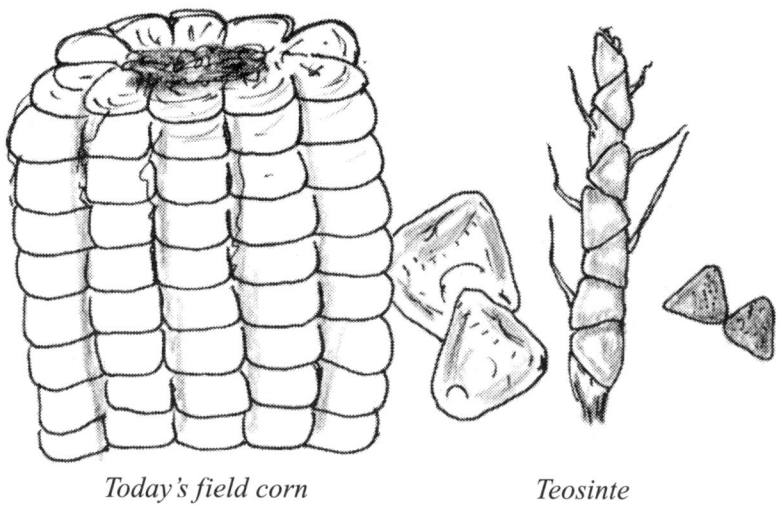

Today's field corn   *Teosinte*

But, let's return to corn as we have known it for thousands of years. Perhaps we should take a few minutes to explore some of they ways the first Americans on both continents used this valuable food resource. The pollen was pressed into cakes, used as flour, and used in a number of religious ceremonies. The scattering of a few grains of corn pollen toward the rising sun was a way to start the day in harmony with the universe and thankfulness to the Great Spirit. Corn pollen was also a part of the treatment program for a number of illnesses.

The silk from young ears of corn was used as a nutritious and tasty snack, while the very young ears continue to be considered a gourmet food. Even the tender young leaves were utilized as a raw salad green or cooked as a pot green. The taste is delightful and different. The side shoots from a stalk of corn produce an abundance of these leaves wrapped inside the older ones, just waiting for their time to grow.

But they didn't live by corn alone. They had beans, dozens of varieties of beans; squash, pumpkins, chile peppers, Jerusalem artichoke and many other crops. They continued to harvest from the land in the hunter gatherer tradition such foods as rice, cattails, jack-in-the-pulpit, wild celery, rose hips, nuts, camass root, Indian turnip, berries and so many more. They found their medicinal herbs in the wild, used the yucca for food and fiber, gathered dye plants and tobacco.

Where the Wild Things Are

Throughout much of the world today wild plants continue to be harvested for food. Often "wild" is a selling point for gourmet foods, wild rice and wild blueberries, even wild mushrooms. However, in many cultures, this "living off the land" is a matter of survival. For millions both agriculture and economics have failed to provide the good life, and, in many cases, have diminished their quality of life, even put their survival in jeopardy. Today we harvest wild forest trees for shelter, in the form of lumber, building and decorative materials. All over the tropics palms and trees are cut for a one time harvest of not only wood but palm hearts, barks and roots for herbal medicines, or even a quick and easy way to harvest the fruit. In certain regions of Africa the entire tree is cut down to harvest the caterpillars feeding on the leaves. The caterpillars are then bagged and transported to the nearest market where the one time harvest brings some desperately needed cash.

The key to improving the quality of life for the people and preserving at-risk forest ecosystems lies in enlightened use, and this can be achieved by creating a symbiotic relationship between plants and people. We cannot retreat into an idealized past that never was glamorous and harmonious, nor can we create human zoos where indigenous peoples can "do their own thing" for the amusement of tourists. The logical course is to work together, learn from each other and through cooperation permit both the indigenous and the industrial cultures to grow. We have a wealth of knowledge hidden in the rainforest, the arid lands, the mountains and plains that make up our global village. It will take respect and restraint to keep from loosing these gifts forever. This is where the hobby horticulturists and the backyard gardeners can make a contribution to the future of humanity and the global environment. By growing the rare and endangered species, by educating ourselves by doing, by sharing our experiences, and by using products made from renewable resources we can do a lot of good.

Clearing the forests to produce crop or rangeland will have disastrous consequences for the global climate, but harvesting wild fruits, nuts and herbs from the forest can help to create jobs, improve quality of life, reduce hunger and third world poverty. We can decrease the poaching of elephants and help to assure the continued existence of the Amazon rainforest by using vegetable ivory made from the seeds of several varieties of tropical palms. The best known is the beautiful "ivory-nut palm," *Phytelephas aequatorialis*, (*Phytelephas* means elephant plant) that is found from Panama to Peru. On the Islands of Micronesia another ivory-nut palm, *Metroxylon amicorum* produces large seeds that look somewhat like a pine cone. Along the Zambezi River in Africa a branching palm, *Hyphaene ventricosa*, produces a fruit with a juicy gingerbread flavored pulp and an ivory hard seed, all this on a beautiful palm. All of these ivory nuts are currently harvested in the wild and are increasingly planted as a cash crop.

We can use handbags, baskets and hats made from the foliage of tropical plants a popular fashion statement, and at the same time enable a family to thrive and be a responsible part of the environment.

There are fruits and nuts that are harvested from the wild, flavorful honeys, flavorful drinks and other edibles that are part of a sustainable natural harvest. The following is a brief list of rainforest products that are eco-friendly. Doing a search of the world wide web will give you a wealth of products and ever changing list of resources. Often these items are harvested from the wild, but in many cases they are produced as a part of an agro-forestry program that is empowering people while reclaiming a damaged environment. Either way we can all benefit.

Tropical nut mixes, dried exotic fruits, gourmet honey, vegetable butter and preserves, breakfast cereals, drinks and teas, flavored chocolates and baked goods are only a few of the rainforest products available.

We see advertised an increasing number of cosmetic and health care products that utilize rainforest materials. This may range from African beeswax to nut oils and fruit fragrances. This may be in the form of bath oils, soaps, candles, potpourri, hair care, skin creams and so much more.

There is an abundance of decorative wear and jewelry that utilizes wild harvested renewable products, such as carved seeds, ivory nut buttons and clothing, shoes and sandals. There is even a latex-cotton fabric that serves as a leather substitute for purses, tote bags, travel bags and more.

Home decor items, art work, weavings and so much more can be found in the responsible marketplace. When we purchase and use the products we are often helping to provide a family's livelihood and encourage wise stewardship of the environment, too.

A Jug of Wine, a Loaf of Bread and Civilization

This trend toward a sedentary life style occurred almost simultaneously in a number of places around the globe. Each researcher has his or her own lists and charts and maps to explain where people became farmers. The fertile crescent of today's Iraq, the Nile river valley, the Indus valley, the Yucatan peninsula, the banks of the Ganges, and several places in China all served as locations for the domestication of humanity. In most of these areas the domestication of a cereal grain is what made larger communities possible. Wheat, oats, barley, teff, millet, sorghum, rice and corn all contributed to the change in diet. Some scientists suggest that we became carbohydrate junkies, that it was this effect on the individual psyche of the first farmers that made them willing to sacrifice independence and tame their wanderlust.

This domestication occurred everywhere between 10,000 and 6,000 years ago. But these agricultural civilizations dined on far more than breakfast cereals. Almost universally, a certain portion of the grains were fermented into beers and other alcoholic beverages. It has been argued that the original fuels of the agricultural revolution were beer and wine. One of the earliest recipes we have from the Egyptians is for beer. Incidently, that beer is again being brewed and sold today. It has been noted that the technology required to produce beer was less complex than what was needed to make a loaf of bread. In "Beer or Bread: Was Beer the First Great Cereal Food?" Andrew Webber explores both the nutritional and technological aspects of the domestication of grains. He points out that the gruel, porridge or mush is where it all began. First we had porridge, then it fermented and we had the earliest beers. This fermented nourishment required neither the production of flour or an oven. Bread probably came much later.

Wine can be made from almost anything, but the industry was founded on the grape. The fermented grape followed ancient trade routes, becoming a medium of exchange before we invented money. Laborers in the early civilizations were literally paid for their work with a jug of wine. Because wine and other alcoholic beverages require time and care, it may be argued that the agricultural revolution was, in fact, based on the brewery and winery.

When we started living together in a relatively small space, we began to pollute our environment, in particular, the water. These alcoholic beverages may have been more than a foodstuff; they may have been used as a safe substitute for dirty water. Perhaps civilization as we know it is the product of all those unknown drunks from the prehistoric past who survived because they chose not to drink the water.

This use of fermented drinks is universal, known to virtually every culture in one form or another. In Mexico they had *Pulque*, made from the sap of an agave; this was later refined into tequila. The Roman army marched on *Posca*, a vinegar water, when they were out of the country and didn't trust the foreign water. Tibet had *Tsampa* made from tea, roasted barley and yak butter, while in Turkey a drink from fermented mare's milk called *Kumass* was the highpoint of an evening by the fire. The Russians enjoy *Kvass* made from a wide variety of potential ingredients ranging from rye to apples. There are web-sites with recipes for this Russian sour beer. In the Orient they enjoy *Kombucha*, basically a fermented tea. To the American colonist cider was the drink with alcoholic content, otherwise it was apple juice. Barrels of cider were set out in the winter to freeze, then the ice was removed from the top to leave a more concentrated brew.

In Eastern Africa the traditional *Pombe*, a beer made by cooking then fermenting millet or sorghum, was, and in many areas continues to be the beverage of choice. *Pito* or *Tchakpalo* is name for this same popular brew in West Africa. It's made by first sprouting part of the grain, then cooking the mash in pots, then giving the liquid a couple days to ferment. Sometimes the pombe is strained to produce a clear drink. In some locales the production of this beverage is the domain of the men, in other areas it is one of the tasks of the women. Regardless of who makes pombe it's nutritious and the strong flavor is enjoyed by all as a basic component of the diet.

A palm wine called *Tembo* is made from the sap of several palms (usually coconut or oil palm). It begins to ferment quickly and must be consumed within a few days before it goes from deliciously sweet to spoiled sour. *Mawa*, or plantain wine is a potent intoxicant made from the peeled fruit mashed, mixed with a little grain or flour and strained into a gourd. In three or four days it's ready to enjoy.

Fermentation has been a traditional way of preserving more than grapes, and, while it almost certainly began accidentally, it was soon recognized as a good idea. We are familiar with pickles, sauerkraut, tofu, and a multitude of other foods and drinks. *Miso* that is such a valuable seasoning in so many Japanese dishes is vitamin rich paste made from fermented soy beans, as are *Tofu*, *Natto* and *Tempeh*. The yogurt that is such a popular part of our diet today is a healthy acidophilus culture. These are all fermented foods that have been produced and enjoyed by peoples vastly divergent in time and space. Not only does fermentation provide a means of preservation, it also changes and enhances the nutritional value of some of these foods. All fermentation requires the action of yeast or bacteria, and in essence we have a partially digested food when they are done. A jug of wine, a fine cheese and a loaf of bread all depend on the work of organisms we can't even see. They are at work making bread rise, producing sourdough, cottage cheese, butter milk, Limburger and all the other cheeses. The MSG that we use as a flavor enhancer and soy sauce are both produced by fermentation. In Scandinavia they even fermented fish, perhaps to sell to the tourist trade.

Perhaps we owe our success as a species to that host of micro-organisms that spoiled our food and soured our milk. Or could it be argued that our survival is based on our body's ability to utilize even rotten vegetables and fermented juices? People are, after all, universal consumers; we will eat virtually everything.

Chapter Three
All People, All Places

*"The fundamental law of human beings is interdependence.
A person is a person through other persons."*
Bishop Desmond Tutu

The success of the human animal lies in our ability to diversify rather than specialize. We didn't have the greatest speed, the biggest teeth, the keenest eyes. At best we are mediocre swimmers and can't fly on our own. We don't even climb trees very well, in spite of the Tarzan stories of Edger Rice Burroughs. But we are among the most adaptable, equal to the roach, the pig and the ant in our ability to make do and change. We are capable of using most of these survival techniques moderately well, making us specialized at being the general practitioners of survival. Throughout the evolution of life on this planet it has been the adaptable species that survived while the specialists were incapable of meeting the challenge of changing environments.

We need to be careful that we don't permit the expression of our humanity to become too narrow, our degree of tolerance to become too limited, or ability to accept change too constrained.

One of the secrets of our success is that we had a varied diet. Humanity is willing and able to dine on the flesh of other mammals, fish and fowl, even mollusks and insects. But we feed on more than flesh. We harvest the vast array of fruits, vegetables roots and shoots, grains and even fungi that abound in almost every forest and meadow, coastline and waterway. We are even capable of being scavengers when necessary. In fact, it has been argued that this willingness to scavenge the kills of other animals and dine on virtually any plant or animal we chanced to encounter is what empowered our proto-human ancestors to make the break from other primates and continue the journey down the evolutionary road to where we are today.

In this text we are most concerned with the produce that can be found on the global dinner table. We all have common needs, but different people in different places have adapted the diet to what was available. The Eskimo and Tinglit in the Arctic Circle consume a far different meal than do the inhabitants of a Peruvian village high in the Andes or the herder in the deserts of Iran. All peoples in all places strive to satisfy their hunger and the appetites of their loved ones and children with whatever resources are available.

We all have a common, and instinctive, bond in the need to gather around the dinner table and share our bounty, or our sparsity. We are a communal animal, even before the fire was tamed to become a safe gathering point, we came together in the field or beside the kill to share sustenance and be social animals. It could be argued that it was the harnessing of the flame that made us different than other animals. It made our domestication possible. It was in this earliest of attempts to share thoughts, swap stories, and break bread together that we began to dominate the landscape.

In the infancy of humanity, these earliest tribal experiments, we had much to learn, and so do we still today. Those who think the human journey is at its end lack a sense of vision, or are mired in their ethnocentrism. As the first families learned to join together for their mutual benefit, and families joined together as clans and clans formed tribes and nations, so this progression will continue as we all learn, by fits and starts to become one big global community. We all share common needs, wants and desires. The beauty of humanity lies in the diversity with which we have developed the means to answer these life and living demands. Once we are able to accept and respect each other's answers and rejoice in the opportunity to learn and share we can all survive and thrive.

Plants as Shelter, a Source of Comfort and Safety

Our primate cousins and our common ancestors found most of their needs supplied in their treetop home. It was shelter against most predators, and our early progenitors continued to occupy trees as safety in the face of danger and darkness of night. Throughout the world today we find this remarkable adaptable human animal putting to good use a wide range of plant material for shelter. Throughout much of the tropics and temperate zones bamboos are the building blocks of civilization. This plant is far more than panda food. We have such a wide variety of bamboo species at our disposal that there is one to answer almost every household need, including the building material for the house itself. Gutters, water pipes, fences, furniture, kitchen utensils, food, fuel, tools and weapons are all made from bamboo. It also controls erosion and serves as a windbreak or screen.

Palms are the symbol of the tropical lifestyle. They too are a multi-purpose class of plant life. From the palms we get building material in the form of timbers and leaves for thatching, fruit, oil, fiber, rope, nets, needles, and a wealth of other household products.

In other places, other peoples have used what was at hand to build their homes. This might range from sod houses to wattle and dab architecture. In the American Southwest today there are experiments with straw bales as a building material. Perhaps the three little pigs were right after all. Plants are used as living fences all over the world, from crotons in the Caribbean to euphorbias in Africa or acacias in Australia.

Healing Plants

Throughout our history on this planet we have enjoyed the plant kingdom as a source of food, but our relationship goes much deeper. We have throughout time used the plants in the healing arts. Until the later part of the 20th century most of our medication in the now industrial cultures came from plants, not petro-chemicals and DNA laboratories. In the manual cultures plants are still the central component of medicine. We have traditionally used plant derivatives for their narcotic effect. Some of these we have declared illegal while others like fermented beverages, coffee and tobacco are sometimes restricted or taxed but generally available.

Unfortunately, the valid and valuable science of ethnobotany has been exploited by a drug culture that is willing to market and use virtually any plant rumored to be mind altering. This drive for a "natural high" isn't what the science is about. Ethnobotany is the study of how diverse peoples utilize the indigenous plant material in every phase of their culture, from shelter to dyes, food, clothing, medication, seasonings, ceremonies, and art. These hardy later day explorers are literally working ahead of the bulldozers to rescue species and preserve knowledge.

There are quests that are universal across all cultures, climates or artificial political boundaries. Every culture quests for that which will delay or reverse aging. Medicinal plants like ginseng, gingko, yahimbi, gotu kola, and so many others throughout the world are sought after, sometimes harvested to the brink of extinction in the never-ending quest for youth, or at least age with wisdom. The second universal sought from the plant world is the aphrodisiac. The list of plants said to be capable of increasing sexual desire and activity is almost endless. There are plants under study now that ancient wisdom claims can cure or control diabetes, cancer and heart disease. It may well be that tomorrow's health will continue to depend on yesterday's medicinal plants, a healthier diet and a lifestyle based on being and living in harmony rather than achieving and acquiring more than we can ever use. It may be that our pathological drive to possess, this obsession that is driven by greed isn't a part of our human instinct, but a negative trait resulting from inner insecurities. Perhaps greed is the root from which the weeds of guilt arise. Perhaps we can treat these emotional diseases of greed, guilt, chronic discontent, frustration and anger with the garden.

Perhaps the medicinal value of plants goes beyond the individual cures from isolated species, and really lies in the totality of what was once called Eden. Our social instincts drive us to create parks with trees, plants, flowers, vistas and venues in an effort to green our city living space. If we are all children of Africa, and the scenery was then as beautiful and awe inspiring as it is today, perhaps the best cure for our social ills can be found in the garden. Horticultural therapists know that being with plants is healing, soothing and a source of hope. The mentally ill have been treated in the garden since the time of the Egyptian pharaohs, a wisdom we are only rediscovering today. The healthy diet for the body is grown in the garden and the garden is also a healthy diet for the soul.

Sacred Plants

It was in this hallucinogenic and narcotic plant material that some of the medicinal and religious practices of many cultures found their origins. Could the shaman in South America have done his or her work without the drug induced trances from datura? Did drugs help some of the earliest religious leaders see visions, contact entities in other realms? It has been argued that much of our religious practice, from incense and censors to the strewing of herbs in medieval churches, was the extension of this "primitive" knowledge. Even the feast days, something almost universal to all agrarian peoples everywhere, focus on a celebration of our people-plant connection.

Around the globe people gather as families or communities daily in what many of us don't recognize as a ritual ceremony of life that is a tradition beyond written history. The sharing of food, of the sustenance of life is found in the mealtime breaking of bread, or a starch based agricultural equivalent. The almost universal mealtime prayers of thanks and Christian communion are religious celebrations of our green connection. Could this universal need to share our bounty be proof of the innate compassion and altruism that resides within the human spirit? Could this be so much a part of our communal instinct that we made it a part of our religious expression?

The sacred plants and trees, mystical flowers and holy foods are common yet diverse. We honor the Christmas tree. In the Orient it's the sacred lotus and Buddha's sacred bo tree, *Ficus religiosa*, the tree under which he sat for years until he received the gift of true enlightenment. The Sub-Saharan Africans have a spiritual connection to the baobab tree. In Australia the Aboriginal population honored the grass trees as ancestral spirits. To the Native Americans the juniper, ceder, white sage, sweet grass and peyote cactus are only a few of the plants with religious significance. In the Arabian Peninsula and Northern Africa frankincense and myrrh were considered a source of spiritual illumination, inner peace, healing and purification. These products from the sap of several trees and shrubs were valued with, and sometimes above, gold. It is logical that these aromatic botanical products acquired great value, for they do bring comfort, soothe the body and stimulate the mind. It's easy to understand why humanity has put such great value on these; the difficult question is why we attach such significance to gold. It isn't the source of inner peace, but rather the cause of stress, strife and the abandonment of the very principles and values that make us human.

To Europe's Druids the mistletoe, oak, holly, ivy and mandrake were revered. Even wheat was a part of the religious ritual as it symbolized sustenance, fertility and renewal. Many of these European "pagan" beliefs and practices were adopted by the Christians as they swept over the continent and the two religions interbred. We see a sheaf of wheat as a part of the funeral ceremony to represent life after death. We see Evergreens hung in the home, entire trees brought indoors and decorated with lights and symbolic ornamentation in celebration of the birth of the Christ child. This list could go on all over the globe.

In Ireland the shamrock was a religious symbol long before St Patrick got there. It was a sacred plant to the Celts because the leaves formed a triad, and the number three was significant to them. It was considered by the Druids to be a cure for snakebite and scorpion stings. Legend claimed that snakes avoided areas where the shamrock was growing, hence St. Patrick's link to the snakes in Ireland, or lack thereof.

When the Spanish were claiming and exploring the new world for cross and crown they carried with them the "apostles' herbs" a collection of twelve herbs including aloe and rosemary that were used in religious ceremony as well as the kitchen and the sickroom.

The famous *Canoe plants* of the Hawaiian and Polynesian travelers and traders are an interesting blend of substance and religion. This collection of 24 species of plants was a priceless cargo. These plants were the basis for their culture, they were what was necessary for survival. Their value went far beyond the foods of taro, gourd, banana, coconut and breadfruit. There were plants valued as building material, clothing, medicine, drink, and religious expression. In this compact "garden in a canoe" they were carrying their civilization.

Plants that sustain life are often the subject of religious ceremony, festival or worship. Native Americans celebrate with corn ceremonies both at the planting and the harvest. The Christian uses sacramental wine. The Hindu have their sacred lotus. We all find diverse answers to the common questions, and it is in this diversity that we can celebrate our commonality. The answer is not as important as the quest. It is the need that is common, the desire is what we all share. How we answer these wants is what makes us all wonderfully different flowers in the same beautiful field.

Sharing Beauty

The use of plants for food, health, religion, shelter, tools, weapons, pesticides, transportation and so much more is very utilitarian. All cultures need all of these things and this makes the plants we either cultivate or harvest very practical. This concept that what we grow, or what we allow to survive must be utilitarian, must have a purpose, is narrow and denies much of that which is human. A sense of beauty is not even the sole domain of humanity. Birds have colorful plumage, some even collect colorful stones or other objects to possess or give as gifts. While people in different areas have different concepts of what is beautiful, all of us possess an artistic appreciation. Without our sense of beauty our ability to explore, define or understand our existence would be seriously limited.

We all, whether we are willing to admit it or not, find beauty in flowers, the colors of seeds and fruit, the texture of bark and fibers. The flowers were religious symbols to the earlier cultures and the instinct remains within us. In the most cathartic moments of our lives, birth, courtship, marriage and death we use the beauty of flowers. Even the Neanderthals buried their dead with flowers. Perhaps this is because a flower is a promissory note issued by nature, literally a guarantee that there will be life tomorrow.

So dynamic is our global need for the beauty of flowers and foliage that we devote a major portion of our resources and energy to the cultivation of this natural art. Even when we don't grow the real flowers we capture them as photos, paintings, jewelry and home decor. The beauty of the flowers is sustenance for the soul, as the fruit is sustenance for the body. It is strange that we are more global in our flower gardens than we are in our vegetable gardens. The lure of the unusual, exotic or unfamiliar flowering plant is a marketable commodity. Perhaps because we sense a safety in the flower, perhaps because we feel the need to share and experience beauty as we feed the soul. Perhaps it's because there is so little threat in the flower that we can relax enough to share the common desire for beauty and the diversity of beauty.

As universal as the cultivation of flowers for their beauty, is the use of the seeds as jewelry and body ornamentation. Something within the human animal drives us all to beautify our bodies with the adornment of jewelry. Some of this is made from precious stones like turquoise, jade, diamonds or sapphires, others use gold, silver, copper or bronze, in some cultures plastic is a popular source of adornment. But for many cultures the seeds, bright colored, shiny or interestingly shaped are the substance of jewelry. Job's tears, vegetable ivory palm seeds, nutmeg seeds, lotus seeds and pods, precatory beans, coral beans, sea beans, wood rose, juniper seeds and pine cones. Henna dyes, herbal and conditioning oils, cosmetics, body paints and lipsticks are some of the ways we enhance the already beautiful human body by employing botanical derivatives.

Botanical Time Keepers

The human animal has always used the cycle of flowers and fruit to mark the approach of seasons as much as the cycle of the heavens. In many parts of the United States children eagerly await the flowering of lilacs because then they can shed their shoes and go barefoot. Spring is celebrated with the flowers of tulips, planting of gardens is timed to the flowering of certain wildflowers. Harvest festivals are among the most joyful times of the year. Native Americans have festivals and ceremonies that follow the cycle of corn. All over the world we mark the growth of our children against the permanence of a tree trunk. We carve symbols of affection, declare our presence, record births and great events on the trunks of trees. In most of the world we mark the flow of the seasons by what is on the dinner table. So ingrained in our cultural memory is this botanical time clock that the smell of certain flowers or fruits invoke images of the season. The appearance of a flower out of season confuses us. The mind rebels at poinsettias in bloom in May, or the taste of fresh cherries in the autumn.

Plants and Flowers Define Who We Are as a Culture

Plants also give us a sense of place. Nations declare official flowers such as the orchid tree *Bauhinia blakeana*, the official flower of Hong Kong that even appears on their flag. In England from 1459 To 1487 The Yorks and the Lancasters engaged in a brutal conflict called the War of the Roses. We see the shamrock as the symbol of Ireland, and the thistle means Scotland. France has the iris, the *fleur de lance*, and Switzerland its edelweiss. Mexico proudly displays a cactus on its flag. Jordan's flag honors the date palm, while other palms grace the flags of Guam and Tokelau. Canada honors the maple leaf while Lebanon graces its flag with the cedar. Norfolk Island proudly displays the Norfolk Island Pine on its flag. Each of our states identifies itself with a state flower and a state tree. Many of the state flags display grains, trees or assorted fruits.

Chapter Four
The Global Salad Bowl

"The only limits are, as always, those of vision."
James Broughton

Throughout the human experience we have eaten almost everything, but today our salad bowl, even in the most exclusive of gourmet restaurants, is meager fare. We enjoy lettuce from Europe, tomatoes from South America, shredded cabbage from Eurasia, and perhaps the popular, or trendy, French and Italian leafy crops like raddiccio, arugela, artichoke, broccoli, endive, frisee and fennel. If we lean toward Oriental cuisine we may experience such delightful flavors as snow peas, bok choy, mizuna, mitsuba, napa and daikon radish.. Perhaps, in a daring moment we will add some of the African foods like okra, Egyptian onions or watermelon. But still, there are hundreds if not thousands of taste sensations, delights to the palate that we have never experienced, either on the table or in the garden. These are edibles that may be pieces of the puzzle of a good meal for everyone on earth. At the very least these uncommon foods can broaden our horizons.

Popeye's Delight

One of the staple leaf crops in the European tradition is a member of the beet family, *Chenopodiaceae*, that we call spinach. Botanically this health food children intensely dislike is *Spinach oleoraceae*. The cartoon sailor, Popeye, found it instantly empowering, and it does contain iron and other nutrients. But "spinach" means different foods in different parts of the world. This is more a generic term for leafy vegetables than one specific plant. Experiencing some of these global spinaches on the dinner table is a true adventure. Growing them is every bit as much fun.

Throughout this book we use the term *potherb* for greens that are boiled in water as we usually do spinach, collards or turnip greens. This is not a term in common use by Americans, but this is what is locally known as a "mess of greens." The term has nothing to do with the slang meaning of the term 'pot' as a euphemism for marijuana. Let's take a look at some of these global spinaches.

African spinach, *Celosia argentea*
Amaranth family, *Amaranthaceae*
Also known as quailgrass
Annual that may exceed 2 m (6 feet) in height
Native to Africa

Value as a food source	6
Value as an ornamental	8
Multi-purpose	no
Continuous harvest	yes
Ease of culture	8
Overall rating	***

    This African cousin to the colorful celosia we grow in flowerbeds and borders is an annual that will reach 2 m or more in a good summer. The leaves are green, or red, or a blend of the two. The plant is both attractive and tasty, both fresh and cooked. A few of the tender young leaves add zest and character to a fresh salad while the more mature leaves can be cooked as a potherb, either alone or with other greens. The leaves can also be added to soups, stews and rice dishes.

    It thrives during the hot humid summers of the tropics and sub-tropics and provides a continuous harvest. As the days shorten it produces pink and white flower spikes that can add much to a dried arrangement. It will set seed with gleeful abandon so that you may never need to plant it again. It can also be started from cuttings. In fact, a few stems in a vase of flowers will often have roots within a few days. They prefer full sun but will take light shade. A well drained site is important but they aren't at all fussy about soil type. Regular watering and an occasional feeding will produce the tenderest, most flavorful leaves.

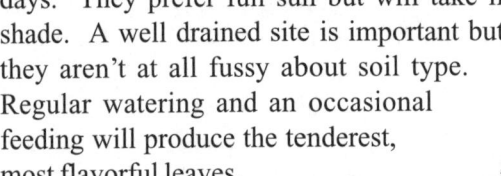

Brazilian spinach, *Alternathera sissoo*
Amaranth family, *Amaranthaceae*
Also known as sissoo
Perennial, frost sensitive, growing to 20 to 30 cm (10 to 12 in) tall
Value as a food source　　　5
Value as an ornamental　　　6
Multi-purpose　　　　　　　no
Continuous harvest　　　　　yes
Ease of culture　　　　　　　5
Overall rating　　　　　　　**

 It makes a great edible groundcover in tropical and subtropical regions. In temperate climates a few starter plants can be held over on the windowsill and set out again in the spring. It contains phytochemicals that may help to prevent cancer.

 It's happy with full sun or light shade in a well drained site. Regular watering and an occasional light feeding will keep the leaves tender and plentiful. Slugs can be a problem in warm weather, but a dusting of chili powder will control them. If they are grown in an area where there is high humidity and poor air circulation there can be some fungus problems.

 Fresh young shoots can be used raw in a salad, more mature leaves and stems can be cooked or steamed. The flavor can range from bland to bitter depending on growing conditions and variety.

Chinese spinach, *Amaranth gangeticus, also A. tricolor*
Amaranthaceae family
Also known as Xian Cai in Malaysia, Yin-choi in China and Pungkirai in Thailand
Annual, warm season crop to 1 m (2-3') tall, some varieties much taller
Asian native
Value as a food source　　　6
Value as an ornamental　　　5
Multi-purpose　　　　　　　no
Continuous harvest　　　　　yes
Ease of culture　　　　　　　8
Overall rating　　　　　　　***

One of several varieties of amaranth that make a flavorful green. It grows well in summer heat, providing a great summer substitute for lettuce and other cold season crops. This plant's use as a part of the southeast Asian diet began thousands of years ago. Like many other amaranths, it's a weed that grows readily on disturbed sites. Because amaranths contain small amounts of oxylates they shouldn't be consumed in excess, but normal portions are both safe and nutritious. The seed germinates in less than two weeks and grows so quickly that the first leaves can be harvested five to six weeks after seeding. Young foliage and growing tips can be gathered continuously to encourage branching and more new growth. Harvesting can begin about a month from germination.

This attractive vegetable does well in a container or raised bed with well drained compost rich soil. Chinese spinach does best in full sun but will tolerate light shade. Growth and flavor are best if the roots are kept evenly moist. As with many other leaf crops it can be beneficial to intercrop with beans to supply nitrogen to the soil.

Chinese water spinach, *Ipomoea aquatica*
Morning glory family, *Convolvulaceae*
Also known as swamp spinach, ung choi (Cantonese Chinese), and kangkong (Filipino), rau muong (Vietnamese), pak bung (Thai).
Perennial vine
Pan-tropical

Value as a food source	7
Value as an ornamental	3
Multi-purpose	no
Continuous harvest	yes
Ease of culture	9
Overall rating	*** Where it can be grown without becoming invasive. This plant is illegal in Florida and some other states.

There are several varieties of this aquatic, or semi-aquatic vine. Those with arrowhead shaped leaves (Pak quat) usually grow in the water while the narrow leaf form (Ching quat) grows on moist soil. It's a perennial vine that roots at leaf nodes with uncontrollable enthusiasm. This makes it an invasive problem in many areas outside of its natural habitat, but a valuable food resource in many areas. Young leaves and shoots are eaten fresh or cooked with oil and herbs. The flavor is bland but not unpleasant.

Cuban Spinach, *Montia perfoliata*
Purslane family, *Portulacaceae*
Also known as miner's lettuce, Miner's spinach or winter purslane
Self-seeding annual, perennial in some locales
grows 15 to 20 cm (6 to 8 inches) tall.
Native to North America and Caribbean

Value as a food source	5
Value as an ornamental	5
Multi-purpose	no
Continuous harvest	yes
Ease of culture	5
Overall rating	***

    This cool season crop is at its prime in the spring. The disk like leaves appear threaded on the stalks, making it an attractive plant as well as a delicious meal. While it's considered a cool season crop, it has little tolerance for freezing weather. It does seed itself readily however. It's easily propagated from seed sown in compost rich moist soil. It prefers light shade and can be container grown. It isn't at its best in summer heat, but makes a fast growing spring and fall crop.

    This plant was a life saver for the prospectors during the California Gold Rush of 1849. That's where it got the name, miner's lettuce. Food was in short supply for those working their claims, and nutritious food was even more difficult to come by. Then they found this plant growing by the stream banks, an easy harvest that could be eaten raw or as a cooked green. It was popular fried with bacon grease.

Duck spinach, *Amaranthus viridis*
Amaranth family, *Amaranthaceae*
Also known as Bayam itek in Malaysian, Ma-see-yin to the Chinese
Annual growing to 20-30 cm
Asian native
Value as a food source   5
Value as an ornamental   4
Multi-purpose   no
Continuous harvest   yes
Ease of culture   7
Overall rating   **

While considered inferior to the Chinese spinach (*A. Gangeticus*) mentioned above it has a slightly sweet taste that enhances soups and stews. The tender new leaves are delightful in a salad but mature leaves and stems are better cooked.

This vegetable thrives in moist soil and tolerates summer heat well. The leaves are sweeter and more tender if grown in light shade. The plant will form a mound of leaves and stems if the central leader is harvested early in its growth cycle. This amaranth, like most of them, will provide a continuous supply of fresh leaves.

Malabar spinach, *Basella alba (or Basella rubra*, red leaf variety).
Basellaceae family
In China it's known as Chan-choi, Saan choi, poi sag and the Thais call it Pasali-kirai. Also called Indian Spinach, Malabar nightshade, Ceylon spinach and climbing spinach
Perennial vine, warm season crop
Asian native
Value as a food source   7
Value as an ornamental   5
Multi-purpose   no
Continuous harvest   yes
Ease of culture   8
Overall rating   ****

This Indian native is popular throughout Asia and tropical Africa as well as being showcased at EPCOT's Land Pavilion. It makes a great hot weather crop when trained on a trellis or wires. Seed germinates quickly and the young plants are so vigorous that harvesting can begin in little more than a month. In Africa it's the job of the youngest children to keep the flower buds pinched off in order to keep the vines more productive. In regions where the summers are short they can be started indoors. It is possible to grow this plant on a windowsill and pluck a few leaves as needed to brighten your salad. Outdoors they respond well to container growing and as a companion planting with scarlet runner or yard long beans. They thrive in compost rich well drained soil in a hot sunny, or moderately shady, location. They are easily propagated from seed or stem cuttings throughout the warm months.

The young leaves and shoots are harvested regularly, mature leaves are tougher and fibrous. There are two color forms, one with green leaves and another with reddish leaves and stems. A few leaves can enhance both the flavor and appearance of a salad. Shoots and leaves can be steamed, cooked as a green potherb, or added to stews and soups. The leaves are great with some chopped onions, a few chiles and a dash of mustard. We were also given a recipe for Malabar spinach leaves and grated ginger.

Mountain spinach, *Atriplex hortensis*
Goosefoot family *Chenopodiaceae*
also known as garden orach.
Annual warm season crop, 2 m (4 - 6 ft) tall
Asian native

Value as a food source	6
Value as an ornamental	8
Multi-purpose	yes
Continuous harvest	yes
Ease of culture	7
Overall rating	****

This colorful multi-purpose vegetable is equally at home in the informal flower garden. It can make an attractive and functional background display of red, green or whitish leaves depending on the variety. This plant is from Asia but it has naturalized in Europe and North America. It has the advantage of being salt tolerant and thrives in any sunny location where there is well drained soil. The seed germinates in one to three weeks with the first harvest of tender leaves about a month after that. The arrowhead shaped foliage is nutritious, with a distinctive taste that can enhance a salad. They can also be used as a cooked green or added to soups and stews. This is another of those ancient vegetables that is in truth little more than a weed, eager to claim its place in the sun on any disturbed site. By trimming off the flower spikes a steady crop of tender greens can be grown. Fresh leaves can be harvested throughout the frost free months.

There are green, cream and red leaved varieties. All make a colorful background plant for the flower border and the flower spikes are a pleasant addition to a floral arrangement.

New Zealand spinach, *Tetragonia tetragonoides*
Tetragoniaceae family
Short lived perennial, hot weather crop
Produces vines 3' or more in length
Native to New Zealand and Australia

Value as a food source	5
Value as an ornamental	4
Multi-purpose	no
Continuous harvest	yes
Ease of culture	5
Overall rating	**

The triangle shaped leaves are attractive enough to make this an effective hanging basket plant. They prefer a well drained sandy soil enriched with compost. They are very frost sensitive, but withstand drought and summer heat well. The best tasting leaves are produced in light shade where the plants have been kept evenly moist.

New Zealand spinach can be started from cuttings or seed. The seeds are slow and irregular to sprout, but with patience and soil temperatures above seventy degrees (F) you will be rewarded. Soaking the seeds in water overnight does seem to speed up the process. In frost free areas they will reseed themselves with reckless abandon. One researcher has been growing a lush crop of New Zealand spinach in a space efficient hydroponic system to provide a continuous harvest of fresh succulent leaves.

Gather only the tenderest growth, the vine tips with about three leaves, for the best flavor in a salad. Don't use too many of these leaves raw because the calcium oxalate content can be overpowering. As a cooked green the mature leaves are a delight. Twice boiled with the first water discarded gives the best flavor. A small amount of diced chile peppers, garlic or onions added to the cooked New Zealand spinach produces a delicious and nutritious green.

Okinawa spinach, *Gynura crepiodes*
Daisy family, *Asteraceae* or *Compositae*
Freeze sensitive perennial forming a mound 1 m or more in diameter
Native to Indonesia or Africa

Value as a food source	9
Value as an ornamental	9
Multi-purpose	yes
Continuous harvest	yes
Ease of culture	7
Overall rating	*****

This is a delightful, and very attractive, succulent shrub that grows with reckless abandon. The fresh leaves and stems are among the favorite greens in our Global Salad. Foliage is dark green on top, and purple underneath. The leaves and fleshy stems can be eaten raw or cooked, either way they have a pleasant pine or nutty taste. In our taste tests everyone enjoyed the raw flavor in salads and children have eaten the shoots and leaves as a snack. If you are using it as a cooked green, steaming the leaves briefly rather than boiling gives a better flavor and keeps them from becoming mushy and mucilaginous. We have added a few of these nutritious leaves to soups, stews and other dishes with great success. In frost free regions this is a vegetable that continues to produce nutritious leaves and stems twelve months a year. In our test garden we harvested every four to seven days. Frequent harvesting tends to encourage more compact bushy growth. We have found that a periodic application of a balanced fertilizer helps to keep it productive. In our "dishwater test" this is one of the plants that thrives on nothing more than watering with waste water.

You can easily propagate this delightful plant from cuttings. These cuttings will root in about a week and are ready for first harvest in about a month. In frost free areas it can be grown in any sunny or lightly shaded area. All it asks is a well drained, compost enriched soil. It will even tolerate sandy soil with little organic matter, but it doesn't produce with as much enthusiasm. This plant is rather drought tolerant and seems to have few insect or disease pests.

In more temperate climates it makes an attractive container plant. There is an added bonus, the flowers attract butterflies.

Okinawa spinach

Strawberry spinach, *Chenopodium capitatum*
Goosefoot family, *Chenopodiaceae*
Strawberry blight or beetberry
Self-seeding annual, warm season crop
Grows 30 to 45 cm (12 to 18") tall
Traditional European dooryard vegetable

Value as a food source	4
Value as an ornamental	5
Multi-purpose	yes
Continuous harvest	yes
Ease of culture	6
Overall rating	**

What a unique old-fashioned plant this is. It's a multi-purpose vegetable producing a tasty edible leaf that can grace a salad or bowl of soup. It has a bonus however, in that the calyx swells to form a miniature strawberry red fruit that can be eaten raw or cooked. This annual is easy to grow and is another one of those continuous harvest plants that makes an interesting addition to the summer garden. Tip from personal experience. If you pinch out the tip of the stem when it reaches about 6 inches tall, it will bush out and form a small mound of nutritious leaves. One word of caution is in order. It is an annual that reseeds itself with enthusiasm.

Surinam spinach, *Talinum triangulare*
Portulaca family, *Portulacaceae*
Also known as Surinam purslane, water leaf
Perennial in frost free areas
Grows .5 m (1.5 ft) tall
Native to the American tropics

Value as a food source	5
Value as an ornamental	5
Multi-purpose	no
Continuous harvest	yes
Ease of culture	6
Overall rating	***

    This is an attractive plant with medium green fleshy leaves and pink to magenta flowers. The leaves and the flowers both have a pleasant mild flavor. They make a nutritious addition to a salad, or they can be steamed, added to soups, pickled or sauteed. They are best of they aren't overcooked.

    While this purslane is considered a plant for the humid tropics, it grows best in moist well drained soil, not bog conditions. The plants are easily propagated from cuttings or seed. It grows effectively in a container garden or raised beds as well. This is another of those vegetables that enjoys hot humid summer weather and will provide a continuous harvest of fresh leaves and shoots with little effort.

Tree spinach, *Chenopodium giganteum*
Goosefoot family, *Chenopodiaceae*
Also known as Magenta lamb's quarters
Annual warm season crop. Often self seeding.
Grows to 2 m or more (5-7 ft)
Originated in Eurasia

Value as a food source	5
Value as an ornamental	8
Multi-purpose	no
Continuous harvest	yes
Ease of culture	7
Overall rating	**

    What a beautiful weed. The young leaves are magenta suffusing to pink as they grow, finally becoming dusty green. If the central leader is pinched out the plant becomes bushy and leaf production increases. It could be equally at home as a background plant in a flower border or informal garden. One catalog lists this as "edible beauty."

This vegetable is popular in Europe. It yields a delicious, slightly tart leaf that is great as a cooked vegetable, but the tender young leaves are even better used raw in a salad where they add beautiful color, texture and flavor. However, raw consumption shouldn't be overdone because they do contain small quantities of saponin. Some make a great deal about this toxin but it's so poorly absorbed by the human body, that it rarely poses a threat, providing we don't overdo it. The group of botanical poisons called saponins are found in many members of the bean family and many other plants. Those plants that contain high concentrations of this chemical are frequently used by indigenous populations as a highly productive way to go fishing. They throw leaves, seeds and sometimes whole plants in pools where the potential dinner is swimming aimlessly while thinking the lofty thoughts only a fish can think. They ingest some of these saponin, loose all sense of balance and float to the top where they can be gathered with ease. To some this may take the sport out of fishing, but sport can come after the belly is full.

The more mature leaves can be cooked as you would spinach, or used in soups and stews. Some harvest the seeds, soak them overnight, rinse then roast them before grinding them with wheat or other grains to make a coarse flour for baking. The flavor is somewhat like amaranth.

This is one of those "weed" vegetables that are almost too easy to grow. Seed sown lightly and barely covered will germinate within a week. All they ask is a sunny location, good drainage and moderately fertile soil. One of the most attractive varieties is a cultivar named 'Magentaspreen.' This will grow rather quickly to 1.5 m or more. They do best during the heat of summer with the finest flavor produced with regular watering. It should be noted that the state of Minnesota lists this plant as a noxious weed.

Beyond Lettuce

Most of us have never tasted such delights as the leaves of the horseradish tree, *Moringia oleifera*, from India, quail grass, *Amaranth tricolor*, from Africa or the leaves and shoots of winged bean or lablab bean, from Asia or miners lettuce, *Montia perfoliata*, from North America.

Many of the tropical and sub-tropical greens are perennial; some of the temperate and mountain foods are also. This is a tremendous advantage when we consider the environmental impact of tilling and the fuel burned to drive tractors and other machinery. It is also a labor and financial advantage to the women trying to provide for their families in areas where war and economic stress have taken most of the men. We will be discussing the rise of perennials in the garden later in this text.

People throughout history have dined on leaves. Humans, like most other primates, are very much grazing animals. In the dawn of the age of Homo sapiens, our ancestors survived by varying their diet, but much of that diet was leaves. They are ever present, easier to catch than a rabbit, and safer to bring to the dinner table than a wooly mammoth. Early in our history, our diet was far more varied. We gathered what we needed when we were hungry, depending on the seasons, terrain and climate to provide something to fill the belly. Then we became "civilized" and began to grow only those foods that were easy and productive. Since the dawn of agriculture there has been a steady decline in the number of species we use as nourishment.

In the European tradition, most of these leaves came from garden plants like lettuce, cabbage, mustard, and a few others. In other traditions there are a number of trees and shrubs that produce edible and delicious leaves. Katuk (katook), *Sauropus androgynus* and chaya, *Cnidoscolus chayamansa escalentis*, are just two of these tropical delights that can be grown as container plants in frost prone areas.

In areas where wetlands and waterways abound we dine on aquatic plants. We think of these as being the fare of poor unfortunate indigenous peoples, but the reality is that such foods as rice and water chestnuts are wetlands produce as well.

Greens as a Second Crop, Multi-purpose Plants

The sweet potato, *Ipomoea batatas*, is valued as a nutritious tuber, but in many parts of the world the young leaves are popular both raw and cooked. The same is true for the most popular euphorbia. No it's not the poinsettia, it's the cassava, also known as manioc, yuca or tapioca, *Manihot esculenta*. While the roots are valued throughout the tropics as a basic table food, the leaves are also consumed, but only as a cooked green because they contain hydrocyanic glycosides which are rendered safe by cooking. It is interesting to note that while the cassava originated in tropical America, the leaves are rarely eaten there but are common table fare in Africa, Asia and the Pacific islands. The indigenous cultures of South

America don't include many greens in their diet at all, while in Asia and Africa it's generally a staple. In Africa it is common practice to dry and powder the leaves of numerous plants so that they can be efficiently preserved for cooking. In the industrialized nations we have leaf crops like lettuce and cabbage and we have other crops grown for their fruit, tubers or seeds, but in Africa and Asia plants are often used for several purposes. This is not only a matter of efficiency, it is a means of survival. The cultivation of multi-purpose plants in the garden is a matter of common sense.

Even the leaves of many common garden vegetables are edible; some are even surprisingly tasty. We regularly harvest a few leaves from the onions while the bulb is forming underground, but in many cultures the young shoots and leaves of the common garden variety ginger are also harvested and used in cooking both for their spicy flavor and their food value.

In Africa the fluted gourd, *Telfairia occidentalis*, and the closely related oyster nut, *T. Pedata* are perennial vines easily grown from seed or cuttings. Vine tips and tender shoots are boiled or added to stews. Often the vines are grown for the greens rather than the fruit. When this is the case, the flower buds are pinched off to encourage greater leaf production.

The bean family also produces a number of edible leaves, although some members also produce toxins in this foliage. The common garden pea, sometimes called English peas, *Pisum sativum*, are valued for their immature and dried seeds, sometimes for the pods, but we rarely dine on the leaves, even though they are delicious. This is a temperate climate green that has been completely overlooked, except in times of famine.

The young leaves of the common green bean, *Phaseolus vulgaris*, are edible as a cooked green and can be more flavorful than the beans themselves. Lima bean, *P. Lunatus*, leaves are also nutritious and they don't have an unpleasant taste either. The fava, or broad bean, *Vigna faba*, is grown in the some areas of the tropics for the leaves as well as the delicious beans. The leaves of cowpeas, *Vigna unguiculata*, when boiled, make a mild and flavorful dish.

The pigeon pea, *Cajanus cajan*, is a perennial shrub that produces masses of delicious seeds, but the foliage can also be eaten. It has a unique flavor that some will say is an acquired taste. The advantage is that it thrives in adverse conditions and has the botanical fortitude to survive drought, poor soil and little care. A couple of pigeon pea bushes can sustain a family through hard times.

One of my favorite legumes is the winged bean, *Psophocarpus tetragonalobus*. The young leaves, beautiful bluish flowers, shoots and immature pods are delicious. This is a perennial vining legume that even produces an edible tuber. It's a plant that deserves more attention.

The lablab or hyacinth bean, *Dolochius lablab*, is not only a beautiful flowering vine, but the beans are delicious and the leaves are edible. The purple or white flower clusters are so attractive that they are grown and sold as cut flowers for the florist trade in some areas. This is also a perennial that produces an edible tuber, and, yes, the flowers are delicious.

Okra, *Abelmoschus esculentus*, is one of Africa's great gifts to the global dinner table. We enjoy the tender young fruit, and occasionally dine on the flowers but in Africa the leaves are also valued for their tart flavor and nutritional value, either raw or as a cooked green. Other members of the hibiscus family also produce edible leaves. Another African delight in the hibiscus family is roselle, *Hibiscus sabdariffa*. It's valued for the delicious deep red flower buds (sometimes called Jamaican sorrel or Florida cranberry) but the leaves are great in a salad or cooked. The seeds have an interesting nutty taste when roasted and are sometimes brewed to produce a coffee substitute. Even the immature leaves of the common ornamental hibiscus from the orient, *Hibiscus rosa-sinensis*, are edible and have served as a famine food.

The sweet pepper produces a healthy crop of leaves that, when cooked retain good color and a pleasant, slightly bitter, flavor. If you grow hot peppers you can cook their leaves as well. They have a hot pepper fragrance when cooked and yield a spicy taste. The leaves are often used in Asian cooking as a seasoning.

The leaves of radishes, beets, mustard, even carrots are edible. Carrot leaves have an interesting, but somewhat bitter flavor and some people develop a skin rash when they eat them, but they are listed as edible in limited quantities.

The young leaves of pumpkins and squash are edible as a cooked green. The popular tropical fruit, chayote, *Sechium edule*, also produces edible leaves and shoots that are rich in iron and other nutrients.

Squash leaves

Some Thoughts on Grazing Your Way Through the Garden

- Be cautious. Don't eat leaves unless you can positively identify them and know they are safe to eat.
- Many leaves contain acids and toxins that are destroyed with cooking.
- Insecticides, fungicides, rodenticides and other pesticides are poisons and difficult to wash off the leaves. If you need to control insects use hot pepper spray, soaps and other safe controls. Keep in mind that just because it's of organic origin it isn't necessarily safe. A rattlesnake is a 100% organic rodenticide.
- Tender young leaves are generally better for the dinner table than mature ones. They are less likely to be fibrous and bitter.
- Harvesting a few of the young leaves is not going to harm most plants because they produce some extra as an insurance policy. To that katuk bush you are just another bug, rabbit or cow out for a snack.
- By harvesting a few leaves, thinning the rows, trimming the shoots and tips of these plants we encourage branching and more compact growth.
- Try unfamiliar greens in small portions. Moderation is always the key. Consuming too much of anything can be the direct route to gastro-intestinal distress.

Oriental Greens for the Global Garden

There is a multitude of Oriental crops grown for the leaves, stems and flower buds, both as a cooked greens and as part of a good salad. Many of these are suitable for continuous harvest and harvesting can actually begin within a month of seeding. The majority of these are cool season crops but you will find that some will continue to produce through the heat of summer. Most are quite easy to grow and are suitable for intensive gardening programs. Because they are ready to harvest so quickly, and can continue to be productive over a period of months, it's easy to have fresh, nutritious greens for the table on a daily basis. With an almost daily harvest it also becomes an easy chore to monitor insects and nutrient deficiencies and remedy them before they become serious problems. Some of these are familiar fair on the global dinner table but others unknown beyond China and Japan. There are also hundreds of others that could have been listed that space simply doesn't permit.

Bok choy, see Pok choy

Chinese artichoke, *Stachys affinis*, sometimes listed as *S. Seiboldii*
Mint family, *Lamiaceae*
Also known as artichoke betony, kan-lu-tsu, tyorogi
Perennial growing approximately 15 to 20 inches tall.
Native to China and Japan

Value as a food source	4
Value as an ornamental	5
Multi-purpose	no
Continuous harvest	no
Ease of culture	6
Overall rating	**

This member of the mint family produces small tubers (about one inch in diameter) that can be eaten raw or cooked. The flavor is almost nutty and these tubers make a flavorful addition to salads or stir fries. While some peel the tubers it isn't necessary. When sliced or peeled they tend to discolor and loose appeal. The young leaves are sometimes harvested and used as a cooked green, but the flavor is rather insipid.

This attractive plant can be grown in a garden, in containers or as a naturalized plant. All it asks is a compost rich, well-drained site that can be kept moist. It will thrive in either full sun or light shade. While this is a plant that will freeze down to the ground with the first frost of autumn the tubers are quite hardy and will sprout in early spring as far north as Pennsylvania (USDA zone 5). This is one of those plants that thrives in the summer heat of the American deep south as long as the soil is kept moist.

They are easily started from dormant tubers or division of growing plants, but starting them from the fine seeds is also easy. The tubers can be harvested as needed throughout the year, even during the growing season. Some prefer to harvest after a frost, leaving a few tubers behind for next year's crop. The tubers can be stored for months in a refrigerator. Traditionally they were stored in moist sand and used as needed. It takes five to seven months to produce a heavy crop.

Chinese kale, *Brassica oleracea* var. *Alboglabra*
Cabbage family, *Brassicaceae* or *Cruciferae*
Also known as Chinese broccoli, Kailaan or Gai lohn
Grown as an annual
Grows 2 to 3 ft tall but is usually harvested somewhat smaller.

Value as a food source	7
Value as an ornamental	4
Multi-purpose	no
Continuous harvest	yes
Ease of culture	8
Overall rating	****

What a delightful vegetable. It produces fleshy, tender flower stalks and loads of leaves. The taste is somewhere between broccoli and asparagus with a distinct sweetness. The flower stalks are best harvested when they have just a few flowers opening. The flower stalks and leaves are great raw in salads, added to soups and stews, boiled as a potherb, steamed or included in stir-fries. There are blue-green and light green varieties available.

While this is often grown as a cool season vegetable it withstands summer heat quite well and can be grown and harvested all year long in most locales. First leaves are ready in about 35 to 40 days; if flowering stalks are cut multiple new stems will grow. Chinese kale is easily grown from seed lightly sown and barely covered in a compost rich loose soil. Thinning can be done by harvesting and transplanting when well started. Flavor is best if it is kept evenly moist and fed frequently.

Garland chrysanthemum, *Chrysanthemum coronarium*
Daisy family, *Asteraceae (Compositae)*
Also known as Shungiku, Chop Suey Plant
Round leaf and small leaf varieties are available
Annual reaching to 2-3 ft, grown as a cool season vegetable.

Value as a food source	6
Value as an ornamental	8
Multi-purpose	yes
Continuous harvest	yes
Ease of culture	7
Overall rating	**

This edible ornamental quickly produces succulent, tender leaves that have a pleasant spicy flavor and the ability to enhance a salad or provide zing to mixed pot of herbs. They're also great in soups and stews, added to a stir-fry, rice dish or even a baked potato. A boring sandwich can become a gourmet's delight with the addition of a few leaves. The bonus is in the cheerful yellow flowers that are equally great in a long lasting bouquet or a salad. A single flower floating in a bowl of soup can add an artistic touch to the meal. This is a great multi-tasking, continuous harvest, cool season plant for the Global Garden

It will grow with little effort from you throughout the cool months. You can either sow seed where it is to grow, or start them in a controlled environment and transplant when they have a good start. Spacing about 6 inches apart will give them room to grow and form a healthy mound. You can begin to harvest the leaves individually in about 35 to 45 days and continue to use the leaves, stems and flower buds until warm weather does them in.

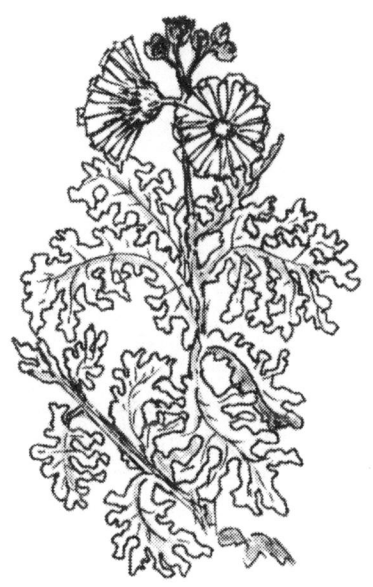

Hon-tsai-tai, *Brassica rapa*
Cabbage family, *Brassicaceae (Cruciferae)* closely allied to the mustards.
Value as a food source	8
Value as an ornamental	7
Multi-purpose	yes
Continuous harvest	yes
Ease of culture	8
Overall rating	***

    This is a delightful and easy to grow vegetable with purple leaves, stems and flower stalks. It's a cool weather crop with great flavor. Both leaves and flower stalks are tender and delicious. The cooler it gets the deeper purple they become. Great steamed or in stir-fries, soups, stews and salads or as a potherb. Grows quickly and easily from seed sown lightly and barely covered. The young leaves are great in a fresh salad. Begin to harvest when about 4 to 6 weeks old. You can thin as you harvest and nothing is wasted. This is another continuous harvest vegetable.

Komatsuna, *Brassica rapa* var. *Komatsuna* or *Brassica rapa* var. *pervidis*,
Cabbage family, *Brassicaceae (Cruciferae)* allied to the mustards and turnips
Sometimes called Japanese mustard or Japanese spinach.
Value as a food source	8
Value as an ornamental	5
Multi-purpose	no
Continuous harvest	yes
Ease of culture	8
Overall rating	****

    This delightfully flavored green can be grown year round in most locales. In mild areas it will take both heat and cold, some varieties being more tolerant of heat than others. Komatsuna can be continuously harvested beginning about 30 days after seeding. The seed can be sown lightly on a compost rich well drained soil and lightly covered where they will germinate in 3 to 5 days. It grows amazingly fast, reaching 20 to 30 cm (8 to 12 inches) in less than a month. Thinning and harvesting can begin in 3 weeks from seeding. Keep well watered and a few plants will keep you well supplied. This is a great, full flavored green in salads and stir-fries. It is also an excellent potherb.

Laksa plant, *Persicaria hydropiper* or *Polygonum hydropiper*
Buckwheat family, *Polygonaceae*
Also known as Smartweed, water-pepper, Yanagi-tade
Also known as *daun kesum* in Malaysian and *laska-yip* in Chinese
Perennial shrub, 3-5 ft
Native to Southeast Asia

Value as a food source	3
Value as an ornamental	5
Multi-purpose	no
Continuous harvest	yes
Ease of culture	7
Overall rating	**

    Laksa's peppery flavored leaves are used throughout the Orient as a seasoning. The young leaves and stems are boiled as a potherb or roasted with other vegetables. Seedlings are used as a garnish. The Japanese use it with raw fish (sashimi) tempura and rice or vegetable dishes. The leaves can also be lightly steamed and served with vinegar. In some Oriental markets the seedlings are sold in bundles. They are also used as a spicy addition to sprouts.

    There are a number of varieties of this fine plant, some are low growing, others have red leaves, and still others have spicier flavors. All will thrive at the water's edge or barely covered with water, much like water cress. They thrive in almost any soil type and will grow in full sun or light shade. The seeds can be scattered lightly and barely covered where you want them to grow, or you can grow them in pots kept in a watering tray or saucer to keep the soil soggy. The plant will naturally trail and root at the leaf nodes. This means they will root easily from cuttings as well.

Mibuna, *Brassica juncea*
Cabbage family, *Brassicaceae (Cruciferae)*

Value as a food source	6
Value as an ornamental	5
Multi-purpose	no
Continuous harvest	yes
Ease of culture	8
Overall rating	***

    While this is often considered a cool season crop, some newer varieties can be grown and harvested all year in milder climates where extreme heat isn't a problem. To keep it at peak production occasionally cut the plant off just above the soil line, give it a good feeding and watch it grow. This delightful green has a flavor not unlike water cress, but with a hint of sweetness. It grows quickly from seed sown lightly and barely covered. Harvesting can begin about a month after seeding. Young leaves are best for use in salads, but as they mature they also make an excellent cooked green.

Michihili, *Brassica rapa* var. *Pekinensis*
Cabbage family, *Brassicaceae (Cruciferae)* more closely allied to the turnips
Sometimes called Chihli, many varieties

Value as a food source	8
Value as an ornamental	5
Multi-purpose	no
Continuous harvest	yes
Ease of culture	8
Overall rating	****

This is a Chinese cabbage with a cylindrical head growing about 45 cm (18") tall. Easily grown from seed sown lightly and barely covered. Seedlings can be thinned by harvesting or transplanting. The outer leaves can be harvested when the plant is less than a month old but the heads aren't ready for the table until they have been growing 60 to 80 days. These are relatively mild flavored and are ideal as a steamed vegetable, used in a stir-fry or soup. The young leaves are good raw in a salad.

Mitsuba, *Chryptotaenia japonica*
Carrot family, *Apiaceae (Umbelliferae)*
Also known as Oriental celery or Japanese parsley

Value as a food source	6
Value as an ornamental	6
Multi-purpose	yes
Continuous harvest	yes
Ease of culture	7
Overall rating	****

The young leaves are aromatic and frequently used as a seasoning with fish, sukiyaki and many other dishes. As the plant matures the leaf stalks are traditionally blanched the same way the Europeans blanched celery, by mounding soil around the plants. First leaves are ready for harvest in about a month, but the real harvest begins in about two months. The flowers, seeds and roots can also be used as a culinary herb. This is one of the Orient's best kept secrets, but the Native Americans gathered and used a close relative called honewort, *Crytotaenia canadensis*, as both a culinary herb and a vegetable.

This is a hardy perennial (USDA zones 4 through 9) that can thrive in the shade. The plant forms a rosette of leaves, the younger, more tender ones being light green. As they mature they may reach 30 to 60 cm (12 to 24") in length and turn darker in color. This is a vegetable that can add much to the ornamental landscape as well as gracing the dinner table. Young leaves can be continuously harvested or the entire rosette can be cut about 2 months from seeding. Because this is a perennial that will continue to produce leaves, flowers and seeds for several years it might be best to simply gather leaves as needed.

Mitsuba is grown from seed sown lightly and barely covered in a compost rich, moist soil. The seed germinates in 7 to 14 days and within three to four weeks you can start thinning or transplanting. The tender young leaves can be added to the salad. You can do a continuous harvest after this by cutting the stems when they reach 10 to 15 cm (4 to 6"). Use raw in salads, or cooked as a potherb or in soups, stews and other dishes.

Mizuna, *Brassica rapa* var. *Nipposinica*
Cabbage family, *Brassicaceae (Cruciferae)*

Value as a food source	8
Value as an ornamental	7
Multi-purpose	no
Continuous harvest	yes
Ease of culture	8
Overall rating	****

A culinary delight that should be grown far more than it is. The white stalks and feathery leaves have a rich flavor, produce abundantly and can be continuously harvested all year long. It is easily started from seed sown lightly and barely covered. Germination is well underway in a few days. The first leaves can be harvested in about 30 to 35 days. They can be used raw in a salad, or cooked in stir-fries, soups and stews. As a salad green mizuna is far more nutritious than common lettuce, and much more flavorful too. There is a bonus with this plant. Because it is so attractive with its mound of lacy deep green foliage, it's great as a container plant or comfortably at home in a flower bed or border.

Napa, or Won bok, *Brassica rapa* var. *pekinensis*
Cabbage family, *Brassicaceae (Cruciferae)* more closely related to the turnip.

Value as a food source	8
Value as an ornamental	5
Multi-purpose	no
Continuous harvest	yes
Ease of culture	8
Overall rating	****

This is a Chinese cabbage that produces a blunt, barrel-shaped head about 15 cm (6") wide and 30 cm (12") tall. The flavor is mild and the young leaves can be used raw in salads or as a potherb, the heads are great steamed, in a stir-fry or any other dish where cabbage is the vegetable guest of honor. The outer leaves can be continuously harvested rather than waiting for the plant to form a head.

As with most members of the cabbage family, napa is easily started from seed sown lightly and barely covered. The crop can be thinned by harvesting or transplanting. Regular watering produces the most succulent and tasty crop.

Perilla, *Perilla frutescens*
Mint family, *Lamiaceae*,
Also known as Japanese Shi-so

Value as a food source	5
Value as an ornamental	8
Multi-purpose	no
Continuous harvest	yes
Ease of culture	8
Overall rating	**

Commonly available in green leaf (*ao-shiso*) and red or purple leaf *(aka-shiso)* varieties. Many others can be found and enjoyed. Looks like a coleus, matures at about 2-3 ft, forming a very attractive mound with tasty leaves and flower spikes for salad or cooking. The purple varieties will give rice a beautiful pink color. Some have a cinnamon flavor while others have the scent of cumin. *Kkaennip* is a Korean variety that produces leaves that often exceed six inches (15 cm) in diameter with a mild cinnamon aroma. These are eaten raw with rice or cooked with sesame oil as a side dish. Sometimes the leaves are wrapped around meat and batter fried. In some parts of Asia the leaves are fermented into a *kimchi*. The flowers are valued both raw and in cooking. This attractive annual readily reseeds itself and will grow in a variety of soils in full sun or light shade. The more sun the richer the color of the leaves. It will appreciate a drink during drought.

Pok Choy, or Pak-choi, *Brassica rapa* var. *Chinensis*
Cabbage family, *Brassicaceae (Cruciferae)*
Also known as Bok choy, bok choi, taisai, wong bok, celery mustard, Chinese white cabbage and spoon cabbage.

Value as a food source	9
Value as an ornamental	5
Multi-purpose	no
Continuous harvest	yes
Ease of culture	9
Overall rating	*****

There is so much variety that names get confused. They are often divided into four groups, distinguished by their growth habit.

▶ White petiole (leaf stalk) types: produce beautiful vegetables with deep green leaves and white or pale green leaf stalk, forming celery-like heads. The young leaves can be continuously harvested for salads and steaming.

▶ Green petiole types: produce deep green leaf and somewhat lighter green leaf stalk. Many varieties to choose from. These form celery-like heads. The young leaves can be continuously harvested, too.

- Baby pak-choy: These are sometimes called dwarf pak-choy. They don't develop the size of the above two types and are ideal for continuous harvest.

- Bunching pak-choy: many varieties are available, some form loose bunches, some are upright in growth habit. All are great for continuous harvest of the young leaves for use in salads, soups or other dishes. The entire "bunch" can be cut above the soil line and the plant will produce again.

Regardless of the type, or types, of pak choy you choose to grow in your garden, all are easy. Most are best treated as a cool season crop, but there are many baby and bunching varieties that will continue to produce well throughout the year. All are easily started and grown in loose, compost rich soil. Sow the seed lightly and barely cover. In 3 to 5 days you will have most of them sprouting. In 3 to 4 weeks you can begin to harvest by thinning the crop. Then it's a continuous harvest of the outer leaves, or the patience to wait 2 to 3 months for the mature heads on the larger growing varieties.

All of these Chinese cabbages are a valuable crop for the garden and a reliable source of vitamin A, folic acid and potassium. They can all be used raw, steamed, baked, boiled or stir-fried. Many are pickled, diced, sauced, creamed or prepared in wonderfully diverse ways. Enjoy.

Tasoi, or tatsoi, *Brassica juncea*
Cabbage family, *Brassicaceae (Cruciferae)* most closely allied to the mustards also called spoon mustard

Value as a food source	8
Value as an ornamental	6
Multi-purpose	no
Continuous harvest	yes
Ease of culture	7
Overall rating	****

This is a small plant that grows well in the cool seasons and can even be harvested in the snow. It forms an attractive rosette 15 to 30 cm (6 to 12") of dark green leaves that lends itself to small space gardens such as roof tops, patios, even as a border along a walkway. Seed germinates in 3 to 5 days when sown lightly and barely covered. The first leaves can be harvested in about four to six weeks and from then on it's a continuous harvest. It does best in a loose, compost rich well drained soil. Grow it the same as you would cabbage.

Tasoi is an underplanted vegetable with a delicious mild cabbage flavor. Raw or cooked it's a nutritious delight. It's also a great stir-fry vegetable.

Yu choy, edible rape
Cabbage family, *Brassicaceae (Cruciferae)*
Value as a food source   7
Value as an ornamental   4
Multi-purpose   no
Continuous harvest   yes
Ease of culture   8
Overall rating   ***

Grown for the tender young leaves and flower stalks, this flavorful vegetable can be continuously harvested. They are great raw in a salad, steamed or boiled as a potherb. This can also be a tasty addition to soups, stews, stir-fries and rice dishes.

It grows best as a cool season crop with harvesting beginning in 30 to 40 days from seeding. Yu choy will tolerate a wide range of soils but prefers a loose, compost rich site that's well drained. Regular watering produces the highest quality yield, but it will withstand some drought.

The Tropical Salad Bowl

Algerian Salad, *Fedia cornucopiae*
Valerian family, *Valerianaceae*
Also known as African valerian, horn-of-plenty
Native to North Africa
Tender perennial reaching .5 m (12-18") in height

Value as a food source	6
Value as an ornamental	8
Multi-purpose	no
Continuous harvest	yes
Ease of culture	6
Overall rating	***

    This perennial is at home in the vegetable garden where the leaves make a delightful addition to any salad, but it also produces beautiful purple branching stems that will literally form a mat as the season progresses. It also produces masses of pink flowers above the leaves.

    It will thrive in average garden soil in full sun where it will grow with little care. It can be cultivated in temperate climes as an annual. While drought tolerant, the leaves are more flavorful if the plants receive water on a regular basis.

    Algerian salad starts easily from seed, usually germinating in seven days or less. In a bed of its own, it will self seed. Harvesting can start in 40 to 50 days and continue on a regular basis.

    This can be an attractive container plant or addition to a low maintenance flower bed as well as the salad garden.

Butterbur or **Sweet coltsfoot**, *Petasites japonicus*
Daisy family, *Asteraceae (Compositae)*
Also known as Fuki or Huki in Japan
Perennial reaching 1m (2-3') high and 1.5 m (4-5') wide
Native to Japan, China & Korean peninsula

Value as a food source	7
Value as an ornamental	8
Multi-purpose	yes
Continuous harvest	yes
Ease of culture	9
Overall rating	***

    This is a multi-tasking plant long valued as a medicinal herb. It has been used as an anti-asthmatic, expectorant, and as a poultice on open sores and wounds. The huge leaves are used by Japanese children as an umbrella. The leaf stalks are frequently used as impromptu walking sticks.

As a food source it also provides several options for the dinner table. The leaf stalks can be cooked like rhubarb, or boiled and pickled for use later in soups or miso. These stalks can also be fried or baked yielding a delightful dish. The flower buds have a tangy flavor and are frequently cooked and eaten with miso or soy sauce. Even the flower stalks are a flavorful cooked dish.

This is a massive flowering groundcover for shady damp locations, but will grow in almost any average soil. It thrives in shade or semi-shade. In fact it is so enthusiastic that it can become invasive in the wrong site. Roots are difficult to eradicate.

The variety, *giganteus*, produces leaves over 2 meters long but has a stronger flavor, being too bitter for many.

Propagation is generally by division. This is an easy process that can be done anytime during the growing season. It can also be started from seed.

Indian Lettuce, *Lactuca indica*
Daisy family, *Asteraceae (Compositae)*
Perennial that may reach 2 m (6 ft)
Native to China

Value as a food source	6
Value as an ornamental	4
Multi-purpose	no
Continuous harvest	yes
Ease of culture	7
Overall rating	**

    This is a true lettuce. The young leaves and shoots are great eaten raw in a salad. But it can also be cooked or used in soups and stews. Unlike the lettuce of temperate zones, the gardener can continue harvesting this one all year long.

    Indian lettuce is a flavorful, nutritious greens source for the warm humid tropics. It thrives in temperatures in the 80 to 90 degree range. While this vegetable likes lots of moisture, it doesn't tolerate wet feet, preferring a well-drained sandy soil. The leaf production is best in partial shade.

    A few plants can provide fresh greens continuously for a family in the tropics. It is easily grown from seed or cuttings. In fact, once the plant reaches about two feet in height, a tip cutting can be taken. This encourages branching and the production of many more leaves. The cuttings should be about 20 cm (8") long with the leaves removed. Cuttings can be struck in containers or directly in the garden.

    The plants respond well to an occasional application of a high nitrogen fertilizer, rabbit or poultry manure. A good surface mulch will help to keep the roots moist.

Jute, *Corchorus olitrius*
Linden family, *Tiliaceae*
Also known as Melokheya, Saluyot, Krin-Krin and West African sorrel, Jew's mallow and bush okra
Native to West Africa
Annual growing to 1.3 m (4 ft)

Value as a food source	5
Value as an ornamental	6
Multi-purpose	yes
Continuous harvest	yes
Ease of culture	7
Overall rating	***

While we think of jute as a fiber crop, second only to cotton, this one is a tasty addition to the equatorial diet. This is a vegetable that appeared on the table of the pharaohs. It is a great multi-purpose, continuous harvest vegetable. In Sierra Leone the leaves are cooked with beans and okra to make a sauce for rice dishes or added to soups and stews. The young leaves are great in a salad and the mature foliage and tender shoots can be cooked as a warm season spinach. The dried leaves are used to thicken soups or make a refreshing tea. In the Sudan fresh or dried leaves are combined with okra seed, oil, salt and a secret blend of herbs and spices to make a sauce called *mulah*. The immature fruit is a delight in a salad or as a part of a soup or stew.

It willingly grows in a wide variety of soil and moisture conditions, thriving during both the dry and rainy seasons in West Africa. It is often interplanted with other vegetables and harvested on a continuous basis starting about 40 days after planting. Jute can be propagated from seed broadcast on prepared beds, or started in nursery beds and transplanted to the growing site. Seedlings can be thinned to about 12" apart. Late in the season it is the custom in many gardens to let the jute plants produce their bright yellow flowers and set seeds that can be harvested for the next season's crop.

Tree kale, *Brassica oleraceae*
Cabbage family, *Brassicaceae (Cruciferae)*
Perennial often reaching 2 m (6 ft) or more

Value as a food source	9
Value as an ornamental	4
Multi-purpose	no
Continuous harvest	yes
Ease of culture	7
Overall rating	****

We think of the cabbage family as cool season crops for the temperate regions, but tree kale is at home in the tropics. This cousin to the famous European walking stick cabbage could be a significant addition to the diet in hot humid climates. This is a weird, some might even say ugly, looking plant that will grow 1-1.5 m (3-5 ft) tall with a palm like cluster of leaves at the top. Left to its own devices it tends to fall over, root at the old leaf nodes and form a row of new shoots. It's propagated from cuttings. Spacing the plants 2 ft apart works well. A surface mulch controls weeds and encourages healthier roots.

Here is a dooryard vegetable that thrives in almost any soil, as long as it's well drained. Naturally, it does best in compost rich, slightly acid soil. Full sun is good but the best tasting leaves are produced in light shade. Because tree kale is a perennial it can be a constant year long salad bar source for several years, then the stalk is either cut into sections or simply laid over and allowed to root.

Eight to ten tree kale plants can keep a family in greens all year. Production can be increased by inter-planting with beans or other legumes to provide nitrogen to the soil and fruit trees to provide shade.

The young leaves can be eaten raw in a salad, cut into soups, stews and stir-fries. The more mature leaves can be used as a wrap for other foods, much like stuffed cabbage. This is a nutritious food that may contain natural cancer preventing phytochemicals.

Uncommon Leaf and Flower Crops for Temperate Regions

Alpine dock, *Rumex alpinus*
Buckwheat family, *Polygonaceae*
Also known as Monk's rhubarb, mountain rhubarb, Pyrenean sorrel and sorrel
Perennial reaching about 1 m (3 ft) in height and almost as wide
Native to Eurasia

Value as a food source	6
Value as an ornamental	3
Multi-purpose	yes
Continuous harvest	yes
Ease of culture	8
Overall rating	***

This is an acceptable addition to the winter salad in mild regions and it makes an effective cooked green. The leaves will stay green throughout the winter in temperate areas where the cold isn't prolonged or severe. In the cool months the bitterness isn't as dominant and the leaves can add some lemon-tart flavor to a fresh salad. Unfortunately, the leaves get quite bitter in the summer, and must be cooked to be palatable. If you discard the first water after bringing them to a boil, much of the strong taste is eliminated. One source suggests adding onion greens during the cooking process to compliment the flavor of these cooked greens. They can be mixed with other spring greens to make a delightful salad. The leaves can be added to soups, stews, stir-fries and boiled vegetables to enhance the flavor. One old recipe recommends using the leaves to wrap shredded pork and slices of potato or turnip, then baking them. In earlier times the leaves were harvested when the flavor was best and dried for later use. Leaves do contain oxalic acid, as does spinach and rhubarb, so they should be consumed in moderation.

This is an easily grown perennial that thrives in almost any soil, but flavor is best in a compost rich, well-drained soil that is kept evenly moist. A sunny location is preferred, but it will accept light shade. In the summer when the leaves are bitter there are several species of butterflies that use the plant as a larval food.

This Alpine dock is easily grown from seeds sown in early spring. They are also started from divisions taken at any time during the growing season. Cousin *Rumex acetosa* has lemon like flavor and tolerates more winter weather without going dormant.

Bellflower, *Campanula versicolor*
Bellflower family, *Campanulaceae*
Also known as Harebell
Perennial evergreen growing about 1 m (3 ft) tall
Native to Eurasia

Value as a food source	7
Value as an ornamental	8
Multi-purpose	yes
Continuous harvest	yes
Ease of culture	7
Overall rating	***

It's always fun when we can grow beautiful flowers and then use the plants on the dinner table. Well, this is one of those beautiful flowering plants. It produces a rosette of leaves that stay green all winter and can be harvested as needed in mild temperate regions. This is a delicious sweet flavored salad green that some liken to sweet peas. The flowers are also edible; in fact, they are delicious and really brighten a salad. Both the flowers and the leaves are rich in vitamin C. The leaves can be eaten raw or cooked. The fleshy roots are also used raw as a snack or salad addition

Not reliably cold hardy beyond USDA zone 6, it prefers well-drained slightly acid soil and a lightly shaded area. A related variety, *Campanula persicifolia*, has narrow leaves that are just as tasty but will take more cold weather. You can also grow and dine on most ornamental varieties.

All are relatively easy to start from seed sown lightly and barely covered in a greenhouse or cold frame, then set out in their permanent home after frost danger is past. They can also be started from stem divisions with some roots attached.

Chicory, *Cichorium intybus*
Daisy family, *Asteraceae (Compositae)*
Also known as Wild chicory, endive, radicchio, blue sailors, blue wedgewort
Perennial growing from 1 to 1.5 m (3 to 5 feet) in height
Native to Eurasia

Value as a food source	7
Value as an ornamental	7
Multi-purpose	yes
Continuous harvest	yes
Ease of culture	9
Overall rating	***

The leaves are somewhat bitter, but when young make a flavorfully tart addition to a fresh salad. Both young and mature leaves can be steamed, boiled, or used in soups, stews and mixed vegetable dishes. It is common practice in some areas to blanch the stems and leaves to produce a more tender and succulent vegetable. Some of the wide-leaf forms are used to wrap meat, rice or vegetables for baking or roasting. The ruggedly attractive blue flowers are used raw in salads, served as a garnish and pickled in vinegars and oils. The roots can be peeled, sliced and boiled, sauteed or baked as a vegetable. These roots can also be roasted to make a coffee substitute. This was a common coffee additive during WWII, and the practice continues in the Southern United States and many other countries today. In some parts of the Mediterranean a chewing gum base is made from the milky sap.

There are many cultivars available, some with superior sweet leaves that form heads, such as *Jupiter* and *Sugarloaf*. Others, like *Catalogna* are grown for the leaf stems and flower stalks. *Red chicory* is a popular gourmet vegetable often called radicchio. Others are grown for the fleshy roots, while Witloof chicory, or Belgian endive, is a popular forced, blanched leaf crop with a distinctive aromatic quality. The naming becomes confusing because there is a great deal of mislabeling and multitude of local choice varieties. Many of these are heirloom cultivars well worth saving. In temperate regions this is an important ingredient in a winter salad.

The basic chicory has made itself at home throughout most of North America, where it is now considered a wildflower. In enjoys a variety of soils from sand to clay and very acid to highly alkaline. It does prefer full sun and a well-drained site. This is an easy plant to start from seed sown lightly and barely covered where it is to grow, or in seeding flats and transplanted. It can be grown as an annual or a perennial. If you are growing it for the roots, they are sweetest after the first season. After three years they tend to become woody and bitter. Bees and butterflies enjoy the perky blue flowers as much as we do.

Corn salad, *Valerianella locusta*
Valerian family, *Valerianaceae*
Also known as lamb's lettuce, winter lettuce, nut lettuce, fetticus, mache
Annual with mild tasting leaves
Native to Eurasia

Value as a food source	6
Value as an ornamental	3
Multi-purpose	no
Continuous harvest	yes
Ease of culture	8
Overall rating	***

This is a delightfully easy salad green to grow in temperate regions. The mild flavored, tender textured leaves can be harvested continuously throughout the cool months for salads and sandwiches. The raw leaves, flowers and flower stalks make a pleasant and nutritious addition to a wide variety of salads, including potato salad, and complements spinach, dandelion, or Oriental cabbages. The leaves are used to enhance soups, stews, omelettes and cooked vegetables. Not only is corn salad easy to grow, it's highly nutritious as well. It contains 30% more iron than spinach. It was viewed throughout Europe as a 'spring medicine.'

The French have traditionally enjoyed the fine flavor of this rugged vegetable and it has been known by a number of names there, including; *salade de Pretre* because of its prominence in the Lenten diet, *loblollie, doucette, salade de chanoine*.

Most varieties will grow about .3 m (12 inches) tall with a cluster of small greenish flowers at the top of the stalk. The leaves can be harvested individually or entire plants removed from the growing bed, making the harvest a part of the thinning process. The leaves are relatively short lived on the plant so frequently gathering the bottom leaves doesn't impede growth.

This is a winter hardy plant for temperate regions where it will continue to grow under snow or a mulch. It isn't at its best in the hot humid weather of tropical and sub-tropical areas, but as a fast growing autumn through spring crop it's great. Corn salad is so easy to grow that if one or two plants are allowed to flower and go to seed, you have a permanent bed of this carefree vegetable. Some varieties are harvested as 'baby corn' and harvesting can begin in less than six weeks from sowing. Others have large leaves, narrow leaves, spoon shaped leaves, and a variety of shades of green.

All varieties of corn salad are easily grown from seed sown lightly and barely covered. Germination will occur within two weeks and growth is rapid. Compost rich well-drained soil is best, and productivity and quality can be guaranteed when the plants are kept evenly moist. They like full sun but will do quite well in light shade.

Dandelion, *Taraxacum officinale*
Daisy family, *Asteraceae (Compositae)*
Also known as pissenlit, pissabed, priest's crown, swine's snout and radicchiello
Flowering perennial for temperate regions
Native to Europe

Value as a food source	7
Value as an ornamental	8
Multi-purpose	yes
Continuous harvest	yes
Ease of culture	9
Overall rating	****

Pity the poor maligned dandelion, abused because it is so willing to grow for us. What other plant conjures so many childhood memories as does this one, the universal natural toy. We could make chains of the flower stems, make yellow pollen tattoos, shoot floral missiles at unsuspecting friends and launch a multitude of miniature parachutes in one breath. Yet, as a nation, we spend more money trying to eradicate this valuable resource from our lawns than we do to eradicate hunger all over the world. Why would we wage this irrational war to protect a turf that is unfit for human consumption, expensive to maintain and environmentally unsound, not to mention exceedingly labor intensive?

Let's look for a moment at just how valuable the dandelion really is. The fresh spring leaves can be harvested for use raw in salads or as a cooked potherb. The flower buds can be used in a stir-fry, in pancakes, omelettes, fritters, soups and stews. The buds and partially opened flowers can be made into dandelion soup with a cream or cheese sauce. The opened flowers are used in the delightful Arabian cake called *yublo*. The open flowers can be steeped to make a liquid for dandelion jam or dandelion sweet sauce that can be used as a topping for ice cream or shaved ice. The flowers also make a fine wine. Even the seeds, when sprouted, are a nutritious addition to a salad or a flavorful garnish for almost any dish. The pollen is even used as a safe, 100% organic food coloring. The fine dining doesn't stop there because the roots are also valuable diced raw in a salad, grated and added to soups and stews or roasted and ground as a coffee substitute. The roots and leaves can be dried and used to make a tea as well.

This is, as you may have guessed, an easy vegetable to grow in almost any soil. It will tolerate full sun or medium shade, drought or moist sites and thrives on neglect. The plants are usually started from seed sown where they are to grow or in flats to be transplanted at your convenience. One old text recommended tying the leaves of the rosette to blanch the tender inner leaves. Mature leaves can be boiled, the first water discarded, then brought to a boil a second time to eliminate some of the bitterness that is a part of the late season crop.

Dittander, *Lepidium latifolium*
Cabbage family, *Brassicaceae (Cruciferae)*
Also known as Pepperweed, pepperwort, perennial pepperweed, lepidio
Perennial forming a mound approximately 1 m (3 feet) in diameter
Native to Europe

Value as a food source	7
Value as an ornamental	5
Multi-purpose	yes
Continuous harvest	yes
Ease of culture	10
Overall rating	***

This is one of the vegetable/herbs grown and enjoyed in ancient Greece and Rome. In your garden you can experience a bit of history. The leaves are extremely pungent with a super-cress hotness. The young leaves do make a great addition to a salad when used in moderation. Mature leaves can also be added to soups, stews, sauces, mixed greens, stir-fries, baked potatoes, sandwiches and meats. These leaves can also be used anywhere you might use horseradish. The roots are even grated and used as horseradish. The flowers are used as a seasoning and the seeds are frequently used as a condiment or cooking spice. So potent is this plant that a tea brewed from the leaves, stems and trimmings can be used as an insect repellent in the garden.

This is such an easy plant to grow that it is considered an unwelcome invasive in some areas. It spreads both from seed and an aggressive root system. It thrives in sun or shade in a variety of soils. It's even salt tolerant. The only thing that will stop it is drought. It does need to be kept evenly moist. It can be started from seeds sown in flats and transplanted when they have 4 to 6 leaves, or from root divisions taken any time of the year. It has been used as an edible ground cover in shady areas.

Garlic cress, *Peltaria alliacea*
Cabbage family, *Brassicaceae (Cruciferae)*
Perennial growing about .3 m (1 ft) in height
Native to Eurasia

Value as a food source	5
Value as an ornamental	5
Multi-purpose	no
Continuous harvest	yes
Ease of culture	8
Overall rating	***

The leaves have a strong garlic/mustard flavor that brightens up a commonplace salad. They can be eaten raw or cooked and can be harvested even during the winter. In fact, they become somewhat bitter during the heat of summer, particularly if they are allowed to dry out. The flowers are milder and quite tasty. This plant is creeping perennial that will slowly become an effective ground cover for temperate zones.

www.globalgardening.info

It's easily started from seed sown either spring or autumn in a seeding tray or bed, then transplanted as they grow 4 to 6 leaves. They can also be propagated from divisions. Garlic cress likes to grow in a light, fertile, moist soil, in full sun or light shade. This is a very easy vegetable to grow. In fact it thrives on neglect, best crop produced from autumn to late spring, ideal winter salad crop.

Warning, this plant does produce a garlic like scent, that stays on your hands after handling. The plus is that this does tend to discourage mosquitoes, fleas, door to door salespeople, and unwanted suitors.

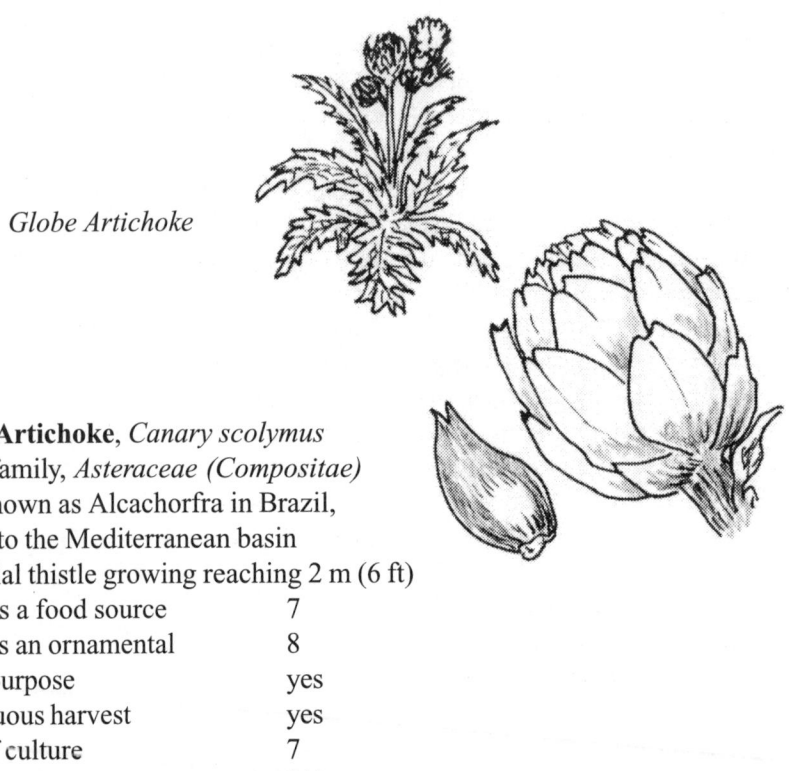

Globe Artichoke

Globe Artichoke, *Canary scolymus*
Daisy family, *Asteraceae (Compositae)*
Also known as Alcachorfra in Brazil,
Native to the Mediterranean basin
Perennial thistle growing reaching 2 m (6 ft)

Value as a food source	7
Value as an ornamental	8
Multi-purpose	yes
Continuous harvest	yes
Ease of culture	7
Overall rating	***

This is an ancient vegetable with edible flower buds. The Egyptians were enjoying the spiny flower buds over 6000 years ago. The Greeks and Romans enjoyed this gourmet food during their classic periods, and the Romans carried them throughout Europe. It wasn't valued only for the ceremonial consumption of the flower buds, but for the medicinal value of extracts from the leaves. This continues to be viewed as a cure for liver and gall bladder ailments as well as snake bite, diabetes, rheumatism and hypertension in many parts of the world.

While some enjoy the flavor of the raw buds and stems, they are usually cooked, but only certain parts of the large thistle bud are edible. They are harvested before their buds open and are boiled, baked or steamed. Only the base of each scale of the flower bud is eaten along with the base, called the 'choke' or heart. The flavor is enhanced when the scale is dipped in melted butter. They are a great companion to lightly steamed mushrooms. This is one of the ritual foods of the Mediterranean region. The very small buds can be pickled, steamed, stir-fried, baked or added to soups and stews. The succulent bud stems can be peeled and eaten raw or added to almost any cooked dish. The raw flavor is pleasantly sweet. Young leaves can be cooked as a potherb but the flavor is somewhat bitter. The leaf stems are also bitter but can be blanched, boiled or steamed. The flavor is great in a saute of mushrooms and young onions.

There has been a long history of use as a medicinal herb. The artichoke leaves have recently been found to possess anti-cholesterol properties and may be of value in treating early-onset diabetes. The leaves were a traditional source for a dark (Lincoln) green dye. The large thistle like flowers were dried and used to curdle milk for cheese making. These beautiful flowers are also popular with a multitude of butterflies.

This is a relatively easy perennial vegetable to grow. All it asks is a place in the sun and some well-drained, compost rich soil. It's even salt tolerant and makes a valuable addition to the coastal garden. It grows best in cooler climates but new varieties have been developed that adapt well to sub-tropical areas like south Florida. In areas of harsh winters there are varieties that can be treated as annuals. *Grande Beurre* is one that produces well as an annual. Seeds started early in a greenhouse or seed flat will germinate within a week and are ready to set out in their permanent home in about 8 weeks. The growing plant also produces suckers that can be divided throughout the growing season and planted in their permanent location.

Good King Henry, *Chenopodium bonus-henricus*

Goosefoot family, *Chenopodiaceae*
Also known as Lincolnshire asparagus, Mercury, smearweed, fat hen, fette henne (German) and allgood
Perennial growing about .6 m (2 feet) in height
Native to Eurasia

Value as a food source	7
Value as an ornamental	5
Multi-purpose	yes
Continuous harvest	yes
Ease of culture	9
Overall rating	***

Let's dispel a myth before we explore this plant. It wasn't named after any of England's kings; the common name 'Good King Henry' is from Germanic mythology. *Henricus* referred to the elves, and the 'Good Henry' was applied to this plant and 'Bad Henry,' *Malus Henricus*, referred to some probably toxic plant whose identity is lost to the ages. The old name *smearwort* refers to the use of leaves in poultices and ointments smeared on minor wounds. In Germany the plant was used as poultry food, hence the name *fette henne*.

This is a vegetable that, unfortunately, has fallen out of favor. But it's steeped in tradition and extremely easy to grow. The young leaves are gathered for use raw in salads or cooked as a potherb. The flavor is rather bland but nutritious. The succulent stems can be harvested after the first year, when about 6 inches tall, boiled and eaten like asparagus. If they are fibrous they will need to be peeled before eating. The seeds can be harvested and used in baking or added to soups. Seeds can also be sprouted and used as an addition to a fresh salad.

Seeds sown in spring will germinate in about 7 to 14 days and grow quickly so that leaves can be harvested in 6 to 8 weeks. They do best in a compost rich well-drained soil, with full sun and regular watering. Like most chenopodiums, Good King Henry thrives in a slightly to moderately alkaline soil.

Kankar, *Gundelia tournefortii*
Daisy family, *Asteraceae (Compositae)* closely allied to the thistle
Also known as *akkub* or *kardi,* and referred to as *silybum* by Dioscorides
Usually grows less than 1 m (3 ft) tall, forming a tumbleweed mound
Native to Near East & Mediterranean

Value as a food source	7
Value as an ornamental	8
Multi-purpose	yes
Continuous harvest	yes
Ease of culture	8
Overall rating	***

Imagine a cross between artichokes and asparagus on a plant that looks like a thistle. That's what you get with this perennial vegetable that is drought tolerant and generally rugged. These flower buds and stems can be steamed, fried in butter or roasted. The multiple harvest potential makes this an extremely versatile vegetable that yields a dramatic palate of flavors. The leaves can be cooked as a potherb, the fleshy roots are valued as a cooked vegetable producing a flavor somewhat like salsify. The seeds can be cooked like rice or toasted and enjoyed as a snack, but the real treat is in the immature flower buds and their stems. The stems and heads are gathered, the thorns at the base of the bud are removed, then they are fried with chopped meats and choice herbs. Some experts claim this is the plant that Christ's crown of thorns was made from. Numerous pollen grains from this plant's flowers were recovered from the Shroud of Turin.

This is a perennial that is easily propagated from seed or divisions. Seed is best started under cover and transplanted to the permanent growing site when they are hardy little plants. Kankar thrives in a sandy, compost enriched soil in a well-drained site. The leaves can be harvested throughout the warm months. A continuous harvest after the flower buds start to form will keep more buds coming.

Warning. In some locations this plant might become an invasive pest.

Lamb's quarters

Lamb's quarters, *Chenopodium album*
Goosefoot family, *Chenopodiaceae*
Also known as white goosefoot, fat hen
Annual growing .3 to 1 m (1 to 3 feet) tall
Native to Eurasia, naturalized throughout North America

Value as a food source	8
Value as an ornamental	5
Multi-purpose	yes
Continuous harvest	yes
Ease of culture	9
Overall rating	***

This traditional European edible weed is closely related to the Mexican epazote, *C. Ambrosioides* and the old-fashioned vegetable, Good King Henry, *C. Bonus-henricus*. Early in the growing season the entire plant is tender, succulent and tasty, late in the season the stalks become fibrous and only the leaves are harvested.

www.globalgardening.info

The flavor remains mild throughout the growing season and the leaves remain a delightful and nutritious addition to salads or cooked greens until a frost brings a halt to production. This plant is in the same family as spinach and can be used in much the same way; in fact it tastes like a mild spinach. It's a good source of dietary fiber and is high in vitamins A & C, as well as iron.

As with spinach there is a warning; don't over feed with fertilizers. The plant stores surplus nitrogen compounds in its leaves in the form of nitrates. The more chemical fertilizers you apply, the greater the risk of making the leaves toxic. Oxalic acid is also stored in the leaves. This is true of spinach also. For this reason both greens should be eaten in moderation, and when consumed as a part of a varied and balanced meal they continue to be a healthy, nutritious vegetable.

As the days begin to shorten the flower stalks are produced with greater urgency and the thousands of tiny black seeds quickly mature. Each plant will produce tens of thousands of these seeds, each in a miniature plain brown wrapper. You can collect the seed heads after a frost and winnow the seeds from the papery chaff. The seeds are a rich source of protein, phosphorous, calcium, potassium and niacin. These cleaned seeds can be added to baking as you would poppy seeds, or ground into a coarse powder and added directly to the wheat flour to make a 'dark bread.' The seeds are also delicious and tasty as a sprout. The sprouts are reddish colored and make a great addition to a winter salad, sprinkled on baked potatoes or added to soups. The seeds can also be added to wildbird seed.

This is one of those vegetables that thrives in almost any soil, in full sun or light shade, as long as the site is well-drained. Avoid the temptation to apply chemical fertilizers. A regular watering during periods of drought is helpful. There are few insect and disease problems to contend with. This is really a weed with flavor. It was brought to the colonies of North America as a potherb and literally raced the colonists across the continent.

They are easily started from seed sown lightly and barely covered. Because they grow quickly in the warmth of the spring sun, harvesting can begin in about six weeks. As the plants grow, don't hesitate to gather the terminal shoots. They're great in a salad. This will make the plant bushy and increase the production of tender new leaves.

French Scorzonera, *Reichardia picroides*
Daisy family, *Asteraceae (Compositae)*
Also known as brighteyes, black salsify, oyster plant, viper's grass and serpentroot
Perennial with leaves reaching .6 m (2 ft) and flower stalks growing slighter taller
Native to mild areas of Europe

Value as a food source	6
Value as an ornamental	5
Multi-purpose	yes
Continuous harvest	yes
Ease of culture	6
Overall rating	****

    This ancient European vegetable has lost favor with both gardeners and diners today, which is unfortunate because it is an easy to grow perennial crop that can provide a harvest over a long period of time. It looks like a dandelion with milder, almost sweet leaves. It's easier to grow than lettuce, as well as being more flavorful and nutritious. Even mature leaves are mild and tender in a salad, or the leaves can also be cooked as you would any other potherb. This is a multi-purpose plant with a delicious bonus. The roots can be peeled and used either cooked or raw, but when eaten raw they have a somewhat bitter taste. These roots are peeled to remove the black outer covering. The flesh can then be used in soups, stir-fries, or mashed.

    This plant is easily started from seed sown in seed flats in early spring and transplanted to the growing beds when they have 4 to 6 leaves. Or you can sow in the permanent bed. This is suitable for a continuous harvest that can begin in about 6 to 8 weeks. Big advantage is that slugs don't like it. Scorzonera grows best in a semi-shady location with well drained, compost rich soil. Once established it is drought tolerant, but prolonged dry spells can reduce the crop. While in many areas it's an effective cool season vegetable, it doesn't tolerate severe winter weather. It will yield continuously in mild areas for 18 to 24 months or more. This is an heirloom vegetable for temperate climates that should be found in more gardens.

Salsify, *Tragopogon porrifolius*
Daisy family, *Asteraceae (Compositae)*
Also known as oyster plant or vegetable oyster
Biennial reaching about 2 ft in height with yellow flowers
Native to the Mediterranean

Value as a food source	7
Value as an ornamental	6
Multi-purpose	yes
Continuous harvest	yes
Ease of culture	9
Overall rating	****

What a delightful and under planted vegetable. This is one of the European multi-purpose plants that we should grow far more often because it gives us so many options, not to mention that this is a "survivor" vegetable that thrives on neglect and abuse.

We traditionally dine on the oyster-flavored roots, either raw in salads or sauteed, baked, stir-fried, even added to soups and stews. These roots can be grated and pressed into cakes that can be baked or deep-fried for a delightfully different flavor. The young shoots, flower buds and flowers can be eaten raw in salads; the flower stalks can be prepared like asparagus. The flower buds can be pickled and used as a flavorful condiment, the flowers can be fermented into a fair "dandelion wine." The milky sap can be partially dried and flavored with fruit or berries, then enjoyed like chewing gum. The seeds can be sprouted and added to a salad.

The goats-beard, an alien wild flower found throughout much of the United States, is a cousin to the domesticated salsify and can be used the same way. There are bonuses with this versatile plant beyond the dinner table. The seed head is a delight for children of all ages with its intricate parachutes. This is a beautiful plant that can grace the flower bed as well as the garden, where it will produce cheerful yellow flowers throughout the warm months.

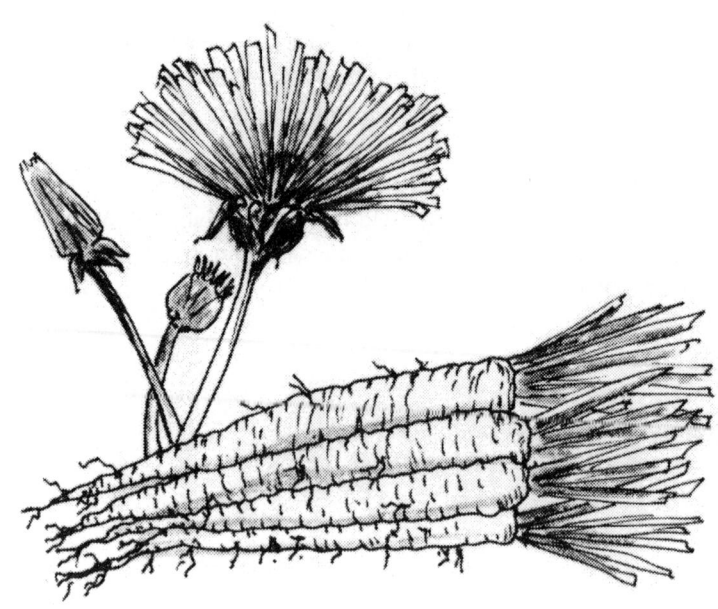

Chapter Five
Treetop Garden

"Don't be afraid to go out on a limb. That's where the fruit is."
Anon

    The European-American gardening style focuses on short term or annual vegetables. Seeds are sown in the spring and after a few weeks or months we harvest and the cycle is completed. In the tropics the leaves of many trees and shrubs are better crops to be served on the salad bar. These are plants that provide a continuous harvest. Continuous production makes these plants valuable as a food source, but the fact that they are perennial makes them labor efficient and environmentally sound. Many of these edible trees and shrubs are legumes that help to build or replenish the soil. All are multi-purpose and provide fruit, medicines, fuelwood, livestock fodder or other non-food crops. Often these trees can serve as a living fence, privacy screen, erosion control, shade for crops like the Madre de Cacao (*Glircidia siliqua*) that is traditionally used to shade the chocolate plants. Even the *Leucaena leucocephala*, that most popular of alley cropping legumes produces leaves that can be eaten in modest quantities if necessary as a famine food.

    Among the trees that serve as a minor or emergency food source are a number of acacias, some cassias, orchid trees (*Bauhinia sp.*), The carob, also known as St. John's bread, is valued for its edible leaves as well as the seed pods that provide a chocolate substitute. Because of the efficiency, productivity and multiple benefits, these plants deserve a far greater application and researchers are busy developing the best varieties and growing techniques.

    Most of the following trees and shrubs are best suited to tropical or sub-tropical regions, but they can be grown as container plants and wintered over indoors or in a greenhouse in colder regions. Because they are usually kept trimmed to a height of 2 m (6 ft) or less the average sunroom or even bay window will accommodate them.

Australian grasstree, *Xanthorrhoea australis*
Grasstree family, *Xanthorroeaceae*
Perennial branched plant reaching 1 to 2 m or more in height
Australian native

Value as a food source	4
Value as an ornamental	9
Multi-purpose	yes
Continuous harvest	no
Ease of culture	3
Overall rating	**

Some plants are the dynamic stuff of lore and legend and these natural scarecrows hold a special place in the history, religion and culture of the Aborigine population. Not only is there a traditional spiritual connection with this dramatic plant, it has a unique history of its own. With arms lifted toward the sky they stoically withstand drought, plagues of insects, the poorest of soils and any other challenge nature can deliver. Brush fires trigger the bloom cycle in these tough guys of the outback.

As an edible it takes some effort to secure a meal but it offers a variety of foods. The soft pithy inner stems can be eaten raw or cooked. The flavor is somewhere between nutty and pine. This stem can be used as a source of sweet sap. The base of the leaf has a sweet to tart flavor. The tough serrate leaf itself can be used as a knife. The flowers produce great quantities of sweet nectar that was traditionally collected with bark sponges. These flowers can also be harvested and cooked to produce a thick honey-like syrup. The roots have been eaten on occasion but not considered a choice food. The dried flower stalks are tough and sometimes gathered for use as spears, but the real advantage is the large shrimp shaped grub that is found at the base of the dead flower stalk. The plant also produces knots of sap/resin that the natives used as a cement.

This is a rugged, determined plant, but it doesn't adapt well to high humidity or wet feet. It thrives in poor well-drained soils in a sunny location. This isn't a plant for frost prone areas. It can be started from seed, which may take months to germinate and tends to rot if kept too moist. A friend's success with this came when the seed was planted in the cactus garden and forgotten. They thrive on neglect and grow slowly, so this cannot be considered a significant garden vegetable, but it is a fascinating plant for the collector.

Bamboo, *Phyllostachys dulcis* and a large number of others
Bamboo family, *Bambusaceae*
Woody stemmed perennial

Value as a food source	7
Value as an ornamental	8
Multi-purpose	yes
Continuous harvest	yes
Ease of culture	9
Overall rating	****

This is far more than panda food. Few plants are used in so many ways. The tender shoots are a valuable food source in Asia, Africa and parts of the Americas, but the stems are used as a building material, utensils, water pipes, weapons, tools, fuel, fencing, irrigation, plant supports and so much more.

Bamboo shoots as a part of dinner come from a tremendous number of different species, each ideally suited for its region, climate and conditions. Most bamboo spread from underground roots, or rhizomes, that serve as erosion control.

Unfortunately, they often become invasive as they enthusiastically seek to claim new territory. The young shoots (soon to become the jointed stems called culms so typical of bamboo) are the parts usually harvested for the dinner table. This is usually done when they are beginning to emerge from the soil. For many varieties soil is mounded around the base of the plants, much as celery is blanched, to keep the sunlight from the sprouts. This gives them a far sweeter flavor and encourages tenderness.

When the shoots are harvested they somewhat resemble ears of corn. The outer husk, or sheath and the woody base is removed and used as fuel or compost. The remaining tender parts can be cut into thin slices and prepared in a multitude of ways. Some varieties are sweet and tender, so they can be used raw in salads or eaten as a snack food. Some require a brief steaming to make them palatable. Still others may need to be boiled for 20 to 30 minutes, with the water changed once or twice, to remove the bitterness and make them tender enough to eat.

Bamboo shoots can be pickled, salted, fermented, canned, smoked or dried. They can also be used in salads, soups, stews, stir-fries, as a side dish or prepared like potato chips and eaten as a snack food. The sap of many species can be collected and used as a sweetener or fermented into an alcoholic beverage. Some bamboo rarely produce seeds and when they do this completes their life cycle and they die. This can be so widespread as to cause starvation among pandas and other animals that depend on them as a food source. Other species of bamboo flower regularly and the seeds are harvested and roasted as a snack or brewed into a coffee substitute.

Almost all edible varieties of bamboos are started from root divisions. These segments of root, or divisions of plants with growing culms are planted at the proper depth for that variety and kept moist while they are becoming established. Cultural needs can vary greatly with the variety being grown. Some require constant moisture, some are very cold sensitive, some will need to be tightly controlled so they don't invade regions of the landscape where they are unwelcome. Because there is so much diversity within this fascinating group of plants we recommend that you consult a text devoted to bamboo before selecting and cultivating them.

Baobab, *Adansonia digitata* and seven other species
Balsa wood family, *Bombacaceae*
Also known as the upside-down tree
Native to Africa, the Malagasy Republic and Australia

Value as a food source	10
Value as an ornamental	10
Multi-purpose	yes
Continuous harvest	yes
Ease of culture	6
Overall rating	****

In the ageless markets of Cairo this dramatic tree is known as *bu hobab*. This may have been from the Arabic *bu hibab* which can be translated as "a many seeded fruit." What a tree this is. Baobabs look like a science fiction writer's wildest fantasy. It defies the imaginations of Lewis Carroll and Jules Verne. It looks like it's growing upside down because for much of the year it doesn't do leaves. The obscenely obese trunk holds so much moisture that the trees have been used as a water supply. They have been hollowed out to serve as shelters, jails and storage pantries. Because of the way it grows there aren't annual rings to determine age and the largest trees may simply be closer to a reliable water source. The oldest living baobab is at least 1,000 years old.

There are eight species and all of them live in the most inhospitable of climates where drought and desert are the norm. Yet some of these are endangered because of development, mining and agriculture. Especially those in the Malagasy Republic. This tree is related to some of the great trees of commerce, the kapok, balsa wood and the foulest smelling of all fruits, the durian. Many of these have beautiful flowers and the baobab is no exception.

It's only natural that such a bizarre looking tree would be the subject of myths, legends, and folk tales. G. E. Wickens, in *The Baobab: Africa's Upside-Down Tree* (a Kew Gardens Bulletin), describes a number of these such as the following. It seems that the Creator, when planting the first global garden, placed the baobab in the Congo Basin. The tree complained that it was too wet there. Then the Creator transplanted it to the mountainsides of the Ruwenzori Range. There the baobab complained about the excessive humidity from living in the clouds. Finally, angered by the tree's constant whining, the Creator seized it and threw it as far as possible. The baobab landed upside-down in dry plains of Africa, and there it has remained until this very day.

In the Transvaal baby boys are washed in a decoction of baobab bark so that they will grow up mighty and strong, just like the tree itself. In other areas the trees are considered the home of the spirit people and offerings are left to guarantee good fortune or a good harvest. Few plants offer as much individuality as the baobab. Even within a single species there will be variations in trunk, branch pattern, leaf form, season of defoliation, color and shape of flowers, size and shape of the gourd-like fruit.

Few tropical plants are as multiple-tasking as the baobab. David Livingston described a tree in Mozambique that was hollowed out to serve as shelter for an entire family. Cavities can be cut into the trunk to serve as water storage. Baobabs can be stripped of their bark and in a few months grow it anew. This is a good feature for the tree because the bark yields a fiber used to make everything from rope, clothing and hats to strings for musical instruments. Even the pollen is used to make a rather effective glue. Almost every part of the tree is used medicinally in one way or another to treat everything from a fever to asthma and kidney disease.

The nocturnal flowers are striking and overpowering in their fragrance. Some species are pollinated by bats, one species employs lemurs and the Australian species use moths. The flowers are valued as a food source even though there are superstitions in some areas that eating the flower will provoke an attack by lions.

The leaves are edible and tasty both raw as a salad or cooked as a potherb. I have tried these and when young the flavor is subtle and delightful. As they mature they become more bitter and fibrous. The fruit is also eaten and the seeds are used to produce a condiment valued in African cooking as a meat tenderizer.

The baobab isn't for the average backyard, but they can be grown as container plants or trained as a rather unusual bonsai. In frost free areas where there is good drainage they will thrive with little care. They start easily from fresh seed and after the first year leaves can be harvested for your dining pleasure. On a global scale several species may well depend on collectors, botanical gardens and global gardeners for their survival.

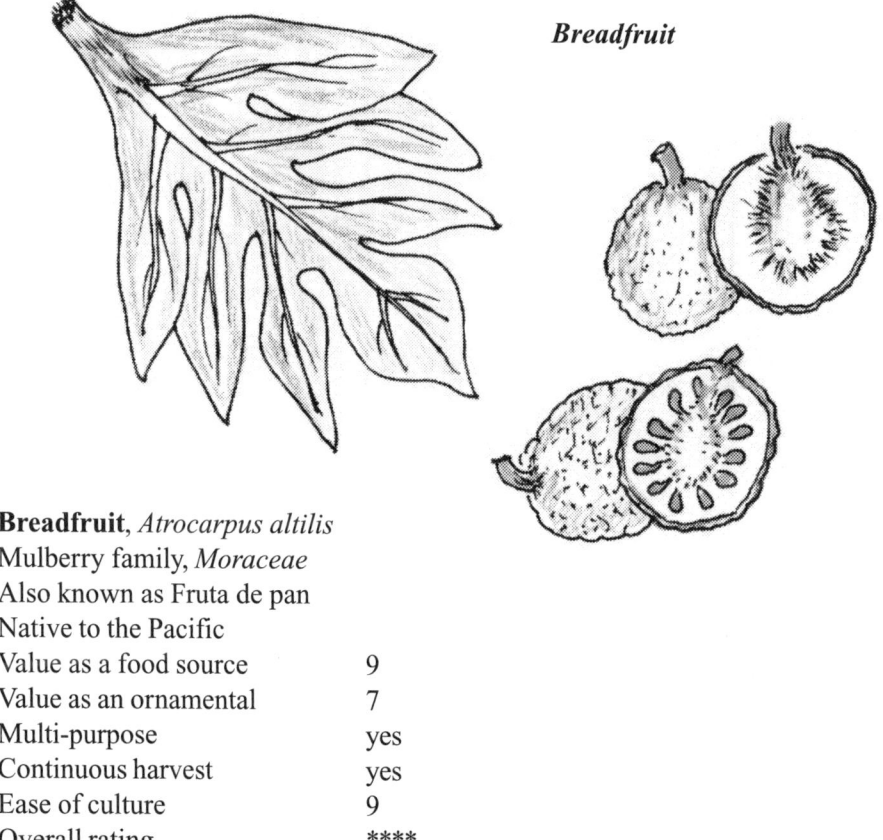

Breadfruit

Breadfruit, *Atrocarpus altilis*
Mulberry family, *Moraceae*
Also known as Fruta de pan
Native to the Pacific

Value as a food source	9
Value as an ornamental	7
Multi-purpose	yes
Continuous harvest	yes
Ease of culture	9
Overall rating	****

Breadfruit, is a legend in its own clime. Have you ever eaten breadfruit? This is one of those tropical fruits that can become lunch at almost any stage of maturity. Ripe it is treated as a fruit, before it is fully ripe it can be used as a vegetable. This oversized fruit can be prepared so many ways it has been called the equatorial equivalent of the potato. There are many varieties of breadfruit, some are seedless while others produce a large edible seed. The seeded varieties are considered more nutritious. Once they start bearing they produce fruit almost constantly, yielding a harvest of between 50 to 200 fruit per year.

Ripe fruit can be baked whole in a large pan with a little water for one to two hours. The traditional method of baking was to place in a pit of hot coals or heated stones, you can use the oven. The core can be removed and the cavity filled with butter and coconut, or salt and pepper. In the Philippines they enjoy the fruit cooked with coconut and sugar. In Malaysia peeled fruits are sliced and fried in palm sugar until crisp. The pulp can be scraped or shredded and mixed with coconut, sugar and milk to make a pudding. Other versions of this can include eggs, cinnamon, rosewater, rum, allspice or nutmeg. The flesh can also be pickled or candied. In some areas of the Pacific the flesh is soaked in sea water for several days, mashed or baked, then wrapped in banana leaves to ferment. This process ultimately produces a pasty substance called *masi*. The fermentation process can take a year or more.

Unripe breadfruit, peeled and diced, can be cooked in the stewpot or used to make breadfruit soup. This is the favorite way to eat green breadfruit in the Caribbean. Cooking sherry, brandy or rum can be added to taste. In Hawaii breadfruit chowder is a favorite. This is made by adding milk, bacon and any available vegetables. Green or ripe breadfruit can be sliced, dipped in flour or batter and fried. In fact the fruit can be eaten almost any way you would eat potatoes, eggplant, or apples, except that they should not be eaten raw.

In the good old days poi was made by filling a pit lined with banana or ti plant leaves with peeled and washed fruit. After a couple of years it was ready. Today the fruit is cooked, sliced, hammered into a paste and strained through a cloth. It can be combined with taro to increase the nutritional value of the poi. The ripe fruit can be sliced and dried to be ground into flour or fried as chips.

ULU is what the Hawaiians called this dramatic tree and its 10 pound fruit. This is one of those trees of myth and legend, its past is deeply entwined with the history of people throughout the tropics. As the courageous Polynesian explorers traveled from island to island throughout the Pacific this was one of the twenty-four plants they carried with them as their survival kit. These plants were collectively known as the "Canoe Plants." Many of these plants had more than merely food value. Breadfruit was the symbol of immortality, and the official fruit of the god *Hawaii Nei*. Because of the productivity and nutritional value of this fruit it was known as the "Polynesian staff of life."

Many other parts of this beautiful and exotic tree continues to be valued in the Pacific as a source for medicines. Leaves have been used to lower blood pressure and cure sore throat. The flowers are used to relieve toothache and gum inflammation. The milky latex sap has been used to eliminate rashes and ease insect bites, or drank to cure diarrhea. The fruit has been mashed into a paste for topical applications to reduce swellings and inflammations or treat skin infections.

The wood from the 40 to 60 foot tall trees is termite resistant and light weight. The traditional Hawaiian drums used for their dances are made from the trunks of these trees. Because music is so necessary to the human animal almost all plants that have been traditional sources of instruments are considered sacred and the ulu is no different. The leaves are used as forage for cattle, horses and other livestock.

Breadfruit trees produce a thick milky sap called latex. This has been cooked and used as caulking for boats and mixed with pigments to yield a long lasting paint. The latex was used to trap birds in past centuries so that the feathers could be harvested for robes and ceremonies. The sap was spread on branches or posts. Birds landed there and were stuck. After the feathers were plucked the latex was softened with oil and the birds released to grow new feathers. The inner bark is one of several sources for a fiber called tapa. A breadfruit cousin, the paper mulberry, provides the best quality tapa fiber.

This is a tree with a dramatic history. In 1787 a sea captain who was a legend in his own time collected over a thousand young breadfruit trees in Tahiti and set sail for the Caribbean. The European explorers of the Pacific were impressed with the strength of the natives and attributed it to the breadfruit. The enterprising Capt. Bligh was going to plant these trees for the slaves in Jamaica and other islands in the British West Indies. The goal was to plant the trees, let the slaves care for them and grow their own nutritious food in their spare time at no further expense to the landowner. Breadfruit is a heavy drinker and soon exhausted the water on board. Bligh rationed the water for the sailors so that his cargo could be kept alive. Fletcher Christian objected, Bligh was set adrift with a few who remained loyal to him, and the trees were thrown overboard sort of like a Pacific version of the Boston tea party, and the rest is history, a good book and a couple of movies. Bligh did eventually get a cargo of breadfruit to the West Indies only to find that the slaves refused to eat this strange food.

Actually, a French entrepreneur, Sonnerat, brought some of the seeded varieties from the Philippines to the French West Indies in 1772. Today the seeded varieties are still the most common in Haiti. The USDA introduced breadfruit to the Canal Zone and Panama in 1906, and numerous attempts have been made to grow these delightful trees in south Florida. While some thrive on Key West, success has been marginal in the rest of the state. Several botanical gardens have specimens and several individuals are growing them but currently Florida has no commercial cultivation of breadfruit. It continues to be a valuable crop in the true tropics where it can have deep fertile soil and about 40 to 60 inches of rainfall a year. Some varieties are drought tolerant and willing to withstand salt spray.

The seeds, of those varieties that produce seed, have to be started soon after harvest because the viability lasts only weeks. The breadfruit will grow quickly with beautiful deep green leaves and a tropical look. Some of the newer varieties are even quite drought tolerant. Its biggest drawback is its inability to handle cold weather.

Carob, *Ceratonia siliqua*
Cassia family, *Caesalpiniaceae*
Also known as St. John's bread, & locust bean
Can grow to be a large tree
Native to Africa and Arabian Peninsula

Value as a food source	8
Value as an ornamental	10
Multi-purpose	yes
Continuous harvest	no
Ease of culture	8
Overall rating	****

This is far more than a chocolate substitute. Within these beanpods is a whole meal. When John the Baptist was living on a diet of locusts it wasn't the plagues of insects that periodically ravages that region of the world, it was the fruit of this tree. Granted, in many areas the insect type locusts are a high protein source and are included in the seasonal table fare, but that's not what John was munching. Let's look at what John was getting from this great tasting seedpod. Raw, either green or ripe and dried they are sweet and filled with fiber. The pods are about 50% sugar and 10% protein. They are made into a syrup called *pasteli* or *dibs el kharoub* that can be used any way we might use Hershey's Syrup. This thick, sweet chocolate-tasting liquid can become a delightful alcoholic beverage. The dried pods can be ground into a flour used in cooking and baking, making candy and drinks. The flour is also used in the cosmetics industry as a facial care compound.

The seeds are over 60% protein and have very little sugar or starch. They can be boiled as we do beans, or baked, added to soups and stews, or ground into a flour for healthy baking. The seeds also have the chocolate flavor. The seeds can be roasted and ground as we do coffee to produce a delightful hot or iced drink with a roasted chocolate flavor that ought to be available in supermarkets and coffee shops. Gum tragacanth is also obtained from the seeds and is used as a thickening agent and in the production of egg substitutes.

The seeds are very uniform in size and weight and were the original jeweler's 'carat.' A mature tree can produce over 800 pounds (400 kilos) of seed pods a year.

The carob does well in a wide variety of soils as long as they are well drained. It will tolerate an alkaline soil and will withstand salt spray. It can survive rocky, sandy or gravel type soils as long as they are moderately fertile. This tree is very drought tolerant and feels at home in arid lands in mild temperate zones. Named varieties are available as grafted specimens. You can start them from seed by soaking them in warm water for 24 hours, or until they have begun to swell. Then plant in 4 or 6 inch pots and keep lightly moist, not soggy. Germination will usually begin within 2 weeks with some seeds taking as long as two months.

Chaya

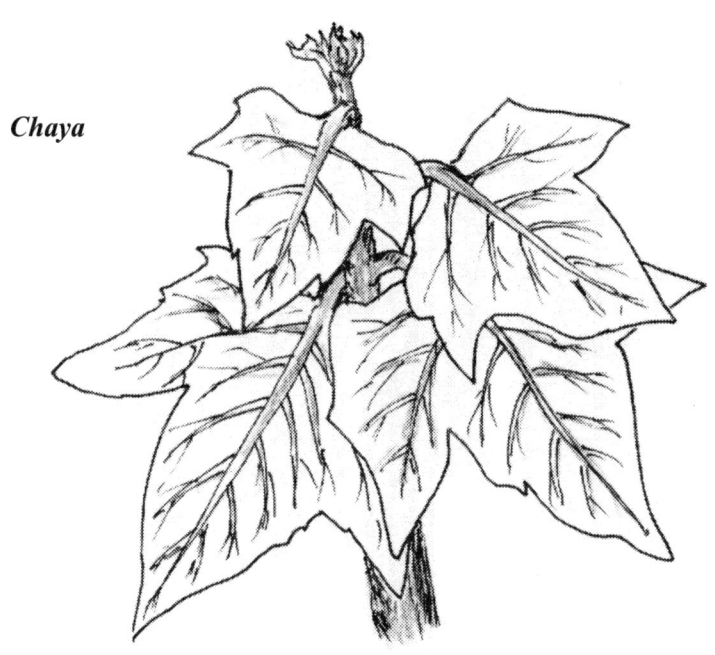

Chaya, *Cnidoscolus chayamansa*
Poinsettia family, *Euphorbiaceae*
Also known as tree spinach, chaya col, kikilchay and chaykeken
Native to Central America
Shrub reaching 3 to 5 m (9-15 ft)

Value as a food source	8
Value as an ornamental	6
Multi-purpose	no
Continuous harvest	yes
Ease of culture	8
Overall rating	****

This is such an attractive shrub that it deserves space in the aesthetic tropical garden as well as the vegetable plots. Crisp green maple-like leaves on a stocky well rounded plant make it ideal as a background, specimen or container shrub.

The young shoots and leaves are cooked and eaten as a potherb. In fact the taste is somewhat like spinach when cooked. This is an excellent source of protein, vitamins A, C, niacin, riboflavin and thiamine, iron, calcium and phosphorous.

There are smooth leafed varieties that are better for the dinner table because they contain less hydrocyanic glycosides (destroyed by cooking) and don't have the irritating hairs on the underside of the leaf. In many indigenous cultures raw chaya leaves are consumed in moderate quantities without negative affect but this isn't recommended.

This is another of the tropical plants that is being tested for medicinal properties. In rural areas it has traditionally been used as a diuretic, laxative, as an aid to digestion and to improve circulation. Teas and extracts have been used in cosmetic compounds to harden fingernails. There have been traditional uses of chaya tea as a beneficial drink for diabetics. Several tests done at Texas A & M-Kingsville seem to confirm potential value and the need for further study to see just how much the blood glucose levels are lowered and the mechanics of these results.

This is an easy plant to grow in a wide variety of situations. It will tolerate poor soils and drought. We have trialed it in sun and shade. The only things that seems to slow it down is cold weather and water-logged soil. We have grown it very effectively in containers and in garden beds.

Chaya produces little in the way of flowers and almost never sets seeds. This isn't a problem because it starts readily from cuttings (in a Cellugro test we have rooted cuttings in three weeks and were harvesting fresh leaves in eight weeks). This is a garden vegetable that ought to be grown far more than it is currently.

Chinese cedar, *Toona sinensis*, also listed as *Ailanthus flavescens & Cedrella sinensis*
Ailanthus family, *Meliaceae*
Deciduous tree growing up to 20 m (50 to 60 feet)
Native of China and much of Asia, temperate regions

Value as a food source	5
Value as an ornamental	9
Multi-purpose	yes
Continuous harvest	yes
Ease of culture	7
Overall rating	**

The Chinese value the tender leaves and new shoots from this tree as a culinary delight. They are usually boiled as a potherb, sometimes added to stir fries or soups. Regardless of how they are cooked they yield a flavor not unlike mild onions. The leaves contain about 6% protein along with a few vitamins and minerals. The leaves can also be used fresh or dried to make an interesting tea that is reminiscent of onion soup. Eating the leaves raw isn't recommended. In some locales the fruits are harvested and cooked but the flavor is reported to be harsh.

The wood is aromatic and fine grained so it's frequently used in cabinetry and fine furniture. A pleasant incense is made from the wood and twigs. The bark and twigs are used medicinally for a variety of ailments. Dried wood chips, bark and twigs can be used as a room freshener, potpourri or deodorizer as the perfumed volatile oils are released. Beyond all these practical applications is the fact that this is also a very attractive tree with masses of fragrant white flowers. It is both long lived and fast growing with a natural resistance to most insects.

This tree is best started from seed that has been stratified for at least three months. They can also be started from cuttings. It responds well to a compost rich well-drained site and will tolerate limestone.

Coconut, *Cocos nucifera*
Palm family, *Arecaceae (Palmae)*
Tree ranging from 6 to 20 m (18 to 60 ft) tall
Pan-tropical

Value as a food source	10
Value as an ornamental	10
Multi-purpose	yes
Continuous harvest	yes
Ease of culture	7
Overall rating	*****

A single coconut equals about a 1/4 pound steak in protein. They can be eaten raw, dried, grated, cooked in a multitude of ways or pressed for oil. The fruit of most varieties contains a liquid, referred to as coconut milk or coconut water, that is a nutritious drink, often used as a meat tenderizer in the tropics. One variety from the Philippines, *Makapuno*, produces a fruit with a jelly-like substance rather than the coconut milk inside. This is considered quite a delicacy, being enjoyed raw with a spoon or made into ice cream. *Nawasi* is a variety with an edible husk. The flowers are eaten as a vegetable, used as a sugar source and made into wines and vinegar. The terminal buds are roasted and eaten, the roots are cleaned and roasted to produce a drink similar to coffee. There is a spongy mass that forms inside a germinating coconut that is called the apple. This is also considered a gastronomic delight. Seed sprouts are valued as a delicacy as well. A book could be written on the fermented foods and drinks that are made from coconuts. Virtually every culture that uses coconuts employs fermentation as a means of serving and preserving this valuable food.

The coconut has been used for thousands of years, not only as a food source, but as a building material in the form or thatch and logs, valuable oil for cooking, lamps and food preservation. The husks can be used as a cooking fuel, burned to charcoal, shredded for erosion control, surface mulch, soil conditioners and growing mediums. *Coir* is the husk fibers, and this is being used today as a renewable alternative to sphagnum peat as a growing medium for plants in nurseries and greenhouses. The mats of this fiber are used extensively in erosion control, reforestation projects, road cuts and as a surface mulch in parks, orchards and groves. *Copra* is the dried meat of the coconut. It stores well and can be pressed to produce coconut oil. Even the trunk can be turned into construction timbers or a drum.

While cultures throughout the tropics have for thousands of years valued the coconut much as the plains Indians of North America once valued the bison, it wasn't known to the Europeans until Marco Polo returned with descriptions of it growing in India. It has spread across the Pacific in all directions, island hopping to the American tropics.

There is a problem called lethal yellowing disease that is wiping out coconut plantations all over the world. Many of the dwarf varieties such as the *Golden Malayan Dwarf* and *Red Malayan dwarf* show a strong resistance to this disease. *Laccadive Dwarf* is a variety that begins bearing in less than 3 years and will at maturity yield 200 to 250 fruit a year. The dwarfs have the added advantages of beginning to produce when only a few feet tall and maturing at less than 30 feet. This makes harvesting much easier.

If you wish to grow a coconut from seed it is best to start with a fruit that is still in the outer husk. Place it flat and about half buried in a sand and compost mix in a three gallon pot. Keep watered, but not soggy and wait six to nine months. The roots may well be forming for several months before you see any activity on the top. Be patient, it will happen. In frost prone areas a warning is in order. They aren't cold hardy but can make a great subject for after dinner conversation for several years. They're relatively easy to grow as a container plant until they get too large.

Katuk, *Sauropus androgynous*
Poinsettia family, *Euphorbiaceae*
Also known as sweetleaf bush, & katook
Shrub or small upright tree to 7 m (20 ft) Usually trimmed to 2 m or less.
Native to India and Malaysia

Value as a food source	9
Value as an ornamental	7
Multi-purpose	yes
Continuous harvest	yes
Ease of culture	8
Overall rating	*****

    This is a plant with leaves that are far more nutritious than lettuce. It tastes better than lettuce too. In many areas of the tropics this can be grown as a dooryard plant where it's kept trimmed to 1-2 m (3-6 ft) The leaves, both young and mature, the young shoots, the flowers and the pink fruits all appear on the dinner table. The young leaves and shoots have a delicate almost nutty flavor when eaten raw in salads. They can also be cooked as a potherb, used in soups, stews, stir fries or steamed. These leaves are a valuable source of vitamins A and C as well as protein and iron. The small, tasty flowers and fruits can be candied and used as a dessert dish.

    There are studies currently in progress exploring the potential of katuk as a means of lowering blood glucose. This could be of tremendous benefit to diabetics. This is one of the best tasting pick and eat snack foods we have in our Global garden.

    The plant can be used as a hedgerow, living fence, support for beans and a privacy screen. It does best in light shade. We have trialed it in dense shade and gotten good results.

www.globalgardening.info

The plants are propagated from seeds or cuttings. They thrive in an evenly moist compost rich soil because they have a symbiotic relationship with certain fungi and the organic material seems to encourage this partnership. In the author's trials it was found that a compost rich soil mix increased the rate of growth markedly. We grew them in containers and in garden beds with equal success. Rooting of cuttings was done in a Cellugro bed with transplants ready in 4 to 5 weeks.

We used perennial peanuts as a ground cover and kept the katuk trimmed to a heigh of 3 to 5 feet. This produced an ample amount of leaves and shoots and required neither stooping or climbing to harvest. The peanuts are a nitrogen fixing plant and this has been a tremendous benefit to the katuk. The more frequently the shoots are gathered the denser the growth is. Feeding occasionally with a nitrogen rich fertilizer or aged manures seems to encourage growth.

The only problem frequently encountered is slugs, which seem to delight in dining on newly struck cuttings. It should be noted that while this is an evergreen shrub, it is frost sensitive. It should be noted that permanent lung damage can occur with excessive ingestion, as is the case with the Japanese weight loss fad that was based on massive intake of raw katuk juice.

Linden, European common linden, lime tree, *Tilia europacea* or American basswood, *Tilia americana*
Linden family, *Tiliacea*
Tree common to temperate regions throughout Europe; basswood is found throughout temperate North America.

Value as a food source	5
Value as an ornamental	9
Multi-purpose	yes
Continuous harvest	yes
Ease of culture	9
Overall rating	****

Here is a tree whose leaves found their way to the European dinner table. Linden honey, made from the delightfully fragrant flowers, is considered fine dining. In Russia they make a sweet flavorful beverage called *Lipez*. Even the sap is used as a sugar source, much like the maple, and is also fermented into a country wine. The sap from wounds semi-dried is a sweet 'manna' that is enjoyed by both children and adults. If you want a real taste treat collect some of the flowers and either eat them whole or crush them into a coarse paste. The flavor is somewhat like sweet chocolate. The same can be done with the seeds, but they don't seem to be quite as sweet. A handful of fresh or dried flowers can also make a naturally sweet tea. The flowers are also a valuable addition to salads, sandwiches, ice creams or any other sweet treats.

The young leaves are delightful raw in salads or sandwiches, or simply chewed by the handful as a 'fresh from the tree' snack.

This tree is easily grown and makes a valuable addition to the landscape. It will get large and it makes a dramatic shade tree.

Malabar chestnut, *Pachira aquatica*
Bombax family, *Bombacaceae*
Also known as Guiana chestnut, provision tree, & saba nut
Tropical tree reaching 20 m (60 ft) in its native habitat
Native to Mexico, Central America and Amazon Basin

Value as a food source	7
Value as an ornamental	9
Multi-purpose	yes
Continuous harvest	yes
Ease of culture	7
Overall rating	****

While this is a respectable sized tree in the jungle, when planted in such locations as Florida or California it rarely exceeds 15 feet in height and can be pruned and trained to 8 or 10 feet and grown as a container plant. It will survive temperatures in the mid 20's but will drop every leaf it owns. Like its cousin the baobab, the tender young leaves can be cooked as a potherb, very young ones can add flavor to a fresh salad. The mature leaves will reach 60 cm (about 24 inches) in length but by the time they are mature they are too tough to be edible.

The flowers are striking and it will bloom as a container plant once it has reached about 2 m (6 ft) in height. The blossom is about the size of a softball with the petals recurved to show off the mass of stamens that give the appearance of a gigantic shaving brush. The flower buds and flowers are edible, possessing a sweet delicate flavor when used raw in a salad. They are also steamed, baked, boiled or added to soups, stews, rice or corn dishes.

The fruit looks like a small coconut, but it's packed with seeds about ° inch in diameter. When ripe the seeds burst the pod and fall to the ground. They taste almost like peanuts when eaten raw and will keep with little care for months. When they are roasted they taste very much like chestnuts. The roasted nuts are frequently ground into flour for baking. A most delicious sweet bread is made from this flour. The seeds can be toasted and ground, then brewed to produce a flavorful warm beverage, that is still no substitute for coffee.

Even if the Malabar chestnut didn't produce delicious flowers, leaves and seeds it deserves consideration because it is a very attractive plant for any tropical landscape or even sitting in front of a large window looking out on a snow covered lawn. It is easily started from seed sown individually in 4 or 6 inch pots and kept evenly moist until they sprout, usually within 2 two weeks. They can also be started from cuttings, but this isn't nearly as easy as propagation from seed. They will grow and thrive in almost any well-drained soil but a compost rich mix seems to work best. They like to be kept evenly moist during the growing season and slightly drier during the cooler winter months.

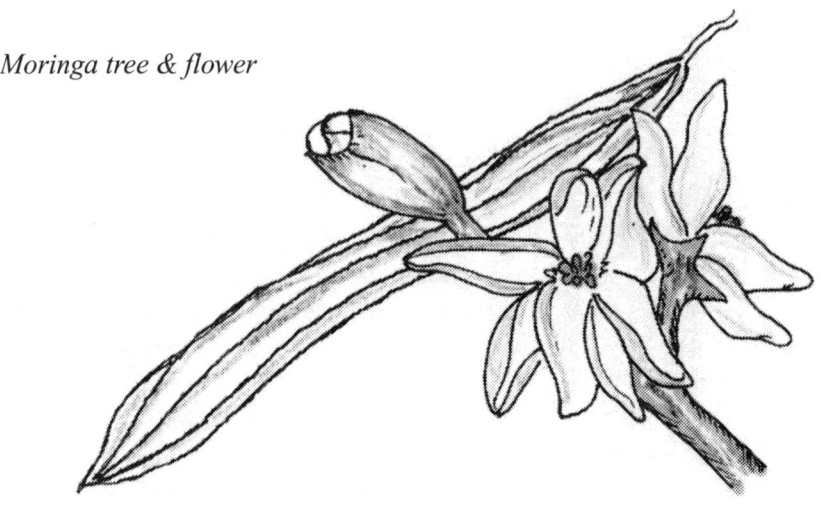

Moringa tree & flower

Moringa. *Moringa oleifera* and *M. stenopetala* (African horseradish tree)
Moringa family, *Moringaceae*
Also known as Horseradish tree or drumstick tree, or Sahjan
Native to India and the Arabian peninsula
A rugged tree reaching 12 m (35-40 ft)

Value as a food source	10
Value as an ornamental	8
Multi-purpose	yes
Continuous harvest	yes
Ease of culture	9
Overall rating	*****

    This is a miracle tree for many areas. Not only is it fast growing, drought tolerant and pest resistant, it is the ultimate in a multi-purpose plant. They call it horseradish tree because the roots actually taste like that popular European seasoning, but this is more than just a seasoning source; this tree can saves lives, by the thousands.

    The leaves are delicious and nutritious. They have an almost spicy taste. Many insist that *stenopetala* is better flavored, but I suspect that this is a matter of personal opinion. These leaves can be harvested daily from a few trees growing at the dooryard or along the garden. Because this foliage is so high in protein and vitamins A & C it is literally a life saver. They are sometimes eaten raw as a salad green but most often used as a potherb or added to soups, stews and other dishes.

Mike Sullivan at ECHO in Florida told us a story about some missionaries from Haiti that were touring their research facility in Fort Myers. They had been mourning the fact that food was in such short supply at the orphanage they directed, that children and infants were malnourished to the point where disease could claim its deadly toll. As they strolled Mike mentioned the moringa and the missionaries asked to see this remarkable tree. When they reached the point in the tour where the moringa were growing they were aghast. The tree was growing in their orphanage courtyard. Because it grew so fast they frequently harvested the branches to use as firewood for the cook stoves. Since then the leaves have saved the lives of many children.

The flowers are eaten raw or cooked and the bees make a delightful honey from them. The flowers can be batter fried and have a taste similar to mushrooms. The immature seed pods are cooked and eaten like green beans or used in a stir fry. These diced pods can also be roasted, boiled or steamed.

The winged seeds are used to purify dirty water. Along the Nile valley it is known as *shagra al rauwaq*, or "tree for purifying." The seeds are crushed into small pieces and wrapped in a cloth and tied. This is then placed in the bucket or container of water where the seeds act as a flocculent. Research is currently being done in Africa using powdered moringa seed in a larger scale water filtration system.

The seeds contain about 30-35% oil. This sweet tasting oil can be extracted in a simple press and used for cooking, lubrication, soaps and cosmetic creams. Because the oil burns without smoke it's also ideal for lamps. This oil doesn't turn rancid and can be used in food preservation. It produces a heavy crop of these seeds, sometimes amounting to over 100 pounds per tree, seed production starts at an early age and continues over a long season. Ben oil, used by artists in mixing their paints, is made from moringa seeds. Since the oil is chemically similar to jojoba seed oil there may be potential as a machine oil and engine fuel.

The bark produces a sappy gum that is used in cooking and food preservation. Each part of the tree has a whole list of medicinal applications from stomach ache to eye infections, blood pressure to diabetes. Most important is the value in combating malnutrition. This fast growing tree (it may reach 10' to 15' in the first year) produces a lightweight wood that makes an acceptable fuel for stoves and if left to grow several years it becomes a useful lumber source.

The plantings can serve as poles for beans, yams, vanilla, pepper and other vining crops, a wind break against the harsh semi-desert breezes, shade to help preserve moisture in the gardens and fields and fodder for the livestock. They can be used as living fences, privacy screens and erosion control. The dried pods and leaves also make a valuable surface mulch on its way to becoming compost.

The moringa is propagated from seeds or cuttings and grows quickly in almost any well drained soil. They cannot survive waterlogged soils, however. While it's drought tolerant, as a defense against a prolonged dry spell it will drop its leaves. It willingly accepts an annual rainfall from 20 to 140 inches (500 to 3500 mm).

It will freeze back to the ground in a severe frost but if well mulched will come back from the roots without a problem. It grows best in full sun but will tolerate light shade. In shady situations it produces fewer leaves and grows with far less vigor. There seem to be few pest and disease problems other than root rot in soggy soils.

A periodic application of a balanced fertilizer encourages growth but in many areas of the world dishwater or wash water provides all the nutrients needed.

Orchid Tree, *Bauhinia purpurea* and *B. Variegata*
Cassia family, *Caesalpinaceae*
Also known as Mountain ebony & Camel's-foot tree
Native to Southeast Asia

Value as a food source	4
Value as an ornamental	9
Multi-purpose	yes
Continuous harvest	yes
Ease of culture	8
Overall rating	***

There are many varieties of these beautiful flowering trees. When in bloom the small tree is covered with pink or lavender flowers that do resemble orchids. Not only are these blossoms beautiful, they are both delicious and nutritious, making them a valuable and attractive addition to salads, or cooked as a potherb, added to potato and rice dishes, or cooked as a vegetable side dish. In India the flowers are added to curries. In Nepal they are cooked with potatoes and tomatoes and selected spices. The unopened flower buds are cooked as a side dish or pickled like capers. The leaves are also cooked as a potherb, or added to other vegetables where the sour lemon-lime flavor can add much to the flavor. The seeds can be cooked or roasted and are used in a variety of dishes.

This is a tropical tree that has little frost tolerance, but will accept a wide variety of soils, as long as there is good drainage and full sun or light shade. Once established most bauhinias are even somewhat drought tolerant. In USDA zone 9 they will often freeze to the ground and spring into rampant new growth with warm weather, with tender new leaves and flower buds. Most bauhinias are easily started from seed sown in seedling trays or individual pots. They will germinate within two weeks and grow rapidly. They can be grown as a container plant in more northern climates and will survive cold winters in a sunny windowsill.

West Indian Pea Tree, *Sesbania grandiflora*
Bean family, *Fabaceae*
Also known as Agati (Figi), Katurai (Guam), Corkwood tree, Hummingbird tree, Vegetable hummingbird & Sesban
Small tree or shrub reaching 10 m (30 ft)
Native throughout Asia, now pan-tropical

Value as a food source	6
Value as an ornamental	7
Multi-purpose	yes
Continuous harvest	yes
Ease of culture	8
Overall rating	**

    The beautiful and colorful flowers make this a popular ornamental in many parts of the tropics and subtropics. These horn-shaped blossoms (resembling a hummingbird in appearance, if you have a good imagination) are found in white, pink or red. It's fortunate that they are produced over an extended season because this hummingbird tree turns into an ugly duckling when not in bloom. The white and pink flowers are used fresh in salads. Red flowered varieties are reported to be too bitter to be eaten raw. Before eating the center is removed to reduce the bitterness and expose the sweetness. All colors can be boiled, batter fried, added to curries, soups and stews or vegetable dishes. The flavor is almost sweet mushroom-like. These flowers are a better source of iron than our traditional spinach. The young leaves can be cooked, used in curry dishes or eaten raw in salads. These leaves are nutritious but eating too many at a time can cause diarrhea. The mature seeds and pods aren't edible but the young beanpods can be used in soups, stews, stir fries, or as a cooked vegetable.

    In Asia it has long been valued for a wide range of medicinal properties. The juice of the flowers is recommended to alleviate headaches, congestion and a stuffy nose as well as a treatment for sore or tired eyes. The leaves are used as a poultice for bruises or rheumatism. They are also a source of fever control, and the juice from the crushed leaves is used for sore throats and as an oral disinfectant. The seeds and seed pods are used as a laxative, and they're also considered intellectually stimulating. The bark has been used in diverse areas as a treatment for dysentery and ulcers, as a laxative and emetic, even scabies. The roots are valued too, as a treatment for rheumatism, epilepsy, gout, leprosy and severe itch. In the Hindu religion this is one of the sacred flowers of Shiva.

    A red gum that exudes from wounds is used to strengthen fishlines and nets. The fast growth makes this a valuable pulp and phalloid source in many regions. The foliage and new growth make acceptable fodder for livestock and the soft wood is also used in construction and the production of cork floats. The trees are used as a nurse crop to provide shade for coconut seedlings, timber crops and fruit tree nurseries. It has been used effectively as a living support for pepper vines (*piper nigra*).

The greatest value in developing countries and areas where efforts are being made at reforestry is this plant's rapid growth. This ability to grow quickly and reseed itself can also make it an invasive problem in areas like Florida and Hawaii. The litter of seedpods can make an effective surface mulch but tends to compost slowly.

Sesbania is an edible flowering tree that's easily started from seed or cuttings. Good compost rich soil gives the best results but it will grow almost anywhere. This will thrive in frost free areas and does quite well as a container plant. It prefers well drained sites and accepts near desert to rainforest conditions. It can, and should be, kept trimmed to a workable height. When left to grow to its natural size it becomes leggy, shallow rooted and prone to wind damage.

There are reports that an extract from the bark is toxic to cockroaches and other insects.

Chapter Six
The Underground Garden

We have this image of starving nomads desperately trying to dig a root from the barren soil to provide their first meal in days. True, before humanity was domesticated by wheat, rice, maize and millet, our ancestors ate a lot of tubers. In North America this included several members of the bean family, *Apios Americana* along the eastern coast of NA and *Psoralea esculenta*, locally known as prairie turnip or scruff pea, in the great plains. (See the profiles below) Beyond these beans there are lilies, wild onions, Indian turnips and many others. Edible cannas and cattails were harvested in the wetlands, Buffalo gourd tubers in the southwest. Actually, the diet of the average hunter-gatherer was far more varied than ours is in this contemporary industrialized society.

For centuries before we invented refrigeration, edible roots, tubers, bulbs and rhizomes kept quite well thank you in the soil where they grew, or, if harvested, were again covered with sand or soil to keep them from drying out or decaying. Nature designed these tubers and roots as a way for the plant to survive the harsh weather of winter or drought. Our ancestors simply took advantage of this, and so do many cultures today.

Most of us in the industrialized world hire others to do the grubbing of our favorite tubers like carrots, potatoes, turnips, onions, beets, radishes, sweet potatoes and more. We then let the professionals clean, sometimes treat with preservative chemicals and store the raw food in a virtual underground we call coolers or the home refrigerator until we are ready to use it.

Now let's take a look at some interesting residents of the "Underground Garden" elsewhere in our global home. You might want to try some of these in your own garden, or you might want to help support the research and development agencies that are striving to eliminate hunger all over the world.

More Than Beans

Beans are among the most basic of our foods, but many of them also produce edible tubers. The winged bean is a universal food. We can eat the flowers, leaves, tender shoots, immature pods, and dried beans. But it also produces a storage tuber that's delicious. This is another of those perennial vegetables. Unfortunately it isn't freeze tolerant but the North American prairie turnip (see detailed information below) is as hardy as a plant can be. The peanut and a wealth of root and tuber crops were grown thousands of years ago in the Andes and other regions of South America. Africa gave us the Bambara groundnut, *Voandzeia subterranea.* Let's look at some of these in greater detail.

Apios americana

American groundnut, *Apios Americana*
Bean family, *Fabaceae*
Perennial small shrubby vine with white, lavender or purple flowers
Native to eastern North America from Nova Scotia to Florida

Value as a food source	5
Value as an ornamental	5
Multi-purpose	yes
Continuous harvest	no
Ease of culture	7
Overall rating	***

    Before there were French, British and Spanish flags fluttering in the American breeze the Native peoples were dining on the seeds and tubers of this plant. There is evidence that they transplanted or started them near their villages but may not have truly cultivated them. They boiled, baked, roasted, dried, grated and powdered the tubers and the seeds were boiled or pounded into a pasty gruel. It was listed in a French garden guide in 1597 and in the 1840's it was being considered as an alternative to the potato during the famine in Ireland. Today there is much study being done on this delightful plant well known to the Native Americans. The tubers that form along the roots are small, usually less than two inches long, but the crisp white flesh is delicious. After the colonists began to settle the North American continent this was one of the native foods taken back to Europe along with corn, pumpkins and beans. The French cultivated it as a prized delicacy while the American settlers used it as both famine food and wild harvest.

It likes to grow in moist locations with poor clay or sandy soils, but will perform well in compost enriched soil as long as we keep it watered. There have been some experiments done growing them in containers with success. Apios Americana does well in full sun but will accept light shade. In poor soils, regions of short summers or where they receive limited attention it may take two seasons to get usable tubers. They grow best from tubers, seeds take an extra year to produce.

The plant is dug when the tops begin to die back and the beans have ripened. The tubers are collected, washed and used as we would potatoes. The smaller ones can be replanted for next year's crop.

The flowers are attractive when it is in bloom and the dried seeds were used by the Native Americans as a soup bean. These seeds are small but possess an interesting flavor. They work well in combination with other dried beans, or cooked then used cold in salads.

Bambara groundnut, *Voandzeia subterranea*
Bean family, *Fabaceae*
Also known as njugo bean, voandzou, nzama, indhlubu, Congo goober, Madagascar groundnut, baffin pea and earthpea
Annual bushy plant .5 m (1 ° foot) mound
Native to Africa

Value as a food source	9
Value as an ornamental	5
Multi-purpose	yes
Continuous harvest	no
Ease of culture	8
Overall rating	***

This is an African version of the peanut, very popular in sub-Saharan regions. The immature seeds are eaten raw. Ripe seed is boiled, roasted, added to soups, stews, meat and vegetable dishes, ground into a flour and used in baking or porridge. One source says the mature seeds can even be popped like corn. The seeds are frequently roasted and used as a coffee substitute. Nigerians mix the ground seeds with spices and oil, then roll this dough into balls called *bakuru*. The young pods are added to stews and other boiled vegetables. The young leaves are also edible as a potherb, usually mixed with other, more flavorful vegetables.

The seeds contain sufficient quantities of proteins, fats and carbohydrates to be considered a nutritious and almost complete food. In areas where there is no refrigeration, it stores easily and can be used in a variety of ways. The leaves are also used as fodder after the harvest. This is a nitrogen-fixing legume and is valuable as a soil building plant.

The Bambara groundnut tolerates drought, poor soils and all the extremes that can be found in its native habitats.

Breadroot Scruf Pea, *Psoralea esculenta*
Also known as Indian breadroot, Prairie turnip or tipsin
Bean family, *Fabaceae*
Perennial
Native to North American great plains

Value as a food source	8
Value as an ornamental	8
Multi-purpose	no
Continuous harvest	no
Ease of culture	7
Overall rating	****

The tuber is sweet and starchy, making it a delight to eat raw as a snack or a valuable addition to a salad. It can also be baked, stir-fried, boiled, toasted, roasted or deep fried into chips or French fries. The root can be grated and added to soups for flavor and as a thickening agent. The tubers can be dried and ground into flour for use in baking or puddings.

Historical note: This is one of the plants that Lewis & Clark brought back from their great adventure. For over a century before that the French fur traders and Jesuit missionaries had been dining with the Native Americans on this *pomme de prairie*. This was a favored food by many of the original inhabitants of the North American prairie because the 3" by 1" tubers form only about 3 or 4 inches below the surface and are easily harvested. This is a plant that deserves more attention for use in northern climates. The foliage is a favorite for grazing livestock, and it thrives under less than ideal conditions such as drought and unseasonal cold.

Earth pea, *Lathyrus tuberosa*
Bean family, *Fabaceae*
Also known as Earth chestnut, tuberous vetch, Everlasting pea, perennial pea, gesse tubereuse, chataigne de terre and Dutch mice
Perennial sprawling plant
Native to Eurasia, naturalized in North America

Value as a food source	4
Value as an ornamental	7
Multi-purpose	yes
Continuous harvest	no
Ease of culture	9
Overall rating	**

This is one of those vegetables that is less efficient to grow, but it has such a great flavor that, if space is available, it's worthwhile. The tubers are not produced in great quantity but the sweet chestnut flavor is pure delight. They can be roasted, baked or toasted. Some recipes call for boiling in sweetened water. The cooked tubers can be sliced or grated and added to breads, cakes, puddings, soups and salads. One resource described a "Dutch mice pie" made with these tubers, chicken and assorted vegetables. The seed pods are also edible and make a mild flavored addition to a soup or stew.

While they may be a little light in the yield, they are easy to grow. The seeds, or small tubers can be planted in the spring, in temperate zones, after danger of frost. They thrive in a variety of soils but the best production is in compost rich, well-drained, evenly moist soil in full sun or dappled shade. The pink to violet sweet pea-like flowers appear from June through September in its native habitat and parts of North America where it has successfully colonized. Because it is so cold hardy it is considered as naturalized weed in Ontario. Once it has been started in the garden, you will never need to plant it again because it is almost impossible to harvest all of the potato-like tubers. They often form 15 inches or more underground.

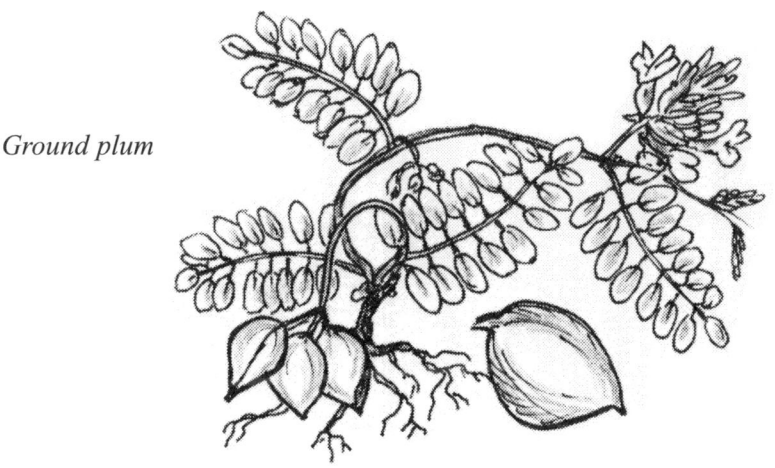

Ground plum

Ground plum, *Astragalus crassicarpus*
Bean family, *Fabaceae*
Also known as Groundplum milkvetch, buffalo pea
Perennial, low growing
Native to Great Plains and western North America

Value as a food source	6
Value as an ornamental	8
Multi-purpose	no
Continuous harvest	no
Ease of culture	7
Overall rating	***

www.globalgardening.info

The seedpods look somewhat like Green Gage plums about 1 inch in diameter. These pods form on short flower stalks and are semi buried much like peanuts. The fleshy immature pods are eaten raw or cooked. They are usually consumed pod and all just like sugar peas. They can also be cooked and added to soups, stews, stir-fries or meat dishes. It was once common practice to pickle them for winter use.

To grow well they require a well-drained sunny site with occasional watering. Once established they will take considerable drought. They are best started from seed that has been cold stratified then soaked in water for 24 hours. They can be started in seed flats or individual 4" pots then transplanted to their permanent site when they have grown into husky plants. They don't transplant well so once they settle in they shouldn't be disturbed. This isn't one of the easiest vegetables to start but it is well worth the effort. There is a Mexican variety that produces even larger pods, but in smaller quantities.

Jicama, *Pachyrhyzus tuberosus* (sometimes classified as *P. Erosus*)
Bean family, *Fabaceae*
Also known as Yam bean, potato bean, Mexican water chestnut & Mexican turnip
Perennial in warm climates. Vigorous vine that will climb trees.
Native to Mexico, Central & South America

Value as a food source	8
Value as an ornamental	6
Multi-purpose	no
Continuous harvest	no
Ease of culture	9
Overall rating	***

The turnip-like tubers of this legume have a delightful lightly sweet flavor and a crispy texture much like a water chestnut when eaten raw. Individual tubers may weight several pounds the first year and are delightful peeled and eaten raw in salads, cooked in stir-fries, boiled, roasted, used in soups, stews or as a side vegetable. Because the tuber is high in starch it is even ground for use in puddings and custards. The tuber can be sliced thin, as you would potatoes, and seasoned with ground chiles, salt and lemon juice then eaten chilled or baked. They can even be deep fried as we would French fries, or made into great tasting chips just like potato chips.

This plant produces clusters of lavender to purple flowers followed by 6-8" beans. These beans are used in the tropics as a rodenticide. While the beans aren't for eating the tuber is completely safe and nutritious. It should be noted that while unharvested tubers will continue to grow in size and eventually weigh 20 pounds or more they become woody and far less desirable for the dinner table.

Jicama grows best in a sandy compost enriched soil in a well drained site. They will tolerate considerable drought, can be grown as a container plant, and when planted in shade they simply climb to the top of the trees to claim their share of the sunshine. They can be grown from seed or by planting small tubers purchased at the grocery store. One source advises starting the next plant by slicing off the top of the tuber you are about to have for dinner and planting it as you would a potato eye.

Marama bean, *Tylosema esculentum*
Cassia family, *Caesalpiniaceae*
Perennial, sprawling vine
Native to the Kalhari Desert, Africa

Value as a food source	8
Value as an ornamental	7
Multi-purpose	yes
Continuous harvest	no
Ease of culture	6
Overall rating	****

    This is one of the few movie stars we discuss in this book. If you have ever seen the movie "The Gods Must Be Crazy," you may remember the scene where the natives squeeze water from a big tuber they have dug from the earth. If they gave Oscars for botanical movie stars, that marama bean tuber should have won. It is an interesting plant that stores water in that underground canteen so that it can survive the months and years of almost no rainfall. This tuber may contain up to 90% water and has been a traditional source of water for the Kung and Hottentotts. These tubers can weigh as much as 20 pounds or more (over 10 kg), and they are, according to ECHO, 90% water and about 9% protein. They can be sliced and fried or roasted much like giant potato chips or a slice of bread. The basketball size tubers can also be baked, roasted whole, diced into soups, stews, vegetable dishes and dried as a snack food.

    The large beans shouldn't be eaten raw, but they can be cooked in a variety of ways. Roasted they have a flavor not unlike cashews or almonds. The Europeans in southern Africa grind the roasted seeds and use them as an almond flavoring substitute. In Africa the shelled beans are boiled and ground with corn meal to make a porridge or thicken soups. These seeds have a high percentage of protein (up to 40%) and they yield a high quality vegetable oil (35 to 45 % by weight) making this a valuable crop in areas where little else will grow. The beans can also be roasted and ground for use as a nutty flavored seasoning in cooking and baking, or brewed as a coffee substitute. The beverage produced tastes nothing like coffee, but it does have a pleasant almond-amaretto flavor with the addition of a sweetener. One of the big advantages with this bean is that after harvesting it can be stored without refrigeration for several years, and still remain edible and viable for planting.

    The marama bean is designed by nature to thrive in what we consider the harshest of conditions. When we try to grow this delightful vegetable we often do it in by pampering it to death. Propagation is by seed. Experts recommend starting them in one gallon nursery pots or 6 inch clay pots. The heavy seed coat can be nicked to permit the embryo to absorb moisture, but don't try soaking the seed in hot water. Rather let it gradually absorb the moisture from soil that isn't soggy. Soil temperature must be above 65 degrees. Once growth starts (from 7-21 days) keep the soil moist but not saturated until the plant is well established. After the tubers begin to form they do best watered only when dry. Once established this is a vegetable that will take care of itself.

Full sun and miserably hot weather are ideal for this vegetable. It takes about 90 days for flowering and seed formation, the tuber will reach as much as 12" in diameter the first year. The plant will die back in the fall in cooler climates but if the tuber is mulched it will come back in the spring.

This may well be a vegetable we will hear much more about in the next few years. It's an extremely drought tolerant plant that scientists are hoping can become an important part of the diet in areas with little rainfall. It also thrives where there is more moisture, including areas where the annual rainfall exceeds 32 inches per year.

Winged bean, *Psophocarpus tetragnalobus*
Bean family, *Fabaceae*,
Also known as asparagus bean, goa bean and princess bean
Perennial vine for warm climates
Originated in Asia

Value as a food source	9
Value as an ornamental	9
Multi-purpose	yes
Continuous harvest	yes
Ease of culture	9
Overall rating	****

This is one of the most multi-purpose plants we can grow. It produces beautiful pale blue or lavender flowers, a vigorous vine that graces any trellis or fence, and it's all edible. This is one of those plants with tasty leaves and tender shoots, so that prunings can be harvested for the dinner table. The flowers are also a gourmet's delight, as are the young winged beans. Mature pods are dried and shelled. The dried beans will keep for a year or more without any special care. They can be treated as we would any dried navy or kidney beans. The bonus with this perennial plant is the tuber which is edible, with a taste somewhat like jicama, slightly sweet, slightly nutty. This is another of those vegetables that we can harvest on a continual basis

Winged beans are easy to grow in any sunny, well-drained soil. It will tolerate less than ideal conditions but rewards us with more produce when we provide a compost rich home and regular watering. It does need support for best results. It has another advantage in that it thrives in the heat of summer. Many varieties require short days for flowering and will produce only leaves in the north. There are day neutral varieties that will perform better in more temperate climes.

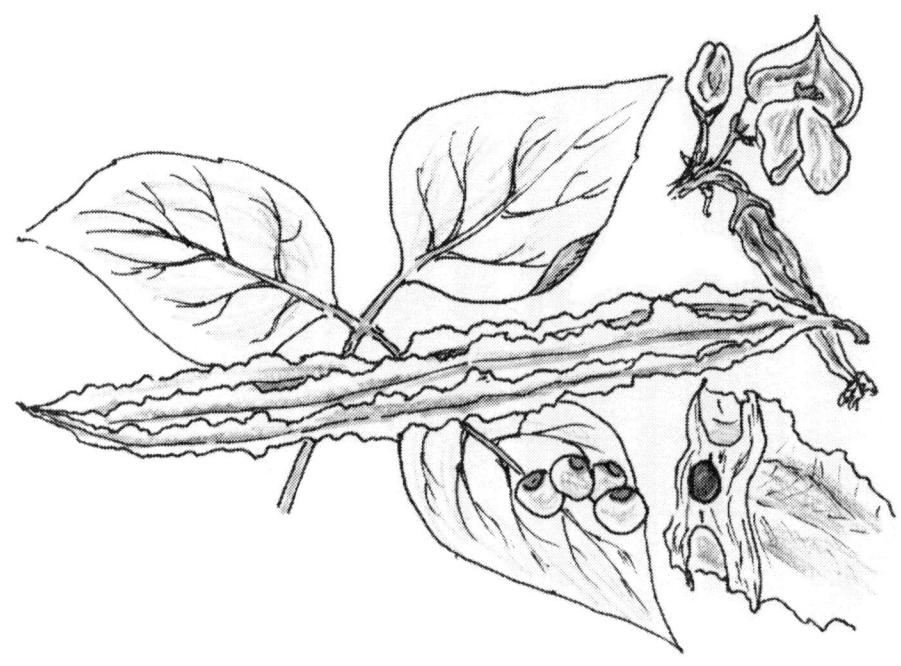

Those Remarkable Andean Roots

The Andean peoples have known some wonderful secrets for thousands of years. We are eternally grateful to these wonderfully adaptable pre-Inca cultures for some great foods that should be common restaurant fare and found growing in the backyard gardens of nations throughout the temperate regions. Imagine oxalis with edible tubers, nasturtiums, black potatoes, and such delightful native names as maca, *Lepidium meyenii*, Arracacha, *Arracacia xanthorrhiza*, mauka, *Mirabilis expansa* and yacon, *Polymnia sonchifolia*. Let's take a closer look at these intriguing plants.

Achira, *Canna edulis*
Canna family, *Cannaceae*
Sometimes called purple arrowroot or Andean canna
Native to Americas
Pernnial 2-3 m (6-9 feet)

Value as a food source	5
Value as an ornamental	5
Multi-purpose	yes
Continuous harvest	no
Ease of culture	8
Overall rating	***

In the Andes this edible canna is commonly used in stews, but because the sugar content increases after it has been stored for several weeks it's often aged then baked or roasted as a dessert. Because of the fine texture and easy digestibility it's used as a basic food for infants and the elderly. The starch has large grains (visible with the naked eye) and it makes a good flour, known as *tous le mois*, that's great for breads and biscuits. In the Orient the starch is used in a popular form of noodles. This is one of many plants that produce a starch commonly marketed as arrowroot.

This is a somewhat tender perennial that will grow where there is an occasional snow, as long as there is a good mulch cover. It likes full sun but will tolerate light shade. It's at its best in a compost rich well-drained soil, with ample water during the growing season. The roots, which can be several inches in diameter and over a foot long, are ready to harvest after a six to eight month growing season. There are few pests other than slugs. Propogation is usually by division or seed.
The plant is attractive, both in foliage and flower. The tender shoots are cooked as a nutritious, protein rich vegetable green and the unripe seeds are cooked into tortillas called, *bocoles*. This is also a source for arrowroot flour in Columbia. The leaves are also used to wrap tamales.

Arracacha, *Arracacia xanthorrhiza*
Carrot family, *Apiaceae (Umbelliferae)*
Also known as Peruvian parsnip, Creole celery, lacachu, oqqe and rikacha
Perennial with semi-fleshy leaf stalks and carrot-like root
Native to much of temperate South America

Value as a food source	5
Value as an ornamental	5
Multi-purpose	yes
Continuous harvest	yes
Ease of culture	8
Overall rating	***

Arracachas were grown before potatoes. It takes eight to twelve months for the root crop to mature but the leaves can be harvested as needed. While they are valued on the dinner table the leaves are also used as animal feed. If left in the ground too long the roots become woody, but some are always left because in the second year flowers are produced. The deep purple flower umbels are attractive and the seeds are used as a seasoning, much like its cousin, caraway.

The plants are started from seeds or side shoots called *pashincas* or *colinas* that form around the base of the *madre*. It can be grown in semi-shady areas and is often interplanted with corn and in coffee plantations. A well-drained compost rich sandy soil is best but it will grow in less. Regular watering is beneficial during drought. There are many varieties with roots ranging from white to yellow, often with purple streaks through the flesh.

Bitter potato, *Solanum x juzepczukii, Solanum x curtilobum*
Tomato family, *Solanaceae*
Also known as luki, ruku, choquepito
Native to the Andes
Value as a food source   4
Value as an ornamental   2
Multi-purpose   no
Continuous harvest   no
Ease of culture   5
Overall rating   **

    This is one of those little known and under used ancient crops. Domestication goes back at least 8000 years. The bitter potato isn't a vegetable for the faint-hearted. They will grow and produce through frost and freeze, (as long as it's not too severe), but the real challenge comes when they are harvested. The tubers contain glycoalkaloids that must be removed or modified before they are safe for consumption. The traditional method is to expose the tubers to several nights of freezing temperatures while drying them in sunlight. This produces *black chuno*. This dried vegetable is a nutritional food source, keeps for a long period and is safe. Bitter potatoes grow well in the challanging climate of the high Andes, making it an important food resource for the Bolivians and Peruvians living there.

    A second food is also produced from the bitter potato, *white chuno*, also called *tunta* or *moraya*. In this process the freezing is followed by a series of soakings in water for a period that can be as long as thirty days. Then they are dried. This is the basic food for festivals and special occasions. Bitter potatoes will grow in a variety of soils and thrive on adversity. They seem to do best in cooler climates in a well-drained sandy soil with some compost added. While they will withstand periods of drought, they produce better with regular watering. They do need full sun. Bitter potatoes are usually propagated from tubers or eyes, but they can also be started from seed, then moved into the garden when they have 6 or 8 leaves.

Maca, *Lepidium meyenii*
Cabbage family, *Brassicaceae (Cruciferae)*
Also known as pepperweed, Peruvian Ginseng and mace
Biennial forming a rosette of leaves
Native to the high Andes
Value as a food source   6
Value as an ornamental   3
Multi-purpose   no
Continuous harvest   no
Ease of culture   7
Overall rating   ***

Over 2000 years ago this plant was grown in Peru, and it continues to be a minor crop planted in small plots, or sometimes intercropped with bitter potato because it tends to repel insects.

This vegetable is high in calcium and iron with about 12% protein. Fresh roots can be roasted or cooked in hot stone pits much like a baked potato. Traditionally these roots are dug then left to dry for three or four days in the sun before storing for future use. Then this dried vegetable can be boiled, then mixed with fruit juice and milk to make a pleasant tasting and nutritious thick soup. A fermented drink is also produced from the dried roots.

It has been grown as a South American answer to ginseng. The rurales are convinced that it increases fertility in both humans and their livestock. This supposed aphrodisiac quality may make this a marketable commodity for mountain villages. It is also being promoted as an energizer and anti-stress herbal.

The roots of this plant resemble turnips with colors ranging from red to yellow, white or black. They tolerate frost while actively growing and take approximately six to nine months to mature. The second year the plant produces seeds and the roots produce offsets. While maca will grow in poor soil it produces much better when fertilizer, regular watering and wise agricultural practices are employed.

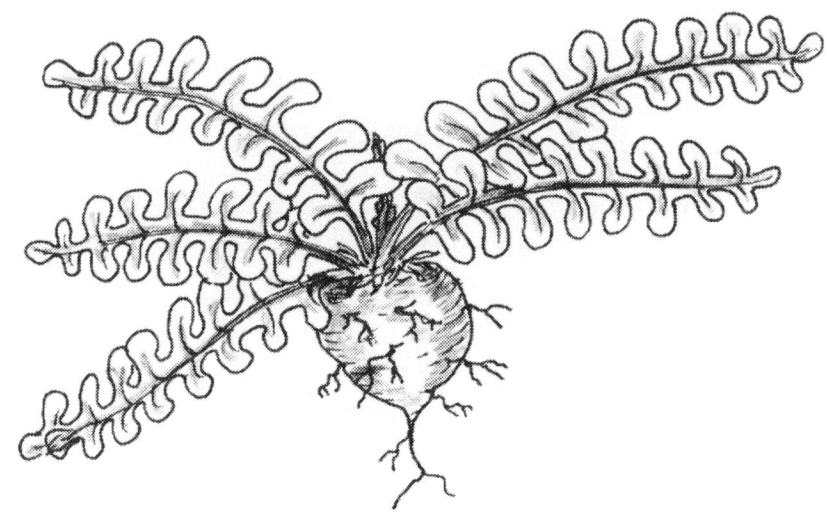

Mashwa, *Tropaeolum tuberosum*
Nasturtium family, *Tropaeolaceae*
Locally known as mashua, mascho, cubio and anu
Treated as an annual, although the tubers make it a perennial
Native to the Andes, spread by commerce through Colombia and Ecuador, Argentina and Chile

Value as a food source	6
Value as an ornamental	3
Multi-purpose	yes
Continuous harvest	yes
Ease of culture	8
Overall rating	***

    Think of this as a nasturtium with small yellow flowers. It has a sprawling vine that may reach six feet or more. This rugged, cold tolerant plant has ornamental value, but the real potential lies in it's ability to out-produce the common potato, even in poor soil, without much effort. The traditional way to grow this plant is to intercrop with ullucu, oca and potatoes because it possesses nematicide and insect repellent qualities. This is one of those plants that we need to experiment with in diverse climates. It might make an interesting edible hanging basket, or informal groundcover in areas of full sun and poor soil. It doesn't take intense summer heat and humidity well, but it will survive light frosts.

    The vegetable has a peppery flavor when boiled, some sources describe it as having an almost vanilla scent. The tubers can be dried or frozen after boiling. It makes a valuable addition to a meal. It's an important part of the diet of many rurales in the high Andes. It takes seven to nine months for the tubers to mature to harvestable size. They are used, like traditional vegetables in stews, soups and roasts. They also set the tubers out to freeze over night then enjoy them the next day with cane syrup or honey. Chemicals in the tubers are said to measurably lower testosterone levels when consumed in excess, and it has been used as an anaphrodesiac with some success. The leaves and flowers can be harvested throughout the growing season for use in salads and sandwiches, or added to soups and stews.

    Mashwa can be grown easily from seed, but is usually started from the tubers. Once it has been grown in an area there will usually be enough small tubers left behind during the harvest to produce the next season's crop. They will accept almost any well-drained soil as long as they have full sun. In temperate and sub-tropical areas where the winters are mild but the summers oppressive this may well work as a winter crop.

Mauka

Mauka *Mirabilis expansa*
Four o'clock family, *Nyctaginaceae*
Known variously throughout South America as chago, miso, yuca, pega pega and taso
Perennial maturing at about 1 m (3 ft) in height.
Native to temperate South America

Value as a food source	7
Value as an ornamental	8
Multi-purpose	yes
Continuous harvest	yes
Ease of culture	8
Overall rating	****

    This is a popular garden vegetable in Bolivia, Chile and Venezuela where it is often grown with squash, melons and other vegetables. The leaves, rich in protein, are used raw in salads or cooked in salsas, soups and stews. The swollen underground stems and roots are harvested parboiled and peeled. It should be noted that eaten raw they can produce an unpleasent sensation on the tongue and throat. In Bolivia the roots are sliced and cooked with molasses or honey. The cooking water is then served as a delightful and unique drink. In Peru they age the harvested roots to increase the sugar content. The roots are 5% to 7% protein by weight, making them particularly valuable in a starch laden diet.

    Mauka is grown easily from seed or pieces of stem. They respond best to a compost rich soil and watering during drought. A well-drained sunny site is best. The roots are ready to harvest in seven to nine months, leaves in about 60 days.

Oca

Oca *Oxalis tuberosa*
Oxalis family, *Oxalidaceae*
Also known as ibia, oqa, ciuba and apilla
Perennial herb growing less than 10 cm tall.
Native to much of South and Central America

Value as a food source	7
Value as an ornamental	5
Multi purpose	no
Continuous harvest	no
Ease of culture	7
Overall rating	****

    The ocas are members of the oxalis family and contain oxalic acid in varying degrees. The campesinos divide all oca into *keni* or sweet ocas, and *luki* or bitter ocas (bitter because of the higher oxalic acid content). Both types are widely grown and highly regarded making ocas second only to the white potato in breadth of cultivation. There is much color variation and some tubers are even variegated in shades of white, yellow, red and purple. They are a great home garden plant because they yield heavily and take little space.

    The watery tubers are often dehydrated in the form of chips called *cavi*, which is eaten raw, served with honey as a dessert or candied like sweet potatoes. These dried chips are frequently ground to produce *caya*, a flour that lasts for months and is economical to store until made into a porridge or added to soups and stews. Left in the sun for a few days the tubers sweeten and the calcium oxalate content declines. They are often eaten raw after this initial drying. Fresh tubers are baked, fried, roasted, boiled or mashed. The fresh leaves are eaten in moderate quantities raw as a snack or salad green or added to soups and stews.

The fresh tubers are about 80% water, but the dried tubers can contain as much as 11% protein and serve as a valuable source of vitamin A, as well as carbohydrates. The leaves are also eaten raw or cooked as a potherb.

Because the yields can be greater pound for pound than potatoes this is a popular crop in the Peruvian hills and mountainsides, but it is also grown in Argentina, Chile, Mexico and New Zealand. There are many cultivars and extensive research is currently underway to develop more productive, adaptable and pest resistant varieties. Because ocas can withstand frost and accepts a wide range of growing conditions, this is a valuable vegetable crop for many parts of the world. They thrive in a sandy soil and respond well to intercropping with several of the other Andean root crops like Mashwa, and uncullo. It requires between 150 and 230 days to mature. They need full sun and a well-drained site. In trials with compost enriched soil the yield increased markedly. They are somewhat drought tolerant but are more productive with evenly moist conditions.

While seeds are produced in limited qualities propagation is usually from the tubers, which are planted just below the soil surface and cultivated once or twice as they grow. Because the plant is attractive it can even be grown as an edible ornamental or as a container plant.

Potato, *Solanum tuberosum*
Tomato family, *Solanaceae*
Also known Irish potato, white potato
Perennial tubers, grown as an annual crop
Native to the Andes
Value as a food source   9
Value as an ornamental   2
Multi-purpose   no
Continuous harvest   no
Ease of culture   8
Overall rating   ****

This is the vegetable that almost took over the world. When it was first introduced to Europe it was not readily accepted and not at all a common appearance on the dinner table. Because of it's versatility, both in cultivation and use it is now the favorite tuber for temperate climates. This vegetable can be served boiled, baked, roasted, fried, deep fried, mashed, made into MacDonald's French fries, Lay's Potato Chips, added to soups, stews, salads and stir-fries. There's even more ways this tuber appears in our global diet. Paper thin slices can be used as a wrapping for meats and other vegetables. In India the potato skins are often eaten in a soup of chickpea flour and various spices. The Norwegians use potatoes to make a flat bread called *lefsa*. Vodka wouldn't be vodka without the modest little potato. In the

Scandinavian countries *Aquavit* is the national beverage of choice. It's made from potato alcohol, orange peel and a blend of herbs and spices. In the potato's homeland it is boiled, sliced and sun-dried to form *papa seca*, a gray chip that is added to soups, stews and a wide variety of dishes. Potatoes can be dried and made into a flour for breads, pancakes, milk substitutes and the list of ways we can use potatoes could go on to fill a book.

The leaves, stems and flowers are poisonous, as are the raw tubers that have been exposed to the sun long enough to turn green. Cooking will render these tubers safe.

In the Andes there are hundreds of varieties of potatoes grown in a tremendous array of shapes, sizes and colors. There are white, cream, yellow, red, blue and purple potatoes with a wide range of flavors as well. What a dynamic vegetable, and it's relatively easy to grow. They will thrive in a variety of soils but accept sandy well-drained soils in full sun. Potatoes are generally started from potato eyes (often referred to as seed potatoes), but there have been a number of varieties that can be grown from seed (now referred to as true potato seed, TPS). These true potato seeds will permit the introduction of potatoes as a viable crop in areas of the world where the transportation of heavy bags of seed potatoes is impossible. The true potato seeds also have a much longer shelf life and there is less likelihood of importing pests and disease.

Ulluco *Ullucus tuberosus*
Malabar spinach family, *Basellaceae*
Known throughout South America as papa lisa, chigua, timbo and melloco
Perennial
Native to the Andes

Value as a food source	6
Value as an ornamental	3
Multi-purpose	yes
Continuous harvest	yes, of the leaves
Ease of culture	8
Overall rating	***

Ulluco is the subject of intense research because of flavor and keeping qualities. The tubers can be found in a variety of colors ranging from green through white to pink, orange and purple. There is evidence that it was grown, or at least harvested in the Andes at least 4,000 years ago. Both the tubers and the leaves are edible. When boiled and fried they taste very much like potatoes. They are locally boiled and served with a vinegar dressing. One of the favorite indigenous dishes is a stew called *chupe*, made with potatoes, ullucu, eggs, cheese and available meat. When you live in the Andes it's easy to freeze dry your vegetables. These desiccated tubers are called *chuno*, and they can be stored until needed, literally for years. The tubers are generally not eaten raw but can be added to soups, stews, boiled, baked or fried dishes. As chuno they are usually added to soups and porridges. The leaves are also edible either raw in salads or cooked as a potherb. There are a number of named varieties available. One of the most popular is 'Shrimp of the Earth' with small pink shrimp shaped tubers and a good flavor. This is also one of the Andean tubers that provides edible leaves. Ulluco leaves can be used both raw and as a potherb.

In Peru it is consumed to ease the discomfort of childbirth. It is also viewed as an anti-aphrodesiac, reducing sexual desire.

The plant rarely exceeds 50 cm ($1^{1}/_{2}$ feet) in height. It can be grown in a wide range of climatic conditions ranging from sandy mountainous soils to compost rich meadow. It thrives in full sun but will tolerate dappled shade. It does need a well-drained site and will tolerate drought once established. It can be propagated from seed, stem cuttings taken during the warm months or by tuber divisions. There is some research being done currently with the hope of expanding its range and productivity.

Yacon

Yacon, *Polymnia sonchifolia*
Sunflower family*, Asteraceae, (Compositae)*
Also known as strawberry jicama, Bolivian sunroot, aricoma and llakuma
Perennial with yellow daisy like flowers that may reach 2 meters in height.
Native to Ecuador, Peru and Bolivia

Value as a food source	7
Value as an ornamental	8
Multi-purpose	yes
Continuous harvest	yes
Ease of culture	8
Overall rating	****

    This South American cousin to the Jerusalem artichoke (sun choke) is an attractive multi-purpose plant with edible tubers, leaves and flower buds. Tender young leaves can be used as a potherb, or added to soups, stews and rice dishes. The very young flower buds can be added to a stir-fry, baked or boiled. The plant is very attractive in flower and the seeds are a favorite of many songbirds.

    The roots have a naturally sweet flavor that is derived from inulin, a polymer based on fructose that our bodies do not have the enzymes to break down. This may have significance for diabetics. The roots are eaten raw and taste more like a fruit than a tuber. After drying the sweetness is enhanced. Numerous products and snack foods are made from this root in South America.

    Yacon is easy to grow in any well drained soil where there is full sun. With compost added the results are even better. It thrives in hot humid climates. Propagation is easy by seed or the dahlia-like tuber.

A Global List of Root & Tuber Crops

The Andes isn't the only part of the globe where roots and tubers constitute a major part of the diet. The native North Americans dined on Indian breadroot, quamash, dog's tooth violets, jerusalem artichokes, yampa and more. Africa has a great many food plants to delight the pallate and intrigue the tastebuds, like bambara groundnuts, Rhazi (Hausa potato), chufa, and marama bean tubers. From the Orient we have *Go*, a member of the burdock family and exotic radishes, while Australia's native delights include yam daisies, potato orchids and vanilla lilies.

Some of these tubers have been a part of human history for so long that their origins are lost in the mists of time, others are historic figures with fascinating biographies. Some of these crops are a part of the past, replaced by new varieties that satisfy the needs of commerce and food production. Others are waiting to be discovered, or rediscovered as acceptable table fare.

Many offer beautiful flowers, landscape potential, medicinal benefits and a multitude of secondary uses. These are plants that adventurous gardeners might want to try in a corner of the landscape or vegetable garden.

African potato

African potato, *Coleus tuberosus* or *C. Parviflorus* or *Plectranthus esculentus*
Mint family, *Lamiaceae*
Also known as country potato, Livingston's potato, Hausa potato, Kaffirpotato, Rhazi and Rizga
Perennial reaching about 1 m (3 ft) in height
Native to Africa

Value as a food source	7
Value as an ornamental	5
Multi-purpose	yes
Continuous harvest	no
Ease of culture	7
Overall rating	***

It looks like a small white potato. It grows like a potato. It even tastes somewhat like a potato. In parts of the world where this was planted by nature, the indigenous peoples ate them raw or cooked them in all the ways we cook a potato in the American cultures. They were baked, boiled, steamed, roasted, fried, mashed, added to soups and stews. They were even dried and powdered to use as a flour in baking and cooking. All this from plants that are first cousin to the decorative bedding plants we know as coleus. There are even reports of the leaves being used as a potherb or added to soups and stews. Unfortunately this productive, versatile and nutritious vegetable has been replaced in most of the world where it once grew by plants introduced by the colonial powers. Again the diversity of our food resources are being reduced.

There is work being done on the preservation and classification of *Coleus parvaflorus, C. Edulis, Plectranthus esculentus* and *Solenostemon rotundifoilus* by Dr. P. M. Kyesmu at Wye College in Britain. Dr. Kyesmu's studies indicate that this is a crop that can play a key role in the battle against hunger in West Africa. It contains almost 8% protein, 6% fiber and 29% carbohydrates, along with sodium, calcium, potassium, iron and other minerals important to human well being. There are also indications that this plant may contain compounds important in the treatment of asthma, hypertension, glaucoma and some cancers. Dr. Kyesmu and a colleague, Dr. S. H. Mantell, are working on ways to propagate this valuable plant through tissue culture in the hope of developing a program for cultivation and improving the productivity.

This is a frost sensitive plant that thrives in the hot humid tropics of the Congo Basin and the semi-arid regions of Western Africa. It can grow in full sun, but is content with a semi-shady location where it can calmly go about its business of producing tubers, leaves and flowers for the bees and butterflies. They are best propagated from small tubers, but can also be started from seed. Unfortunately this isn't a plant readily available. In fact it is headed toward extinction in many parts of the world where it was once common. Dr. Danforth, an agricultural missionary working in the Congo is cultivating this plant as a productive indigenous crop.

Cassava, *Manihot esculenta*
Poinsettia family, *Euphorbiaceae*
Also known as yuca, manioc, mandioca
Native to American tropics, now pan tropical
Shrubby perennial reaching 2 to 3 m (6 to 9 ft) in height

Value as a food source	9
Value as an ornamental	8
Multi-purpose	yes
Continuous harvest	yes
Ease of culture	8
Overall rating	*****

Cassava is the staple food of over 500 million people, and it's so productive that more calories can be harvested per given area than nay other crop with the possible exception of sugar cane and cattails. Not only does it produce that starchy root, and nutritious leaves, it's also the source for tapioca. All this in a root that contains cyanogenic glucosides that our digestive process breaks down into cyanide. This means that the harmful compounds have to be removed before the tubers can be used as the "potato of the tropics." You will find cassava listed as "sweet" or "bitter" with the sweet containing far less of this toxic compound. Often the distinctions blur, but with proper processing or cooking these compounds can be leached out.

The peoples of tropical America and the Caribbean worked out a system thousands of years ago that is still in use today in some remote areas. First the roots are peeled with a knife then grated into a pulp of juicy flakes. This pulpy mass is then stuffed into a special woven, tube shaped basket sometimes called a *couleve*. This finely woven basket is flexible and closed at one end. After this tube is filled it's stretched and twisted to squeeze the poisonous juice out of the pulp. The pulp is then dried and ground into a flour or placed in sieves and rinsed in water to remove any remaining cyanic compounds. In some areas of the world the pulp is simply dried, or the cassava is chipped and soaked in water to remove the poison, but simply cooking will render this food safe.

Few food resources are consumed in as many different ways. Each culture has a favorite manioc or yuca dish. It can be baked into breads or cakes, roasted, boiled, fried, made into a potato chip substitute, used in soups or stews mashed, made into a gruel or breakfast food, fermented into drinks and tofu like foods, or made into puddings and starches like tapioca and arrowroot. In fact tapioca is the cassava product that people living in more temperate are most familiar with. When this tapioca is in the form of large starch grains called tapioca pearls it can be used in soups, puddings, dumplings and sweet cake. The powdered form is called *goma de tapioca* or simply tapioca flour. This flour is used as a thickening agent for soups, sauces, gravies and all the other uses people all over the world have for arrowroot or corn starch.

The juices that were squeezed or washed from the roots are boiled to produce a condiment called *cassareep* that is a key ingredient in the tropical American dish called pepperpot. This boiled juice can also be fermented into *chicha* or other alcohols, some of which are an acquired taste, and vinegars. One popular drink is a blend of fermented yuca juice and chile peppers.

The root itself is popular in Africa mashed and whipped into a side dish called *fufu* or *dumboy*. This is the equivalent of mashed potatoes and is served with meat dishes and stews throughout Western and Central Africa. It can be made from cassava flour, or yams. The flour is mixed with cold water and brought to a boil. Then butter is added and this is whipped until it is completely smooth. Then the fufu is shaped into fist sized balls and served with the main course.

One of the great advantages of growing cassava is that there is a continuous harvest of leaves that can be cooked as a potherb. These are 11 to 39% protein and contain B Vitamins and several minerals making them a valuable addition to the diet. For this the younger leaves are best, and it is recommended that they be boiled for at least fifteen minutes. In the Congo *saka-saka* is a popular way to prepare the leaves. You begin by shredding the leaves and boiling them for thirty minutes to an hour. Then add diced sweet peppers, onion, okra, eggplant, a little garlic, chile peppers, salt and pepper to taste and a dash of vegetable oil. Bring this to a boil then let simmer for at least thirty minutes without stirring. You will have a flavorful almost sauce that can be served with fufu, chicken or fish.

The tropical Amerinds were growing and preparing cassava over 4,000 years ago, possibly gathering it and cooking both roots and leaves as much as 10,000 years ago. It was taken to Africa in the late seventeenth century along with the chile pepper and tomato. All three soon became a significant crops there, with the sweet potato appearing soon after. There is some dispute among anthropologists about how and when it spread through the Pacific, but it is grown throughout the tropics.

Because manioc grows in poorer soils and provides a continuous harvest it is one of the most popular family garden crops, but because it doesn't store well and has a very short shelf life there is little commercial marketing of this vegetable. It is easily started from stem cuttings struck where they are to grow or started in a nursery. It will grow in a wide variety of soils and will do well in full sun or as an understory crop. It takes between six and fourteen months for the roots to mature, but leaves can be gathered as needed. The leaves are also used in some areas as forage for cattle. The greatest danger to this vegetable comes from frost. It will freeze to the ground, but usually will recover from the roots.

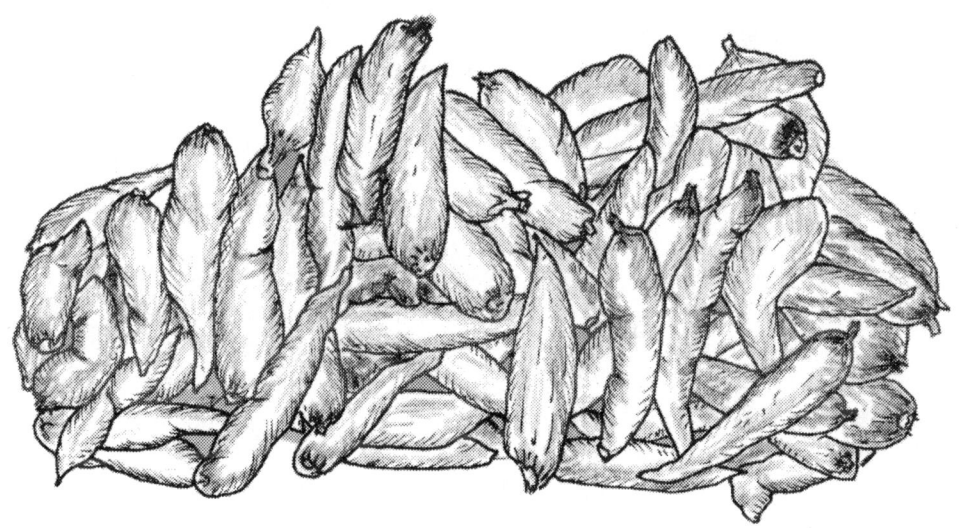

Cassava

Chufa, *Cyperus esculantus sativus*
Sedge family, *Cyperaceae*
Also known as Tiger nuts, earth almond, Zulu nut, ground almond & edible rush
Perennial reaching 1 m (2-3')
Native to Africa

Value as a food source	5
Value as an ornamental	2
Multi-purpose	no
Continuous harvest	no
Ease of culture	9
Overall rating	**

If you like water chestnuts you'll like the tubers produced by this relative, and they don't have to grow in the water. The small tubers can be roasted, baked, boiled, stir-fried or mashed into a paste. They can be squeezed to produce a nutritious milky liquid called 'Tiger's Milk' popular in Spain and some areas of north Africa.

We are accustomed to pulling sedge from our lawns as a weed, and many varieties are. The problem is that they spread by the underground tubers and set seed with reckless abandon. However, the variety *sativus* doesn't produce seed. This is the only variety I can endorse, as others can become dangerously invasive in many areas of the world.

This plant is almost too easy to grow. It will take a wide variety of soils and wet feet are no problem. It likes full sun but will thrive in partial shade. Grown with encouragement in compost rich sites it will produce in abundance. This 1/2 to 3/4 inch tubers can be harvested in about 90 to 120 days. In warm climates you can keep a crop coming on all year.

Day lily, *Hemerocallis lilio-asphodelus*
Lily family, *Liliaceae*
Also known as lemon lily, yellow day-lily
Perennial flowering plant reaching .5 m (15 to 20 inches) or more
Native to China

Value as a food source	6
Value as an ornamental	9
Multi-purpose	yes
Continuous harvest	yes
Ease of culture	9
Overall rating	****

This is one of those multi-purpose plants that provide us with an edible flower that can be eaten raw in a salad, as a snack or stuffed with seafood, cheeses, or sweet meats. The buds and flowers can be batter dipped and fried. The flowers can even be dried for later use in soups, rice or noodle dishes or stir-fries. The young shoots can be consumed raw as a snack or steamed and eaten like asparagus.

The fleshy roots can be boiled in salt water to yield a flavor somewhere between sweet corn and salsify. The roots can be added to soups, stews, stir-fries, or roasted, baked, batter fried, mashed or eaten raw.

This is an easy plant to grow in a wide range of locales. It is cold hardy enough to grow throughout the Orient and Canada, yet it will grow in the sub-tropics. All it asks is a place in the sun and well-drained, compost rich soil. It isn't fussy and will grow in nutrient poor sandy soil as long as it gets enough water.

There are many different species of daylilies and many are grown as ornamentals. It should be noted that for all of the true daylilies, the flowers, roots and succulent new shoots are edible. They are all propagated best from divisions, but some will set seeds.

Indian potato, *Orogenia linerifolia*
Carrot family, *Apiaceae (Umbelliferae)*
Also known as Great Basin Indian potato, or Great Basin potato
Perennial reaching about 15 cm (6 inches) in height
Native to Rocky Mountains of North America

Value as a food source	6
Value as an ornamental	5
Multi-purpose	no
Continuous harvest	no
Ease of culture	6
Overall rating	**

This is a plant harvested for the fleshy roots which, even though they are in the carrot family, taste more like a potato. This is only one of many tuberous plants referred to as Indian potatoes. The tubers can be harvested as needed at any time of the year and boiled, baked, stir-fried added to soups and stews or grated into a thick porridge.

It is worthy of greater study as a rugged perennial crop for northern climates. Once established it will perpetuate itself with little care. It thrives in a compost rich well-drained soil in full sun, but it will tolerate light shade. Evenly moist soil is best but it will withstand periods of drought, sometimes by going dormant.

This uncommon vegetable is propagated from seed or root divisions.

Iron cross oxalis, *Oxalis deppei*
Oxalis family, *Oxalidaceae*
Also known as Deppe's wood sorrel
Perennial tuberous plant reaching 15 to 20 cm (6 to 8 inches) in height.
Native to Mexico.

Value as a food source	4
Value as an ornamental	8
Multi-purpose	yes
Continuous harvest	yes
Ease of culture	7
Overall rating	***

Many members of this family have found their way to the dinner table in one form or another. Others have been grown as decorative ornamental plants for flowerbeds, ground covers and windowsills. This plant gives you both purpose and beauty. It produces deep violet leaves with lighter markings and impressive deep pink flowers. These leaves and flowers possess a tangy lemon taste and add flavor, color and nutrition to a salad, sandwich, soup, cream sauce, corn porridge or rice dish. More delight lies just beneath the soil in the form of fleshy white and pink tubers. The flavor of these cooked tubers is spicy with a hint of lime tartness. They are usually boiled but can also be added to a stir-fry, vegetable soup, meat stew, or roasted, deep fried or steamed.

The plants are at home in almost any sunny, or only lightly shaded location and will take quite a bit of drought once established. The best performance is achieved with a compost rich sandy soil, even if it's in a container. They don't respond well to overfeeding, but left on their own they will spread and fill in a bed or border. They are easily started at any time of the year from the tubers. Sometimes the seeds are available and they will germinate with enthusiasm. They are winter hardy into the Carolinas, but will freeze down completely with the first frost.

Oxalis

Madeira vine, *Anredera tuberosa* or *A. Cordifolia*
Malabar spinach family, *Basellaceae*
Perennial vine
Native to Tropical Americas
Value as a food source   5
Value as an ornamental   5
Multi-purpose   yes
Continuous harvest   yes
Ease of culture   8
Overall rating   **

    The root is edible raw, but this is an acquired taste as the tender flesh becomes uncomfortably glutenous as one chews and a residue is left after swallowing. They are delicious baked, boiled like potatoes or sliced and fried. The succulent young leaves can be eaten raw in a salad or cooked as a potherb. These leaves can also be stir-fried, added to soups, stews and rice dishes.

    This is an attractive frost sensitive plant that thrives in a compost enriched, well-drained site with full sun or light shade. The tuber can be mulched in frost prone areas and it will survive freezing temperatures quite well. This is a vining plant so it does require something to climb on, such as a trellis, arbor, fence or trees and shrubs.

    They are propagated from seed, stem cuttings taken during warm weather or by dividing the tubers and replanting after or during harvest. This is considered an invasive plant in some regions, a valuable food source or ornamental in others.

Pale vanilla lily, *Arthropdium milleflorum*
Lily family, *Liliaceae*
Perennial flowering bulb
Australian native
Value as a food source   3
Value as n ornamental   8
Multi-purpose   no
Continuous harvest   no
Ease of culture   6
Overall rating   **

    The flowers produced in the spring are beautiful and fragrant, but the tubers growing underground are the real treat. They are small, about radish size and are only eaten cooked. The flavor of the white flesh can vary from sweet to slightly bitter depending on the growing conditions. This is a mild vegetable that's high in starch. It can be boiled, baked, stir-fried, added to soups, stews or meat dishes.

    This is a perennial plant that thrives in a sandy, compost enriched soil in a sunny, well-drained site. To grow and prosper it needs regular watering, and an occasional feeding throughout the growing season is helpful. They work well in the flower border or in containers. They bloom in mid-spring, producing a rich vanilla scent. The same fragrance is released by the leaves throughout the warm months. This plant is about as cold hardy as the common dahlia, and will need to be dug and stored for the winter where the soil freezes.

The pale vanilla lily is propagated by seed sown in seed trays, preferably in a greenhouse, and transplanted to individual 4 inch pots for the first year. After they are large enough to survive they can be planted in the garden site or larger containers. They can also be easily propagated by division.

Pignut, *Bunium bulbocastanum, Apium bulbocastenum*
Carrot family, *Apiaceae (Umbelliferae)*
Also known as Earth Chestnut, Great pignut
Perennial reaching .5 m (15-24") in height
Native to Europe and the British Isles

Value as a food source	5
Value as an ornamental	6
Multi-purpose	yes
Continuous harvest	yes
Ease of culture	8
Overall rating	**

Described by the British as "small and fiddly" this isn't going to be a great cash crop, but there is more to this plant than those smallish tubers that taste like chestnuts when cooked or roasted. The leaves can be used as you would parsley, either as a seasoning in cooking, raw as a garnish or as a spicy addition to a salad. The seeds make an acceptable cumin substitute, and the flowers can also be used as a culinary herb. All parts have been used medicinally as an astringent.

Because of its informal appearance and dill like flower umbel it lends itself comfortably to well-drained beds or wildflower gardens, but the best roots are harvested from compost rich gardens or containers. It is easily started from seed, and even has a tendency to reseed itself if the umbels are allowed to ripen.

Quamash, *Camassia quamash*
Lily family, *Liliaceae*, closely related to the onion.
Produces beautiful flower stalk slightly less than 1 m high
Native to western North America

Value as a food source	5
Value as an ornamental	9
Multi-purpose	no
Continuous harvest	no
Ease of culture	6
Overall rating	***

This was a staple and ceremonial food of Native Americans along the Pacific coast. The tops die down after flowering in mid-summer. At that time the Indians would move into the valleys where the quamash were growing, dig a pit and line it with stone, and build a fire. Others would dig the onion-like bulbs. As the fire burned to hot coals the bulbs were placed over the stones and buried where they would cook for two days. With dancing and music they would then open the pits and feast on the harvest meal. What wasn't consumed was dried for later use.

This plant produces a bulb that resembles a medium sized onion but has a more sweet taste. It can be eaten raw or cooked. The bulbs do not store well but can be dried or kept in sand for several months. Quamash starts easily from seeds or small bulblets. They thrive in average well drained soil and will tolerate light shade quite well. They are cold hardy and drought resistant.

You get delicious produce and beautiful flowers.

Skirret, *Sium sisarum*
Carrot family, *Apiaceae (Umbeliferae)*
Also known as skirwort
Grows to 1 m (3 ft) or more in height
Native to the Orient, popular in Europe

Value as a food source	4
Value as an ornamental	4
Multi-purpose	no
Continuous harvest	no
Ease of culture	8
Overall rating	***

This is one of those antique vegetables that we should see more often. Skirret is grown for the six to eight inch cylindrical roots that have a decidedly sweet taste when grown in good soil with sufficient water. The name, skirret, comes from the Dutch *suikerwortel*, which can be translated 'sugar root.' These ultra-white roots can be used raw in salads where they are great with a light herbed vinegar. They also make a great raw, low calorie snack with a great taste. This is also a delicious vegetable boiled, baked, batter fried, stir-fried, creamed or steamed. They make a flavorful addition to soups or stews and compliment meat dishes well. Skirret can even be mashed and served with gravy or a cheese sauce. These's one more dubious use for these sweet roots. They can be grated and roasted, then used as a coffee substitute that is memorable of not what you might expect from Starbucks.

This would probably be a far more popular if it weren't for the tough, fibrous core. The edible white flesh has to be peeled from this core before using, and the harsher the growing conditions the higher the ratio of core to the good stuff.

This is a perennial usually grown as an annual that can be easily started from seed sown where they it's to grow, much as you would carrots. They can be started early in pots or flats and transplanted to the garden after they have grown into young plants. Skirret can also be started from root divisions much as we do dahlias.

The lacy leaves and white flower umbels make this an attractive background plant for flower borders or containers. For the best quality roots it should be grown in a compost rich soil that is kept evenly moist. They respond well to a regular feeding with increased productivity and sweeter flavor. Harvesting can begin as a part of the thinning process in about three months, but it actually takes about five to eight months before the roots are the optimum size.

Sunchoke, *Helianthus tuberosus*
Sunflower family, *Asteraceae (Compositeae)*
Also known as Canadian potato, Indian potato, Jerusalem artichoke
Perennial reaching 2 to 3 m (6 to 9 ft) in height
Extremely cold hardy
Native to North America

Value as a food source	7
Value as an ornamental	8
Multi-purpose	yes
Continuous harvest	no
Ease of culture	9
Overall rating	****

This was a popular vegetable in North America long before the French and the English arrived on the scene. Early colonial traders carried it back to Europe and it was first cultivated in England in 1617 where it has been a popular garden item since. Although commonly called Jerusalem artichoke, it has nothing to do with Jerusalem. This is a corruption of the French word *Girasola*, which can be loosely translated as 'turning with the sun.' The artichoke in the name is from the flavor of the cooked tuber.

This is an amazingly under used vegetable that doubles as a striking landscape plant. When planted in a row they form an informal fence loaded with small yellow sunflowers from mid summer through autumn. The birds appreciate the seedheads when they ripen. As a vegetable they have the advantage of growing well in the marginal areas where there might be light shade, poor soil or occasional drought. A vigorous plant can produce between 8 and 10 pounds of delicious tubers.

These tubers can be used raw in a salad, or cooked in a variety of ways. Boiled and served with melted butter they taste very much like artichokes without the effort the true artichoke requires as a part of the dining experience. They can also be baked, batter fried, stir-fried, pickled added to soups or stews, even mashed. The immature flower buds can be harvested and boiled or added to a stir-fry, open flowers and individual petals can be used as a garnish and tender leaves can be used as a potherb (the flavor is virtually non-existent). The tubers can be roasted and ground to make an almost acceptable coffee substitute. The seeds can be harvested when ripe, shelled and ground as a flavorful flour additive in baking breads and desserts.

The seeds can also be pressed for their high quality sunflower oil. The tubers were popular as a inexpensively produced livestock feed at one time.

Because the tuber contains inulin, a sugar our body doesn't try to break down (much like its cousin the *yacon*) it's a safe and nutritious food for diabetics. These tubers have also been the subject of extensive experimentation as a source of fuel alcohol.

They thrive in almost any soil and can handle periods of drought as well as moist areas. Naturally the better the growing conditions the greater the yield. There are a number of named cultivars including *Stampede*, producing large white tubers that mature early. *Dwarf Sunray* is a compact plant producing tender tubers that don't need to be peeled. They are commonly planted in early spring and can be harvested when the tops begin to go to seed or freezing weather occurs. In some areas this carefree plant can become invasive, because no matter how carefully you dig the tubers at harvest time, some are always left behind. Even the smallest pieces will sprout and become a new plant. Pieces of the tuber are the most common method of starting new plants. All that is required is to cover the smaller tubers with an inch or two of soil and wait for spring weather. They can also be propagated from seed but from seed the harvest is usually delayed until the second year. Basal stem cuttings will also grow into a new plant with little difficulty.

Taro, *Colocasia esculenta*
Calla lily family, *Araceae*
Also known as coco-yam, kalo
Perennial growing from corms, leaves may exceed m (3 ft)
Native to Asia, now pan tropical

Value as a food source	9
Value as an ornamental	9
Multi-purpose	yes
Continuous harvest	yes
Ease of culture	9
Overall rating	*****

Taro is often referred to as the potato of the tropics, and it is indeed a significant part of the diet for hundreds of millions of people. This is one of the famous 'Canoe Plants' of Hawaiian and Polynesian history. The plant was the direct descendent of *Wahea*, the sky father, and *Papa*, the earth mother, and the name, *Kalo*, means everlasting breath. It has been the survival food of many Pacific Islanders, and continues to be the staple crop in Africa, Asia, the Pacific and the West Indies. Without taro there would be no *poi*, and what would Hawaii be without this cultural foodstuff?

There are hundreds of varieties, many are so beautiful that they are grown as ornamentals. They are often divided into two categories, upland or dry field taro is often called *dasheen*, and wetland taro that thrive with wet feet for at least part of the growing season. The wetland varieties are commonly used to make the poi. This is done by peeling and beating the corm to a pulp with special stones in a wooden trough. The resulting mash is then fermented to produce the characteristic liquid we all know and love as poi. Poi is rated by thickness, one finger, two finger or three finger, and range in color from purple to gray. It is the universal seasoning to Polynesian cultures, much like salsa is to the American cultures.

These roots, or more properly, corms can also be boiled, baked, steamed, fried, roasted, used in soups, stews and puddings, mashed or fried into chips much like we do potatoes. The large leaves can be stuffed like cabbage leaves or cooked as a potherb. In India *patra* is made by baking a bean flour and spice dough in a taro leaf wrap. The young leaves are eaten everywhere as a cooked green in soups and stews called *luau* in the Pacific and *callaloo* in the Caribbean. The large leaf stalk, petiole, can be used as a thickening or vegetable in soups, or cooked and served with soy sauce. The early Hawaiians fed taro to the dogs they were fattening for ceremonial meals. These were called poi dogs. Tender new leaves and stalks could be blanched to produce a vegetable with a delicate flavor almost like mushrooms.

Both leaves and corms of the taro plant contain calcium oxalate, but this is destroyed by cooking. There are some cultivated strains that contain so little of this compound that they can safely be eaten raw, but the authors don't recommend uncooked consumption of any part of this vegetable. Why risk the discomfort? It should be noted that the corms can be boiled and mashed to make an easily digested food for infants and the frail elderly.

They can be grown in a wide variety of soils and are most productive in light shade but will tolerate full sun. They can be grown is USDA zones 8 through 11, and will survive freezes that will kill the tops. Taro is propagated from the small side tubers called cormels or eddos. In six months new eddos have formed and these can be harvested and used while the main tuber, called a mammay or dasheen continues to mature.

Many varieties are sold as elephant ears, and others are marketed as pool side or aquatic plants. One of the most attractive and highly productive varieties is 'Black Magic' with deep purple colored foliage and good quality corms. Some varieties of Colocasia are considered dangerous invasive weeds and there are restrictions on their importation in some areas. Several related plants are marketed as malanga. One of the most common is known botanically as *Xanthosoma violaceum*, which produces delicious leaves and petioles as well as high quality corms. *X. Brasiliense* is commonly known as belembe, Tahitian taro or Tanier spinach. It is grown for the leaves.

Tiger lily, *Lilium lancifolium* (sometimes listed as *L. Tigrinum*)
Lily family, *Liliaceae*
Also known as lance-leaf tiger lily, Tekir kambak, chuen tan, oni-yuri
Perennial bulbous plant growing 1 to 1.5 m (3 to 5 feet)
Native to China, Japan & East Asia

Value as a food source	6
Value as an ornamental	9
Multi-purpose	yes
Continuous harvest	no
Ease of culture	7
Overall rating	***

    Imagine beautiful spotted orange flowers that can grace both the table and the garden. Then add the bonus of a starchy, sweet parsnip flavored bulb. That's what we get with this easy and edible plant. The flowers can be used raw in salads, stuffed with soft cheeses, seafood or other vegetables. They can also be added to soups, rice dishes, stir-fries, or dried for future use. It is recommended that the stamens be removed because the pollen can cause an upset stomach or allergic reactions for some people. The bulbs are cooked, boiled, baked, steamed, roasted, added to soups, stews, stir-fries, vegetable dishes or deep fried. The bulbs can be dried and ground into a flour used as a flavoring, thickening agent or sauce. Make certain of the species before dining on these bulbs and flowers because some bulbs with similar bloom contain toxic chemicals.

    This plant has been used in folk medicine as everything from a diuretic to a decongestant. The flowers have been used as a treatment for morning sickness and the bulbs have been used to relieve the pain of angina pectoris.

    This is an easy plant to grow in almost any compost enriched soil that is well-drained and evenly moist. It will thrive in full sun or medium shade, with little or no care. It will take the harshness of temperate winters without a whimper. It should be noted that while it produces magnificent flowers it rarely produces seeds. Instead bulbils form where the leaves attach to the stem. This is one way they can be propagated. You can also separate the individual scales from the bulb and plant them in a compost rich mix where they will begin to produce small bulbs in a matter of weeks. The bulbs left undisturbed in the ground will form a number of offsets that can be divided after the tops have gone dormant for the cool months.

Yam daisy

Yam daisy, *Microseris lanceoloata* or *M. scapigera*
Daisy family, *Asteraceae (Compositeae)*
Also known as Murnong
Perennial
Australian native

Value as a food source	5
Value as an ornamental	6
Multi-purpose	no
Continuous harvest	no
Ease of culture	7
Overall rating	***

    For the Australian aborigines this was a staple of their hunter-gatherer culture. The women would dig the roots with digging sticks in such quantities that one source calls it "the Aborigine's potato." The fleshy, dahlia shaped roots, about 6 to 8 cm (3 inches) long, were roasted in an earthen oven, or in pits of hot coals. In some areas they harvested the roots all year long, but in other locales they only gather these roots after the plant had flowered, insisting that the flavor is bitter if gathered too early. This is one of those attractive plants that can grace the flower border and the dinner table with equal ease. On the dinner table it adds a moist, sweet flavor somewhere between coconut and sweet potato. They can be baked, roasted, added to stir-fries, batter dipped or sliced and deep fried like French fries. They can also be added to soups and stews. Regardless of how they are prepared, they are Australia's delicious contribution to the global table.

    This perennial produces a rosette of leaves and from that arise stalks, about .3 m (12 inches) with a yellow flower much like its cousin the oyster plant, *Scorzonera hispanica*, from Europe. They thrive in a well-drained sunny location and will tolerate winters to USDA zone 6, with a mulch. They prefer a sandy, compost enriched site, but will accept a wide range of soils. They are easily propagated from seed sown lightly and barely covered. Germination occurs in 10 to 20 days and they grow like dandelions. They can be started in seedling trays, then transplanted to their garden site when they have about 6 or 8 leaves. They can also be harvested and the smaller tubers replanted for the next crop.

Yampa, *Perideridia gairdneri*
Carrot family, *Apiaceae* (*Umbeliferae*)
Also known as yampah
Perennial reaching 1 m (3 feet) or more in height
Native to western North America

Value as a food source	4
Value as an ornamental	5
Multi-purpose	yes
Continuous harvest	yes
Ease of culture	7
Overall rating	**

This is another of those rugged and versatile, but little known Native American vegetables in the carrot family. The seeds are similar in flavor to caraway seeds and can be used in baking, soups, stews, stir-fries and salads. They also can be parched or toasted and used as a seasoning. The young leaves can be eaten raw in a salad or cooked as a nutrition flavoring for soups, stews, meat dishes, even rice and pasta. The root can be eaten raw much like we would a carrot. It has a refreshing, sweet, nutty flavor that makes it a great snack or adaption to a salad. The roots can also be cooked, boiled, baked, roasted or used in any other way you might use a potato. The roots can be sliced and dried for later use or ground into a flour that can be used for breads, cakes, porridges or added to soups and stews. The roots are best harvested after the tops die back for the winter. They can be stored in the ground and gathered as needed.

This is an extremely adaptable vegetable willingly accepting everything from bogs to dry hillsides, sand to clay, acid to alkaline, sun to semi-shade. The highest quality roots and leaves are gathered from plants grown in compost rich soil that has been kept evenly moist. This was one of the staples of the Native American diet, and one that we should be embracing as we look for perennial vegetables.

They are started as easily from seed as carrots, or you can start them by dividing the clumps during harvest and replanting the smallest roots. Left in the ground they will form a large clump with many harvestable roots in 2 or 3 years.

Yams & Sweet Potatoes

Is that a yam or is it a sweet potato? The great confusion over these two basic foods is partly due to the fact that they are both tropical in origin and similar in flavor. The following is an attempt to make the distinctions clear, although marketing will continue to be ambiguous.

First of all, they come from two different families. The sweet potato is morning glory kin, belonging to the *Convolvulaceae* and it's native to the New World tropics. The yam is a member of the *Dioscoreaceae* family. Most of its members are native to the Asian and African tropics.

Columbus introduced the sweet potato to Europe, but it had been grown and used for thousands of years throughout the American tropics. He found it being cultivated on the island of Saint Thomas where the natives called it *batatas*. The Spanish called it *patata* and this became *potato* to the English. In the early days of colonization in the western hemisphere the white potato, *Solanum tuberosum*, was unknown and when someone mentioned potatoes he or she was referring to sweet potatoes. The white potato didn't even find its way to the European farms and gardens until late in the 17th century.

Yams have a far different history. There's a multitude of members of this *Dioscoreaceae* family that provide edible tubers, including some that produce aerial fleshy parts called air potatoes. While these are a valuable food resource throughout the tropics, they are considered dangerously invasive in Florida. The confusion is compounded by the botanical name of the true yam, *Dioscorea batatas*. The word yam came from the African words *njam, nyami,* or *djambi,* which is loosely translated *to eat*. While there are varieties of *Dioscorea* growing in the Americas most of the productive ones came the western hemisphere from Africa along with the slave trade. Sweet potatoes have a higher concentration of Vitamin A than yams, and will grow well in both temperate as well as tropical climates in a variety of soils. The following descriptions should also help you to distinguish between these two vegetables.

Sweet potato, *Ipomea batatas*
Morning glory family, *Convolvulaceae*
Native to Tropical Americas
Perennial vine with a wide variety of leaf forms

Value as a food source	9
Value as an ornamental	8
Multi-purpose	yes
Continuous harvest	yes
Ease of culture	9
Overall rating	*****

The vigorous vines spread over the ground making an effective ground cover, as they produce great quantities of leaves. The young leaves are edible raw as a salad green while the more mature ones can be cooked as a potherb. Some varieties are more bitter than others but by bringing them to a boil then discarding the first water and boiling again the flavor in much improved. Even the leaves of the ornamental varieties with burgundy or chartreuse colored leaves are edible. The leafless stems are used in *kimchi* in Korea. In the Orient there are members of this sweet potato family that are grown only for the edible leaves.

The roots contain over three times the necessary daily requirements of sight saving vitamin A. On the African continent over 2000 children go blind every day because of a deficiency of this vitamin. By cultivating this adaptable plant this tragedy can be avoided. While these roots may take 90 to 140 days to mature the leaves can be harvested daily.

Sweet potato tubers can be eaten raw, boiled, baked, fried, mashed, batter fried, made into chips or dried for later use. They can be fermented into a number of alcoholic beverages including *awamori, chicha* and *shochu.* Candies, cakes, ice cream, breads and sweet treats are also made from these roots. This is the source of Brazilian arrowroot, and the Japanese make several snacks including *imokarinto* and *sembei* from the sweet potato.

There are yellow skinned and red skinned varieties with flesh that can range from white to purple. Sweet potatoes are usually started from stem cuttings, but one of my fondest childhood memories is of starting a sweet potato vine by suspending a small tuber in a glass of water so that the bottom half was in water. They will grow quickly from cuttings and thrive in a wide variety of soils ranging from compost rich to sandy. They are at their best in full sun but can tolerate light shade. Even the ornamental varieties will produce edible tubers, often in a variety of colors.

Yams, *Dioscorea esculenta* and *D. batata* plus many others
Yam family, *Dioscoreaceae*
Also known as name, true yam and greater yam
Vigorous often climbing vine

Value as a food source	8
Value as an ornamental	4
Multi-purpose	no
Continuous harvest	yes
Ease of culture	9
Overall rating	***

The African and Asian yam has been a staple part of the human diet for over 50,000 years, even though it's toxic if consumed raw. There are varieties that produce tubers exceeding 2 meters (6 ft) in length with a weight over fifty pounds. Because yams tubers are so large they are often found in fruit markets and groceries cut into more family size portions and wrapped in plastic. The tubers are more starchy than sweet potatoes are quite low in vitamin A (Beta carotene). The true yam is rarely found in the United States but is popular throughout the American tropics. There are between 100 and 200 varieties in cultivation with great diversity in size, color and texture.

Cultivation is limited to the hot, humid tropics where it may take as long as a year for the tubers to reach maturity. They generally form vigorous vines that will scramble up trees and over buildings. In some areas they can become seriously invasive. Many members of this family produce bulbils, or aerial tubers, as a means of asexual reproduction. These small tubers can be harvested and used in the same way as the tubers taken from the ground. They can be boiled, baked, fried, roasted, sliced, fried, dried, mashed, added to soups, made into chips or flour.

Dioscorea esculenta, also known as goa yam or fancy yam, has a delightfully sweet flavor with a creamy white flesh. An Asian yam, *Dioscorea japonica*, has a fleshy tuber that is grated and added to flour to make *soba*, or served with rice, noodles. This succulent vine tips of this yam are sometimes steamed or added to stir-fries. Cushcush, *Dioscorea trifida*, is delicious smooth textured yam from the Caribbean.

The air potato, *Dioscorea bulbifera*, sometimes called yam potato, is popular in the tropics because it bears bulbils almost all year long, thus providing a continuous harvest. Unfortunately this has become a seriously invasive plant in some areas such as Florida. The bulbils and tubers should only be eaten after cooking, but the flavor is quite pleasant. The flower spikes can also be a part of a good meal if they are boiled, baked or added to soups and stews.

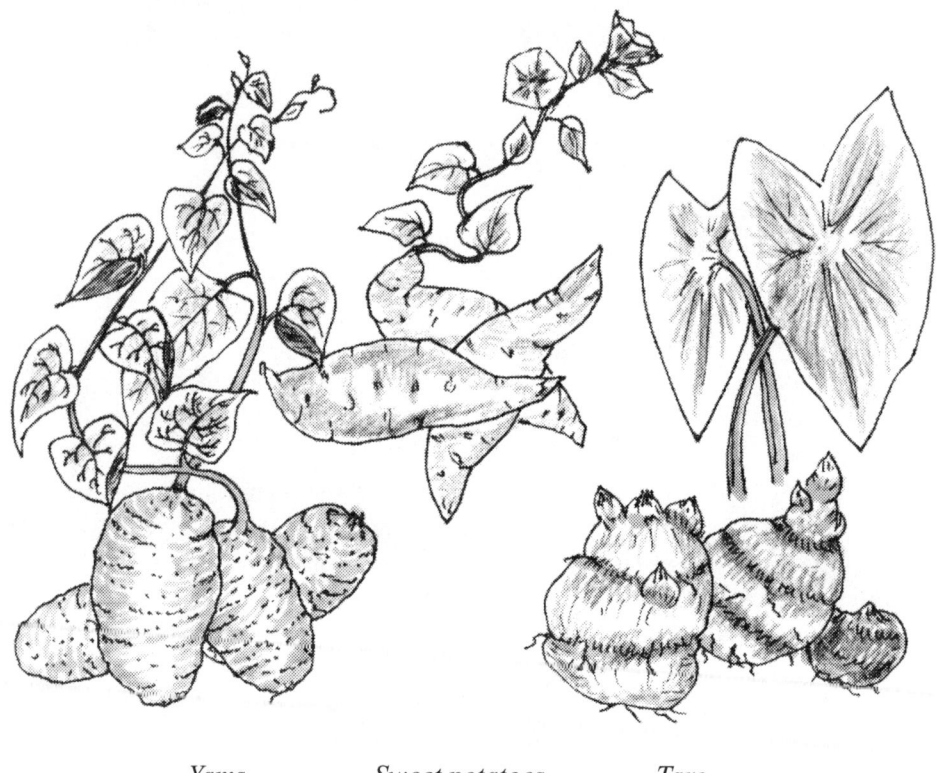

Yams   Sweet potatoes   Taro

Chapter Seven
BEANS, BEANS & MORE BEANS

More than Beans, Peas & Pulses

"Beans are the prime rib of the poor" a friend once told me. Another claims it is the health food of the future and that soybean products will replace red meat in the All-American diet. In truth they are both at least partly right. In cultures where life is measured in sufficient calories to survive rather than stock options, beans are a major investment in the future. The legumes have played a part in our diet from the days of our earliest ancestors on our evolutionary journey. Beans are versatile, store easily, contain protein and vegetable oils, are easier to catch than a rabbit, and safer to harvest than an angry mastodon. Beans grow, in one variety or another almost everywhere that humanity has been able to set up housekeeping.

Beans have always played a major part in the family garden. We all grow green beans, and occasionally the yellow wax beans, and those neat purple podded varieties like "Purple Royalty." Limas, peas, Southern peas, chickpeas, even garbanzo and fava beans find their way into our gardens. We all enjoy chili with its kidney beans. Black beans, navy beans, pinto beans and so many others add their flavor to so many dishes.

Beans are a good choice because they are some of the most productive are extremely easy to grow crops for both garden and field. There is a bonus in that most members of the family add nitrogen to the soil. This nitrogen-fixing habit of legumes makes them valuable far beyond the tasty flavor of their seeds and pods. They become useful in soil building, crop rotation and intercropping.

My gardening heroes have always been the Native Americans who were wise enough to plant corn, beans and squash together. The beans climbed the corn stalks while they fed the corn plant nitrogen. The squash served as a perfect living surface mulch keeping the weeds under control, keeping the soil cool and helping to preserve moisture in periods of drought.

Some tribes in the Southwest, (Zuni and Hopi) planted "waffle gardens" which were series of water reservoirs that held every drop of rain water where it was needed. Other peoples in other places have created extensive irrigation systems, terracing and gardens in the forest. Regardless of where or how, everywhere that people garden, or everywhere that people have harvested or gathered they have valued the lowly bean.

Yet the *Fabenaceae* family also contains some of the most deadly poisonous plants and many of the varieties that find their way to the global dinner table contain toxins until they are properly prepared.

We don't think of dining on the leaves of beans, or the flowers, or the roots, but these parts of the plant not only provide survival food, they yield nutrition, flavor and variety. In the European-American culture we view the garden in three phases, planting, growing, harvesting. The seeds are planted, then we tend and wait months until the produce is ready to harvest. In a hungry world this is an inefficient system. Wouldn't it be better if we planted crops that gave us a continuous harvest? What if we were growing plants that gave us greens or potherbs before the seeds were ready, then roots and tubers after the seed harvest was complete? Many members of the bean family give us this varied menu, but it goes beyond food. Some of these plants give us beautiful flowers, browse or fodder for livestock, shade, fuel wood, timber, medicines, oils and industrial products. Dried beans (pulses) store easily and will keep for a long time making them as valuable as the cereal grains, and that they have a greater nutritional value. Many beans are also an excellent source of oils for a variety of uses. Because of the ability of many members of this family to fix nitrogen in the soil, they are valuable in soil building and erosion control.

Variety on the Global Dinner Table

Let's take a look at some of these dynamic beans beyond the winged beans and maramas mentioned earlier.

Beach bean, *Canavalia maritima*
Also called bay bean and Mackenzie bean
Vigorous trailing vine may exceede 7 m (20')
Native to the Old World Tropics

Value as a food source	5
Value as an ornamental	7
Multi-purpose	yes
Continuous harvest	yes
Ease of culture	9
Overall rating	***

This is one of those seeds you plant and get out of the way. It's a salt tolerant beauty for tropical and semi-tropical areas. The flowers are big, plentiful and rich pink in color making this an attractive addition to the landscape. It makes a great erosion control and good forage for cattle. It is used extensively in dune restoration projects. This isn't the ideal vegetable for every garden but if you live on a coastal dune with extended warm weather give it a chance.

The young pods can be cooked and eaten, it isn't reccommended to eat them raw. In some regions of the world immature seeds are boiled into a delicious pea soup. While the mature seeds can be stored and cooked the flavor isn't as good as some other choices, but the dried seeds can be roasted and ground to make a coffee adulterant and in some cases a caffine free substitute.

The mature seeds, about the size of a healthy lima bean, travel well on the ocean currents and are among the multitude of seeds called "sea beans." These are gathered and polished, carved or made into jewelry.

The plant grows rapidly from seeds scarified and planted in moist soil. In less than one month the vines will be 1-2 m (3-6 ft) long, and that's only the beginning.

Butterfly pea, *Clitoria ternatea*
Also known as kordofan pea, blue pea or Asian pigeon wings
Probably originated in tropical Asia
Beautiful perennial flowering vine

Value as a food source	6
Value as an ornamental	9
Multi-purpose	yes
Continuous harvest	yes
Ease of culture	7
Overall rating	***

This is the forage of choice for livestock in the tropics and makes a great cover crop, but in the family garden it provides a good flavored immature beanpod that can be used like string beans. The leaves are often used in the tropics as a potherb and those magnificent flowers are used to give a blue color to breads, cakes and rice dishes.

This is one of those "show-off" vegetables that is as much at home in the flower garden as the vegetable plot. Trained on poles, trellis or fence the blue butterfly like flowers are a sight to behold. They start easily from seed and grow in average garden soil with regular watering. They are at their best in full sun but will tolerate light shade with only a slight decline in flower production.

Chickpea, *Cicer arietinum*
Also kown as garbanzo, Spanish pea, Bengal gram or ceci
Annual plant reaching 20 to 45 cm (10 to 18 in) in height
Native to Turkey, Asia and the Mediterranean Basin

Value as a food source	9
Value as an ornamental	5
Multi-purpose	yes
Continuous harvest	yes
Ease of culture	8
Overall rating	*****

This is the second most popular pulse crop in the world and it has been cultivated for thousands of years. It was known as the "salted provender" of Isaiah, and was common fare from India to Spain before the Roman legions put on their marching shoes. In some areas it is considered a symbol of poverty, not appropriate food for those who have status. In other regions this is the equivalent to the potato in Ireland.

The dried seeds contain 20 to 24% protein and are easy to digest. They're easy to store without refrigeration and will keep for years if kept bug free. The beans can be pressed to produce a paste or dried as a flour, or they can be cooked and eaten whole. The dried beans can be cooked in so many ways, boiled, baked, in soups, stews and porridges. A flour, *dahl*, made from the dried beans is used in baking and making couscous. The green seeds can also be used in a variety of creative ways. The immature pods can be used as we do green beans. Young leaves, shoots and flowers can be cooked as a potherb or added to soups. There is even a coffee-like beverage made from roasted dried chickpeas. The beans can also be fermented into a *tempeh*, similar to the tofu made from soybeans. In Chile a chickpea milk is prepared from the cooked beans that is both nutritious and easily digested by infants. It is also useful in helping to control diarrhea.

Research is being done on the sprouted seeds as a means of controlling cholesterol levels. There are industrial uses for this crop as well, including an adhesive used in the production of plywood and a starch textile sizing for fabric.

This is the ideal bean to grow in areas that are too arid for most other beans. It requires a well-drained soil and is not salt tolerant. A compost enriched soil is best and clay type soil can limit productivity. ECHO reports that there is some evidence that the chickpea roots release phosphorus into the soil. This is best treated as a cool season bean crop that will mature in about 90 to 120 days. They are easily started from seed sown where they are to grow. Treat much as you would green beans.

Lablab bean or Hyacinth bean, *Dolochios lablab*
Also known as Pharaoh bean, shink, bonavist & Chinese flowering bean
Perennial in frost free areas
vigorous perennial vine reaching 12-18 feet (4-6 m) on trellis or fence
Native to Africa and Asia

Value as a food source	7
Value as an ornamental	9
Multi-purpose	yes
Continuous harvest	yes
Ease of culture	8
Overall rating	****

If I could only grow one bean this would be it. The lavender, pink or white flowers are so spectacular that in the Orient bouquets are sold as a part of the florist's trade. Not only are these flowers beautiful, they're also delicious, tasting like sweet green beans. They make a great garnish addition to salads, soups and stews. They can also be smothered with a lemon flavored cream sauce for a truly delightful side dish. You can also add a handful of these flowers to rice to enhance the flavor and give it a pink blush. The cut flowers are popular in many parts of the Orient for bouquets and as tokens of affection. The love struck young fellow gives the girl of his dreams a bouquet of lablab flowers and she invites him to share a dinner of lablab flowers served in a cream sauce.

The young beans are rich purple in color. They can be used raw in salads or cooked like green beans. When cooked they retain a pink color. As the seeds begin to form and the pods swell, they can be shelled like peas or limas. When cooked these beans have a good flavor. Left to dry on the vine, then shelled, the dry beans can be stored for a long time. The dried black or cream colored beans have a delightful flavor when cooked.

But that's not all. A bonus for all growing this delightful vegetable is in the leaves. Young, tender leaves can be harvested and cooked as a potherb. With bits of bacon or ham they are delicious. They can also be cooked with slices of lemon rind for a different taste.

Wait. There's still more. This remarkable plant also produces an edible tuber about the size of a turnip. Sliced in a mixed vegetable stir-fry it is delicious. Or you can boil, bake, roast or serve this tuber with a cream sauce. This root can be stored in the ground where it was growing until you are ready to use it.

What more can we ask of a plant that grows easily from seed, thrives in a wide variety of soils and loves the summer heat and humidity. It will grow in full sun or light shade. While this bean will take a good deal of dry weather it does best with regular watering. This is an ideal summer vegetable that can begin to flower in 60 days. The first leaves can be harvested in 30-40 days. In frost free areas it will grow and bear for several years.

Pigeon pea, *Cajanus cajan*
Also kown as Congo pea, dhal, ambrevade
Perennial shrub, some varieties reach 3 m or more.
Native to Asia and Africa

Value as a food source	8
Value as an ornamental	8
Multi-purpose	yes
Continuous harvest	yes
Ease of culture	7
Overall rating	****

The very young seeds have a rich flavor and can be cooked and eaten like peas. In Latin America these beans are canned and marketed as *gandules*. The dried seeds can be easily stored and last for a long time. They can be used as we would any other dried bean. They are also fermented into something similar to tempeh. Even the young pods and leaves can be cooked as a potherb or added to soups and stews. It is best to cook all parts of the plant before eating.

This is an easy perennial crop for frost free areas. Once established pigeon peas can withstand drought conditions. They will thrive in a variety of soils but do insist upon good drainage and full sun to bloom and bear well. They are easily started from seed sown as you would green beans. Germination usually occurs in 7 to 14 days. They will begin to flower in less than 90 days and thrive in the heat of summer.

Popping beans, *Phaseolus vulgaris*
Also known as nunas
Annual vine reaching 20 ft or more in length.
Native to the high Andes

Value as a food source	7
Value as an ornamental	7
Multi-purpose	no
Continuous harvest	no
Ease of culture	7
Overall rating	***

Before there were people in the Andes to eat them the nunas were there, and people were gathering and enjoying these beans at least 11,000 years ago. The plant looks like an average pole bean, the seeds look like average dried beans in a variety of colors ranging from white to rust and black. But this is a fun food. When you put some seeds and a little cooking oil in a frying pan and put it over a fire you have beans that pop, almost like popcorn, except that there is less expansion. The flavor is almost like roasted peanuts. These seeds can be stored for years and not only retain their viability, they will pop. Nutritionally it is about the same as our more familiar beans, roughly 22% protein.

This is an ideal addition to the garden in temperate and mountain climates where there is at least 80 days with a mean temperature in the 70's. Their native habitat is between 5,000 and 9,000 ft up in the mountains where it gets at least 20-25 inches of rainfall annually. This isn't at its best in the tropics, although we have been able to grow it in Florida as a cool season crop. Care must be taken that it doesn't freeze. In our trials we found that it grows well through the heat of a Florida summer in partial shade, but refused to set buds until the days began to shorten, then virtually every leaf node sported a cluster of buds soon to become beautiful white flowers.

This is a fun plant to grow and serve along with the story of how it predates the common beans or frijolis, and was one of the first plants in the Americas to be domesticated. Growing this bean is like growing a little bit of history. This plant flowers only during 'short days' and is reluctant to bloom in more northern climates.

Scarlet runner bean, *Phaseolus coccineus*
Also known as scarlet emperor, fire bean, Dutch runner and red giant
Vigorous perennial vine 4 to 5 m (12 to 15 ft)
Native to Central America

Value as a food source	8
Value as an ornamental	9
Multi-purpose	yes
Continuous harvest	yes
Ease of culture	8
Overall rating	****

What a treat, beautiful flowers in colors ranging from red, through pink to white and even bi-colors that are edible as a fresh garnish in a salad. These flowers are followed by young beans that can be cooked as you would snap or green beans, or, after the seeds begin to mature they can be shelled like limas and used in a variety of ways. The mature beans can be dried and stored for an extended period of time as a protein rich food source with a good flavor. The immature leaves can be cooked as a potherb and the tuberous starchy root can also be boiled, baked, roasted, batter fried, stir fried or used in soups and stews. This is a vegetable plant that's as multi-purpose as the lablab and the winged bean.

There are many named varieties available from seed companies where they are often they are marketed as ornamentals, but there is great food value in this plant. While native to the tropics it's adaptable to a wide range of growing conditions and climatic zones. Scarlet runner beans, regardless of the color, are as easy to grow as any other pole bean. They respond well to compost enriched soil and are at their best in a well drained site with lots of sunshine, but will tolerate a great deal of adversity. They will bear well and flower profusely when trained on an arbor, trellis or fence. Many varieties produce a bean larger than limas, and they can range in color from red to speckled or brown and even white. In frost free areas this vine is perennial, but in temperate zones it is treated as a productive annual vegetable and ornamental.

Sword Bean, *Canavalia gladiata*, and closely related **Jack bean**, *C. Ensiformis*
Also known as Coffee bean, Brazilian broadbean & horse bean
Vigorous annual vine
Native to tropical Asia

Value as a food source	2
Value as an ornamental	5
Multi-purpose	yes
Continuous harvest	yes
Ease of culture	8
Overall rating	**

This is a popular vegetable in Southeast Asia and India and it's also appreciated in many other parts of the tropics. The vine is vigorous and will cover a large area if left to run. The pods can exceed .3 meters (12 to 14 inches) in length ant the seeds may be almost an inch in diameter. The young stem tips and leaves are used as a potherb or added to soups. Tender, immature beanpods are best harvested when they are 4-6 inches (10-15 cm) long and cooked like green beans. After they start to swell the green seeds can be eaten, but only after boiling, discarding the water and cooking thoroughly a second time to improve the flavor and safety. They contain small amounts of growth inhibiting substances. Mature or dried seeds should be considered toxic and consumed only after hours of cooking in a succession of waters and the seed coats have been removed. The seeds can be fermented into a *tempeh* as a means of detoxifying. The Japanese slice and pickle the young pods with lotus, radishes, and eggplant in soy sauce.

The sword bean is a source of vegetable protein and starch compounds that can be extracted and used as a food supplement for livestock. The vines also serve well as a green manure.

One of the advantages in using this nitrogen fixing legume is that it will grow quite well in extremely poor soils. This means that it's valuable in reclaiming agriculturally depleted regions.

White lupine, *Lupinus albus,* sometimes listed as *L. Sativus*
Also known as lupino, Beyaz acibaka and white lupin, and sweet lupine
Annual growing about 1.2 m (3 to 4 feet)
Native to Eurasia

Value as a food source	6
Value as an ornamental	8
Multi-purpose	yes
Continuous harvest	no
Ease of culture	8
Overall rating	***

Many of our edible plants also give us beautiful flowers and the white lupine is one of these. This is an almost unknown plant that should be a lot more popular. While most lupines contain a bitter alkaloid that makes them toxic the cultivar *Kiev* has a relatively safe sweet tasting seed, as do *Primorsky* and *Ultra*. There are many other varieties that may or may not taste bitter. If there is a bitterness to the "bean" this indicates the presence of the alkaloids, and they can be eliminated by soaking the seeds overnight and discarding that water. If bitterness persists, you may want to bring them to a boil and discard the first cooking water as well. Many plants are not edible raw (green tomatoes for example) but cooking chemically changes the toxins into harmless compounds.

The seeds are not only delightfully delicious, they're good for you too. In fact they are about 35% protein and 8 to 10% edible vegetable oil. You can cook these dried seeds just as you would any other beans. They make an interesting addition to chili, baked beans, and bean salads. But it gets better. You can lightly roast these seeds and make a snack that tastes better than peanuts. You can grind the seeds into a flour for breads, pastas and breakfast cereals. If you give the seeds a second roasting and put them into the coffee grinder you can make a passable coffee substitute that is absolutely no threat to Starbucks.

This is one of those "Swiss Army Knife" vegetables that have multiple uses. The oil is used to make fine cosmetic soaps. Both the oils and the powdered seeds are used in a number of cosmetics and skin treatments. After the seeds have been harvested the stalks yield a fiber that can be used in the production of both paper and cloth. Bruised seeds soaked in water until they become soft can be mashed into a poultice that was traditionally used in Russia to treat boils, ulcerations and skin infections. It has also been used as a diuretic and a folk control for hypoglycemia.

This is a weed that thrives on disturbed sites, and very acid soils; but will grow even better in good compost rich well drained soils in full sun. While it will withstand some drought it is much happier with evenly moist well-drained soils. Because it is a nitrogen-fixing plant it's often used as a green manure, grown then tilled into the soil. If the tops are harvested for fiber or biomass fuels the roots can be left undisturbed in the soil to enrich it and add nitrogen.

This is an easy annual crop for temperate regions. Planted in the spring after soaking over night the seeds will germinate in about 7 to 14 days, begin flowering in less than two months and be ready to harvest in 110 days from planting.

Jeheb nut, *Cordeauxia edulis*
Native to Western Africa
Also kown as ye'eh
Perennial shrub
Value as a food source   7
Value as an ornamental   5
Multi-purpose   no
Continuous harvest   no
Ease of culture   6
Overall rating   ***

    This is an endangered species that provides both nutritious beans and a valuable cash crop under desert conditions. These seeds are about the size of a macadamia nut with the consistency and flavor of a chestnut. They are delicious raw or cooked, but this is more than just a snack. The seeds can be ground into a paste or roasted and made into a flour that adds both flavor and food value to baked goods, soups, stews and other cooked dishes. The nuts can also be roasted, boiled, baked or added to stir-fries, meat and vegetable dishes, rice and maize meals. The leaves are used to make a mild flavored tea.

    In its native West Africa this is an endangered species, but there is research currently being conducted in Israel, Australia and arid Africa. Aside from the nutritional aspects of the nuts, there is the potential as a source of fine vegetable oil. The shrubs also serve as an erosion control and help to stabilize soils while serving as windbreaks for more delicate crops. It is also a legume that serves its role as a nitrogen-fixer in these barren and inhospitable soils.

    They are started from seed that has been scarified before planting. Germination usually occurs in 2 to 4 weeks and growth is slow for the first year. By the time they are a meter tall they are bearing prolifically and are ready for a commercial harvest.

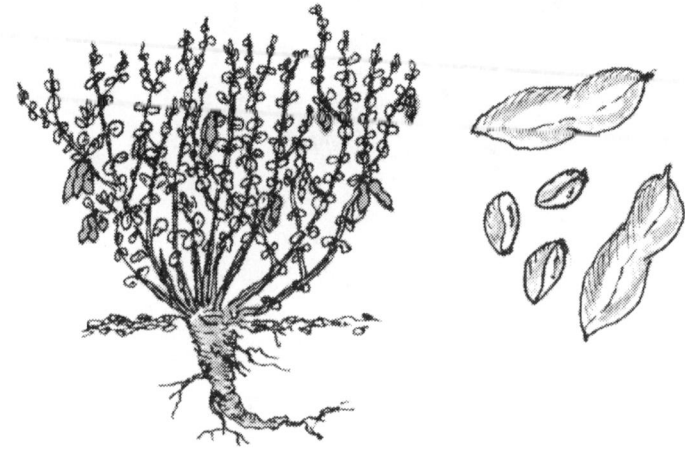

Chapter 8
Melons and More, Vegetable Fruits

We have discussed enough edible leaves to fulfill a bunny's wildest dreams, bushels of roots and tubers, a global bean soup, but we haven't yet explored the wonderful diversity of the fruits that we call vegetables. There are cannibal's tomatoes, sweet peppers and African eggplants, melons and edible gourds, okra, unicorn plants and so many others. Many of these plants require months of growing time before the harvest is possible, but many give us a secondary use, others are perennial and require far less labor and environmental impact. There are delicious and nutritious vegetables from every culture, from every geographic area, every climatic condition, every eco-system. We focus on tomatoes, peppers, cucumbers and a few melons, but there is so much more that we can enjoy both growing and eating. Many of these under used plants, these vegetables of the past and perhaps future, may well be key players in the battle against hunger, malnutrition and starvation everywhere. Let's take a look at some of these.

The Tomatoes and Their Kin

African scarlet eggplant, *Solanum aethiopicum*
Also called mock tomato, Ethiopian nightshade
Perennial shrub, (deciduous) growing 2.5 m (7 to 8 feet)
Not cold tolerant
Native to Tropical Africa

Value as a food source	5
Value as an ornamental	5
Multi-purpose	yes
Continuous harvest	yes
Ease of culture	8
Overall rating	***

The small fruits are a beautiful orange-red color with a somewhat bitter eggplant flavor. In Africa they are used in soups, stews, fried in oils or lard, used as a condiment or pickled. They are sometimes sliced and soaked in vinegar, salt, or sorghum overnight to alter the bitterness before cooking. We could find no reference to it being consumed raw. The immature shoots can be picked cleaned and peeled then chopped into soups or stir-fries. The young leaves can be cooked twice, with the water from the first boiling discarded to avoid bitterness and toxicity. The flavor of the leaves doesn't make them a gourmet's delight but it constitutes a famine food.

This is sometimes referred to as the *tomato of the Jews of Constantinople*. These are the people forced from Timbuktu into Spain in about 1400 AD. They carried this fruit with them into their new home, then Spain expelled them in 1500 AD when they resettled to Constantinople.

The attractive plant is available in several named varieties that give more flavorful fruit and high yield. *Turkish Orange* is a hardy insect resistant cultivar that will give you your first harvest in about 70 to 80 days from seed. The mature fruit are about 6 cm (2 to 2 ° inches) in diameter and deep orange when ripe, but they are best harvested when still green. They have an almost sweet flavor that is popular in several Thai and Italian dishes, curries, and sauces. *Sweet red* is another high performance variety of this vegetable that we ought to know more about. The fruit are small, about 1 inch in diameter and striped like a miniature watermelon when immature. As they ripen the fruit becomes two-tone red. This is a thornless variety that takes somewhat longer to mature, but the small fruit are best harvested while still green.

They are at their best in full sun in a soil that can be kept evenly moist and well-drained. They will tolerate every soil from sandy loam to heavy clay, but produce very well in a compost rich sandy medium. They can also be grown in a large container as an edible ornamental. The lavender flowers and rich green leaves are as attractive as the bright orange fruit. In frost prone areas they can be grown as an annual vegetable.

They are as easy to start from seed as tomatoes and can be grown as a long season annual. The named varieties will bean quite heavily and the fruit is well worth the effort to locate and grow them.

Cannibal's tomato, *Solanum uporo*
Perennial shrub reaching approx. 1 m (3 feet) in diameter
Frost sensitive
Native to Polynesia

Value as a food source	4
Value as an ornamental	5
Multi-purpose	no
Continuous harvest	yes, almost
Ease of culture	8
Overall rating	**

In earlier times, when missionaries roamed the islands of the Pacific seeking souls to save, they were occasionally served at the dinner table of cannibals in Borneo and other locales. Sometimes as honored guests, sometimes as the meal itself. When these reluctant converts made missionary stew they used this little red fruit as the primary seasoning. It was colorful, rich in vitamin C and flavorful. This plant, with such an intriguing history, has been one of the most popular plants in our trial gardens. It is also the source of one of our greatest embarassments. We served this bright red fruit for the first time while guests were present and our first efforts were completely inedible. The small red fruit are extremely bitter unless soaked in saltwater, vinegar or honey and water over night, then cooked as you would eggplant or added to soups and stews, meat sauces or stir-fries. It should be noted that the fruit are meatier and more flavorful if harvested and cooked before they are fully ripe. Unfortunately for our dinner guests, we didn't know this until after that fateful meal. We have since found numerous recipes and advice on serving the fruit. One source told us that the ripe fruit are only palatable when blended with sugar, vinegar, onions and several other seasonings to make a great dip for chips and French fries. The leaves can be cooked and eaten as a potherb. Because they contain solanin, it isn't recommended that you eat either the fruit or the leaves raw.

Cannibal's tomato is an easy and attractive plant to grow in any evenly moist well-drained corner of the garden. It does best in a compost rich soil mix with neutral to slight acidity. It prefers full sun but will tolerate light shade. It will form a mounded shrub with a profusion of pale lavender flowers and rich green leaves. The first fruit are ready to harvest in about 75 to 80 days they continue to bear almost continuously for months after that.

Cannibal's tomato

Clammy ground cherry, *Physalis heterophylla*
Perennial vine
Native to North America, from Canada to Texas
Value as a food source   6
Value as an ornamental   4
Multi-purpose   no
Continuous harvest   no, but extended harvest season
Ease of culture   8
Overall rating   **

    Only the fruit is edible, but what a delight. Each orange-yellow thumbnail sized fruit comes in its own plain brown wrapper. The sweet flavor is delightful raw, but don't eat the "paper bag," really the calyx, because it is poisonous, just like the leaves and stems. Only the fruit is safe to eat, and make certain that your identification is beyond a shadow of a doubt because even the fruit of related species can make you rather ill.

    These ground cherries can be used to make a tasty pie, flavor ice cream, enhance a fruit bowl or salad. They even make a delicious jelly or sweet-tart sauce for the table. The seeds have been used in folk medicine to treat urinary tract infections while a tea made from the leaves has been used to treat a headache. Compounds from this plant are currently being researched for their potential as a cancer treatment.

    Because this is a perennial vine it can be started from seed and transplanted to it's permanent home in either full sun or light shade. All it asks is a well-drained site and at least half a day's worth of sunshine. It can also be started from stem cuttings and divisions.

Cocona, *Solanum sessiliflorum*
Also known as Cubiu, Orinoco apple
Perennial sprawling shrub reaching 2 m (6 feet) in height
Native to tropical Americas
Value as a food source   6
Value as an ornamental   4
Multi-purpose   no
Continuous harvest   no, but extended harvest season
Ease of culture   7
Overall rating   **

    This is a frost sensitive, shrubby, rather ugly plant with large leaves and apple sized orange-red, oval shaped fruit. The flesh is cream-yellow colored and rather acid. These fruits are generally peeled and cooked where they make excellent pies, jellies, sauces and preserves. The flavor has been described as reminiscent of everything from gooseberries to melons to pineapples. The variety, Kendall Gold, produces a sweeter, more flavorful fruit that is suitable for fruit salads. Aside from the value of the fruit in cooking and desserts, there is a tartly refreshing drink made from the juice. In some regions the indigenous population gather the young leaves and cook them as a potherb. The flavor is somewhat bitter, and is probably best considered a famine food.

The plants can be started from seed or rooted cuttings and do best in an evenly moist well-drained soil that is compost rich.

Currant tomato, *Lycopersicon pimpinellifolium*
Also known as German raisin tomato and grape tomato
Generally treated as an annual
Frost sensitive
Native to The Andes

Value as a food source	7
Value as an ornamental	4
Multi-purpose	no
Continuous harvest	no, but extended harvest season
Ease of culture	8
Overall rating	***

This plant produces grape clusters of small yellow, orange or red fruit. These small currant-sized fruit are a delight as a raw snack, colorful addition to a salad or used as a garnish. In some regions they are harvested and dried while in other areas the inhabitants prefer to pickle them, either green or ripe. They make a flavorful addition to soups, stews, pasta and rice dishes. This is one of several members of the tomato family called 'currant tomato,' and this one probably gives the highest yield because it will begin to bear early and continue until frost.

This vegetable is easily grown from seed the same as you would any tomato. It does well in a three to five gallon container or directly in the garden. A well-drained compost enriched soil and a sunny location can assure a good continuous harvest. They don't handle drought well, but do appreciate an occasional application of a balanced fertilizer.

Egyptian peafruit eggplant, *Solanum torvum*
Also known as Pea eggplant, susumber, pokak & Lao green grape
Generally treated as an annual, forms a sprawling thorny plant 2 m tall
Native to North Africa, found throughout the tropics

Value as a food source	8
Value as an ornamental	7
Multi-purpose	yes
Continuous harvest	yes
Ease of culture	8
Overall rating	***

This is another of those multi-purpose plants that can serve the gardener so well. The young shoots can be eaten in a variety of ways. Boiled, stir-fried or steamed they have a pleasant, slightly tart taste. The immature fruit are harvested in the West Indies and cooked with salted fish. In many parts of the world the fruit are added to soups, stews, stir-fries or as a substitute for eggplant. The unripe fruit do have a decidedly bitter quality, that is somewhat diminished as they ripen. They are also pickled in vinegar, or sauteed with mushrooms and chile peppers.

There are several varieties, one of the best is 'Snake Eye,' or Laotian grape, which seems to be the most rugged and productive. It's also the most cold tolerant and resistant to the common insect pests. The plants will exceed 6 feet in height with small thorns every inch of the way. They are easily started from seed, the same as you would tomatoes. They can also be started from cuttings.

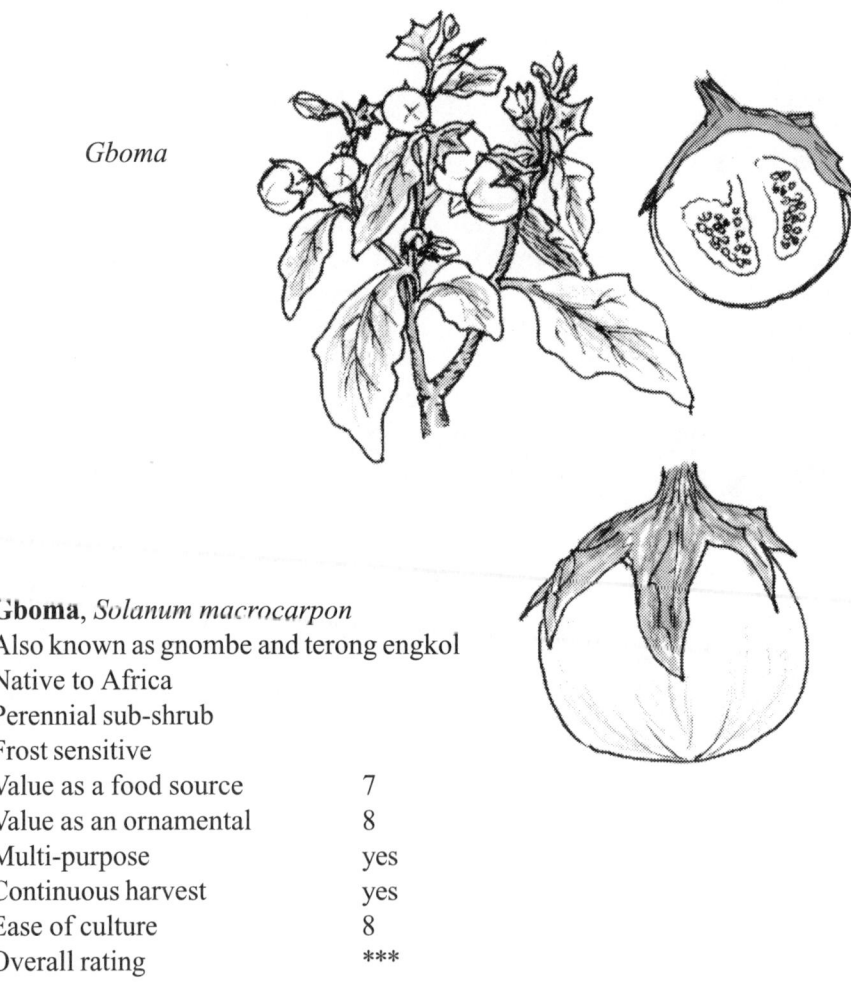

Gboma

Gboma, *Solanum macrocarpon*
Also known as gnombe and terong engkol
Native to Africa
Perennial sub-shrub
Frost sensitive

Value as a food source	7
Value as an ornamental	8
Multi-purpose	yes
Continuous harvest	yes
Ease of culture	8
Overall rating	***

This is one of several 'garden eggs' grown and eaten throughout western and central Africa. The fruit are small and deep yellow when ripe. They must be cooked to make them palatable. This golfball sized egg can be sliced and added to a stir-fry, used in soups and stews, or added to fish or meat dishes. The raw leaves are mildly toxic but they can be harvested and cooked as a potherb. This cooked greens are both safe to eat and nutritious, with a slightly bitter taste that can be easily overcome with the addition of some onions, bacon or vinegar.

This is an easy plant to grow in the tropical or sub-tropical garden as a perennial; in temperate regions it can be treated as an annual. The young leaves can be harvested continuously and it bears fruit over an extended season. In our trials fruit was produced every month but January and February in Central Florida. It grows well in a variety of well-drained soils, responding best to a compost rich site with regular watering. This delightfully rugged plant can withstand periods of drought with little decline and is quite happy in full sun or light shade. You can start it easily from seed sown as you would tomatoes. It transplants with ease and even tolerates growing in a container where it makes an attractive edible ornamental with its blue star-shaped flowers, deep shiny leaves and yellow fruit.

Jaltomate, *Jaltomata procumbens*
Native to Central America
Value as a food source	7
Value as an ornamental	5
Multi-purpose	yes
Continuous harvest	yes
Ease of culture	8
Overall rating	***

This is a great multi-purpose plant. The leaves can be harvested continuously and eaten raw or cooked as a potherb. In Mexico these leaves are frequently cooked and served with eggs. The sweet tasting fruit is marble sized and shiny black. They can be eaten raw, cooked or dried like raisins. Jaltomate fruit are used in soups, with meats, in baking to make sweet breads, and in desserts. Even the fleshy roots can be eaten either raw or cooked. These are great in a stir-fry or in a mixed vegetable dish. The roots have potential as a salad vegetable in the family garden.

They are easily started from seed or cuttings and grow under the same conditions as tomatoes. This is a sprawling semi-vine that can be trained on a support for greater space efficiency and productivity. Note: there are several other varieties of Jaltomate that aren't as flavorful or productive as *J. Procumbens*.

Kangaroo apple, *Solanum aviculare*
Also called New Zealand nightshade
Evergreen shrub reaching about 2 m (5 to 6 feet)
Frost sensitive
Native to Australia
Value as a food source   3
Value as an ornamental   5
Multi-purpose   no
Continuous harvest   no
Ease of culture   7
Overall rating   **

    The unripe fruit, as is the case with tomatoes, is poisonous. Fortunately, once it's fully mature it can be safely consumed raw or cooked. The flavor can vary from super-sweet to acidic bitter depending on growing conditions. The fruit is best gathered after it has fallen, because then it is sweetest. This is one of the traditional Aboriginal bush foods of Australia. The oblong fruits can be baked or boiled with a little honey or sugar added if necessary, or they can be made into sauces, preserves and jellies. They can also be used as a vegetable in stews and with numerous meat dishes. The leaves are toxic and even when cooked are unpalatable. The green fruit contain botanical compounds that are being used in the pharmaceutical industry.

    On a scale of 1 to 10 for efficiency and productivity the kangaroo apple rates about a 4, but it is an attractive shrub that has been used as both a specimen plant and a hedge, even in warmer parts of Great Britain.

    If the temperature drops below freezing it will die down to the ground, but if well mulched this fast growing shrub will come up again when spring arrives. It tolerates a variety of soils ranging from sandy loam to heavy clay as long as the site is evenly moist and well-drained. It doesn't seem to be too particular about soil acidity but yields best with a neutral or slightly acid soil. It isn't tolerant of shade, and will grow spindly with few flowers if subjected to more than a couple hours of shade per day. It also seems to grow best if not overfed.

    Kangaroo apples are easily started form seed or cuttings. It has been reported that cuttings taken from semi-mature wood in mid-summer will root before the seeds germinate, usually within two weeks.

Naranjilla, *Solanum quiteonse*
Also known as 'Golden Fruit of the Andes' & locally called *Lulo*
Native to South America
Value as a food source   5
Value as an ornamental   4
Multi-purpose   no
Continuous harvest   no
Ease of culture   6
Overall rating   **

    Some say this is an ugly shrub, others grow it as an edible ornamental. The yellow to orange fruit are used to produce a popular Latin American juice that combines the tastes of citrus, pineapple and a hint of tomato. The flesh of this fruit is yellowish-green with a refreshing sweet-sour flavor that is often used to make a foamy green drink called *sorbete*. This fruit is also used to flavor ice cream or make jams and jellies. It can also be mixed with cane syrup to make a fermented beverage called *chicha*.

    This is a perennial shrub with ruggedly attractive spiny purple veined leaves and lavender flowers. It will freeze back in a heavy frost, but is otherwise quite hardy. It prefers a compost enriched well-drained site, and once established can withstand periods of drought. To grow well and bear it needs full sun. These are easily started from seed sown as you would tomatoes. It will grow relatively fast, blooming and bearing fruit the first year from seed. There are seedless hybrids available. They can also be propagated from cuttings.

Pepino, *Solanum muricatum*
Also known as melon pear, pepino dulce
Native to South America
Value as a food source   6
Value as an ornamental   4
Multi-purpose   no
Continuous harvest   no
Ease of culture   8
Overall rating   ***

    This is a sprawling plant that produces the most flavorful of fruits. Imagine a scent of muskmelon with a hint or pineapple and a dash of ripe pear flavor. This is a delight to pick fresh and eat out of hand. They also make a valuable addition to a fruit salad, serve well as a nutritious snack food, can be served with wine and cheeses, used as a delicious garnish, or made into jams and jellies. While it isn't used this way in it native habitat, it does make a delicious pie. The fruit can also be used in sauces, fruit drinks, and pastries. One researcher recommends slicing the fruit and drying it for easy storage.

    This is an easy vegetable-fruit to grow from seed. If you are fortunate enough to find one in a specialty food market dry a few of the seeds for a day or two and plant the same as you would tomato seed. They will germinate within two weeks and grow rapidly in a container or in the garden. They like an evenly moist, but not soggy, soil rich in compost. Full sun brings out the best in them. One of the advantages is that they begin to bear early and continue over a long season.

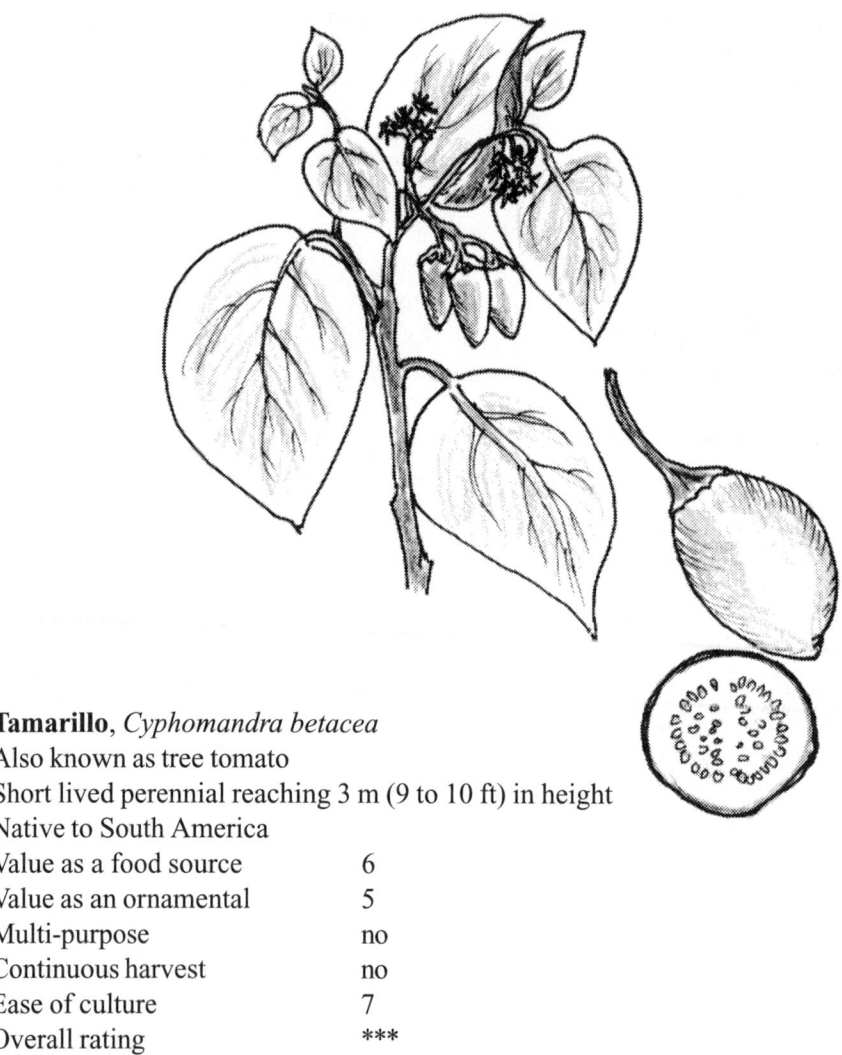

Tamarillo, *Cyphomandra betacea*
Also known as tree tomato
Short lived perennial reaching 3 m (9 to 10 ft) in height
Native to South America
Value as a food source   6
Value as an ornamental   5
Multi-purpose   no
Continuous harvest   no
Ease of culture   7
Overall rating   ***

This is an interesting novelty for the garden in frost free areas, or as a container plant in colder climes. The fruit is red, orange or yellow and about the size and shape of a hen's egg. When ripe this fruit can be picked as needed. They can be enjoyed fresh by cutting the top off and scooping out the sweet, almost tomato-flavored pulp with a spoon. They also make a great addition to a salad. Tree tomatoes can also be cooked in a number of ways, from boiling, baking, roasting or adding them to salsas, stews, sauces for rice and pasta. Great jams and preserves, pies and sweet sauces can also be made from the ripe fruit.

There are numerous named varieties with some of the best research and development being done in New Zealand. All start easily from seed the same as you would the more traditional tomato. Once they begin to grow you will need to give them more room. They will also grow in a large container. They thrive in full sun in a well-drained compost rich soil. They are heavy drinkers and need regular watering and feeding with a balanced fertilizer. While none of our resources mentioned it, this plant responds well to pruning and can be kept to the size you prefer. It can also be propagated from cuttings struck in moist soil or sand.

Wolfberry, *Lycium chinense*
Also known as Chinese wolf berry, Chinese boxthorn, matrimony vine, and gau gei choi
Perennial shrub
Native to East Asia

Value as a food source	6
Value as an ornamental	7
Multi-purpose	yes
Continuous harvest	yes
Ease of culture	8
Overall rating	***

This is a rugged, sprawling vine that can be used in roadside erosion control as well as the perennial garden. It produces small star shaped lavender flowers and great quantities of juicy red fruit. One catalog listed wolfberry as a great plant for attracting wildlife, but it has potential as a food source too. The huckleberry sized fruit have a sweet, licorice-like flavor when eaten fresh from the bush, but they can also be dried like raisins or made into jams and preserves. In China they are added to soups, stews and some rice dishes or fermented and distilled into a sweet alcoholic drink. A related spices native to the American Southwest, *Lycium pallidum* (rabbit thorn or pale wolfberry) was gathered and eaten raw or added to soups, stews, meat dishes or cooked down to a sauce or sweet syrup. This syrup was often dried and stored for future use in cooking or as a snack. A meal made from the dried berries was added to baked goods. A mild, licorice flavored tea can be made from the ripe or dried fruit. The seeds can be roasted and brewed into a drink that some call a coffee substitute, but there is no resemblance to coffee. It is a delightful hot drink in its own right and worthy of our consideration.

The young leaves have a mint-like flavor that can dramatically enliven a salad when added raw. In China the leaves are added to soups with duck eggs, cooked as a potherb, added to rice dishes, pork, fowl and turtle. The leaves are used to make a sweet tea called *Lord Macartney's tea*, considered a tonic by some. There is another wolf berry, *Lycium barbarum*, sometimes called Duke of Argyle's tea tree, whose leaves are used in the production of one of the traditional herbal teas called *Essential Harmony*.

This is an easy shrub for temperate climates where it can get full sun. It needs good drainage but isn't fussy about soil and will survive in almost anything, but does best in a compost rich site. It grows well on banks and slopes. It can be propagated from seed sown in trays or pots and barely covered. Germination will occur sporadically from 2 to 6 weeks. Nurture them in 4 to 6 inch pots for the first year, then give them a permanent home. One source recommends them as a large container plant that can be kept trimmed to shape and size. They can also be easily propagated form 6 inch hardwood or softwood cuttings. Rooting can take place in 3 to 6 weeks.

Dining on Gourds, Melons and other Cucumber Kin

The *Cucurbitaceae* family includes the common garden variety squash, pumpkins, cucumbers and gourds along with some truly exotic fruits, vines and roots. They can be found all over the world and have been appearing in the human diet from that shadowy time when the humanity was little more than a vague concept, a series of evolutionary experiments. Some are highly nutritious, some produce valuable oil seed, some are poisonous. Many members of this family were designed by time and trial to withstand the harshest of conditions, from the Kalahari Deserts to the wet lands of Southeast Asia. Some, like the Zambo melon, *Cucubita ficifolia* v. *Grande*, grow in the Andes. There are members of this family that provide sponges, musical instruments, dyes, edible tubers like the buffalo gourd, *Cucurbita foetidissima*, of the American Southwest, and a whole ethnopharmacy of traditional remedies for many human ailments. Research is currently being done with members of this family on cancer and diabetes treatments and controls. Members of this family are among the most vigorous and productive vegetables we can grow in our gardens, yet some of these are dangerously invasive, like the scarlet gourd, *Coccinia grandis*, and have become noxious weeds. The future holds some interesting possibilities for this dynamic botanical family. By combining the genes of a perennial watermelon cousin, *Citrullus ecirrhosus*, from the Namibian Deserts with our commercial varieties we may get a drought tolerant perennial watermelon. We may well be able to develop significant vegetable oil production from some of these cucurbits and in the process create an economic base for small villages in many parts of the world. As we learn more about the varied crops, growing techniques and ways to use many of these gourds, melons, squash and more we increase the potential for our universal survival. The following are only a few of the interesting *Cucurbitaceae* grown and utilized throughout the world.

Achocha, *Cyclanthera pedata*
Also known as achoccha, pepino de rellenar and korila
Annual vine that may exceed 4 m (12 ft) in length
Native to Central and South America

Value as a food source	4
Value as an ornamental	2
Multi-purpose	yes
Continuous harvest	yes
Ease of culture	8
Overall rating	***

This tropical vine will grow enthusiastically in the warm months, producing a multitude of leaves and tender shoots that can be harvested and cooked as a potherb. These leaves and shoots are great boiled and served with an herbed vinegar, or cooked with diced onions, green peppers and sesame seeds. A few can also be added to a stir-fry. Tender young leaves and shoots can be used raw in a salad as well. The vines begin to blossom as the days begin to shorten and a steady supply of young fruit are available for harvesting. They look and taste somewhat like cucumbers but aren't as crisp. The very young fruit make an excellent pickle. As they mature they become hollow and can be stuffed and baked. They can be filled with meat, cheeses, rice or vegetables to become a key part of a delightful meal. The mature fruit can also be sliced and added to stir-fries, soups, stews. They are delightful lightly fried with vinegar and oil.

This is a vegetable that will thrive in a compost rich well-drained site in full sun. They will bear better if trained on a trellis or other support. Regular watering is also beneficial and a regular feeding will increase productivity. They are easily started from seed the same as you would cucumbers. In Northern climates they can be started indoors and transplanted to the garden after danger of frost. One of the best for salads and pickles is a variety called Fat Boy. Lady's Slipper is a variety recommended for cooking and stuffing.

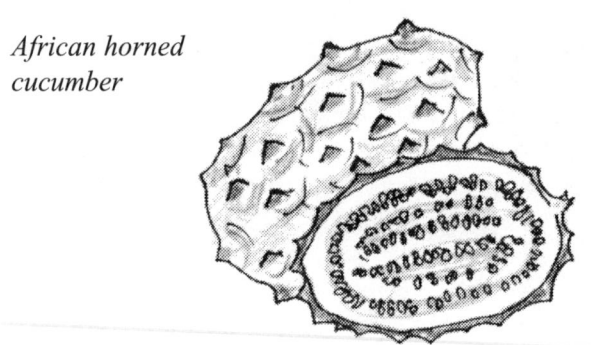

African horned cucumber

African horned cucumber, *Cucumis metuliferus*
Also known as *kiwano*, horned melon, melano and jelly melon
Annual vine
Native to tropical Africa
Value as a food source   5
Value as an ornamental   5
Multi-purpose   no
Continuous harvest   no
Ease of culture   9
Overall rating   ***

So ugly it's cute, the horned melon is often found in the supermarkets as a novelty fruit. The flesh inside the orange rind covered with its blunt thorns is green and juicy with a pleasant, mild flavor. In its native habitat the melons are eaten raw, boiled, baked, roasted or added to soups and stews. They are sun-dried or pickled for storage, although because of the thick rind they have a long shelf life. Some claim the flesh is rather underwhelming while others describe it as being a blend of banana and lime. In our taste trials we found it to be mild and refreshingly cool with a hint of citrus flavor. The French make an iced dessert with it. The leaves can be used as a potherb. In Africa the leaves are fried with a peanut butter sauce or cooked as a potherb.

Because the roots are resistant to a number of diseases and nematodes, the African horned cucumber is being used as a root stock for other melons in some areas. This is a rugged vine from the more arid parts of Africa, from Botswana and Namibia to Malawi and Nigeria. It has been cultivated as a cash crop in Australia, New Zealand, Israel and more arid regions of Latin America. They grow in a wide range of well-drained soils that have been compost enriched and withstand drought very well. Home gardeners often train the vines on trellises or fences to conserve space but commercial growers cultivate them the same as cucumbers or muskmelons. Full sun is a must, and in humid areas powdery mildew can be a problem. It takes about 110 days of warm weather to produce a good crop. Propagation is from seed and it's best to start them indoors in 4 or 6 inch pots or seeding trays at least 4 weeks before they are to go in the garden.

This may be one of those fruits that we will hear more about in the future, as creative chefs discover intriguing ways of serving it. This is a survivor in arid lands. However it should be noted that Julia Morton, in her book *Economic Botany*, warned that is can become a weedy invasive in many areas. It was deleted from ECHO's seed bank.

Bitter melon, *Momordica charantia*
Also known as balsam pear, carilla fruit, alligator pear, bitter gourd
Native to tropical Africa, pan tropical

Value as an edible	5
Value as an ornamental	3
Multi-purpose	yes
Continuous harvest	yes
Ease of culture	9
Overall rating	***

It's the unripe fruit that are the most edible portion of the plant. They are usually harvested fresh, cut in half with the seeds and fibers removed. They can then be boiled, fried, baked, stir-fried, or added to soups, stews and grain dishes. In some regions they are frequently filled with vegetables, meats, or rice much like a stuffed pepper and baked. It should be noted that the name 'bitter melon' is well deserved.

This bitterness is from an alkaloid, *momordicine*, and the more mature the more bitterness in the fruit until it begins to ripen. While there are many varieties that claim to be less bitter, most cultures still soak the cleaned fruits in salt water, or parboil and discard the first water to help moderate the bitterness. The leaves and tender new growth are prepared as a potherb or added to soups, curries, or stews.

This is an easy vine to start from seed, the same as you would a cucumber. Because this is a vigorous vine you will need to provide a trellis, or some support for it. It thrives in a compost rich well-drained soil that is kept evenly moist. Full sun is best but it will produce in light shade. There are many named varieties and hybrids available, some are disease resistant, others yield a more marketable fruit that is less bitter, larger, has a longer shelf life of is more prolific. One variety, *Prodigy*, produces a pale fruit about 8 inches long that can actually be sliced and eaten in a salad. This is a variety that is best described as more tart than bitter. It is also heat tolerant and extremely vigorous.

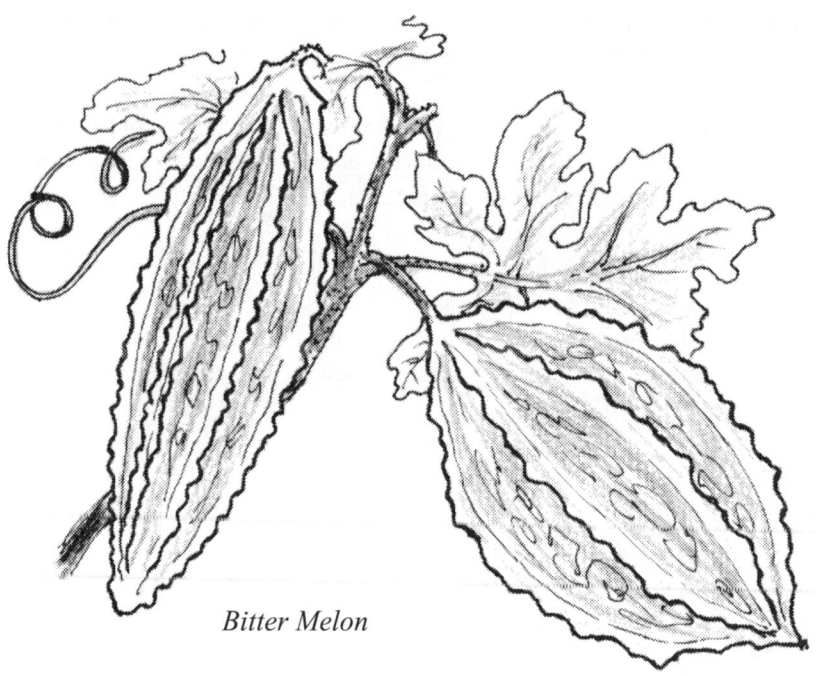

Bitter Melon

Bottle gourds

Bottle gourd, *Lagenaria siceraria*
Also known as calabash gourd, lauki, opo
Annual vigorous vine
Native to Africa, pan global

Value as an edible	7
Value as an ornamental	6
Multi-purpose	yes
Continuous harvest	yes
Ease of culture	9
Overall rating	***

    This is one of those plants we are familiar with as an ornamental, but for people throughout the tropics, this is dinner, and often the serving bowl as well. The young fruit are enjoyed the same as those of us in the temperate regions use zucchini and summer squash. Actually they are a bit more creative with this fruit because they will boil, steam, batter and deep-fry, bake or stir-fry. The fruit will be added to soups, stews, curries, sauces, rice and bean dishes or pickled. In many parts of Asia this is the staple garden vegetable, as versatile and valuable as the tomato is to Americans. The young leaves can be cooked as a potherb. The young shoots can also be prepared in a number of ways, including boiling, roasting, adding to soups, stews, and stir-fries, or simply used as a vegetable side dish. In Africa the seeds are added to soups. The seeds are a source of high quality vegetable oil and in some locales the seeds are ground and fermented into an equivalent to the tofu derived from soybeans.

The young gourds can be carved with designs that become permanent as the fruit matures. These etchings can be painted or dyed and the fruit made into drinking gourds, bowls, musical instruments ranging from guitars to drums and rattles. Dried gourds are also used as storage and cooking utensils.

This is an easy plant to grow in a wide variety of soils, although the best production is achieved with a well-drained compost enriched site with regular watering. Because this is a vigorous vine it will need support, either in the form of a trellis or a tree to clamber over. They will serve as a ground cover if support is lacking, but the quality of the fruit isn't as uniform. It thrives in full sun and longs for the hot humid days of summer. They are propagated from seeds the same as you would squash or melons. There are numerous named varieties available. Long white prolific and summer prolific are two heavy reliable producers.

L. Siceraria 'Clavata' is popular as an edible wrap. The young fruit are peeled and the flesh cut into thin strips that are then dried for storage. They can be softened by soaking in seasoned or salted water for about half an hour. These reconstituted dried gourd shavings are then used as a wrap or packaging in the preparation of other foods, much like the European cabbage leaves used in making cabbage rolls.

Buffalo gourd, *Cucurbita foetidissima*
Also known as mock orange, stinking gourd, chilicote, chili coyote, coyote melon &calabazilla
Perennial vine suited for arid sites
Native to North America

Value as an edible	2
Value as an ornamental	3
Multi-purpose	yes
Continuous harvest	no
Ease of culture	7
Overall rating	**

This is the little gourd found all over the American Southwest and Mexico. Most of the Southwestern Indians considered the fruit fit for coyotes only, but did consume them on occasion. However, they have long valued the seeds that contain about 30% protein and over 30% oil. They are roasted and eaten as a nutritious snack, or ground into a meal, then used in baking, soups, stews and porridge. The tuberous roots are a valuable source of a sweet starch and can be used to make puddings and serve as a thickening agent. The very young fruit itself is sometimes cooked and eaten, but this is usually considered a famine food. I have been told that they can also be sliced and dried then later added to soups, meat dishes and stews. It seems that after drying much of the bitterness dissipates. The flowers are also edible as a potherb or fried like squash blossoms. The early settlers used the crushed root as a cleanser when washing clothes.

The plants thrive in a wide range of soils, withstanding drought extremely well. In humid areas they are subject to powdery mildew and other fungus problems. Experiments are currently being conducted using this perennial plant as a root stock for cucumbers, squash and other cucurbits. This could give people in arid lands an increased production potential and be environmentally sound gardening.

Buffalo gourd

Casa banana, *Sicana odorifera*
Also known as musk cucumber, melocoton and zucchini melon
Perennial vine in the tropics, grown as an annual in temperate zones
Tropical American native

Value as an edible	8
Value as an ornamental	2
Multi-purpose	no
Continuous harvest	yes, of the fruit
Ease of culture	7
Overall rating	***

This is a vigorous vine that produces a large aromatic, sweet tasting fruit. When ripe they can be sliced and eaten raw, but they are also made into preserves, and used as the base for a sweet fruit drink called *cojombro*. The juice can also be used as the base for a popular alcoholic beverage. It is sometimes used to make a sweet sauce, sweet treats and candies. The unripe fruit can also be harvested and used as a vegetable in soups, stews, stir-fries etc. The flavor of the green fruit is somewhat like zucchini. Each large fruit also contains 700 to 900 seeds in the cavity. These seeds are almost 40% oil and 25% protein, making the seeds a valuable resource as well as the fruit. These seeds can be eaten roasted as we do pumpkin seeds or boiled, pressed for oil and pulp, dried and ground.

This is an easy vegetable to grow in almost any tropical or temperate garden that has at least 110 frost free days. The vines will scramble over a wide variety of well-drained soils, but productivity is increased in a loose compost rich site. Full sun is necessary for efficient growth. This melon isn't as drought tolerant as many in this family are. Because the young fruit can be harvested on a continuous basis this is one vegetable that lends itself to a continuous harvest. They are easily started from seed sown as you would pumpkins or squash. They can be started indoors to get a jump on the growing season or sown where they are to grow. This is one of those plants that deserves a broader audience and further research as both a family garden vegetable and a cash crop.

Chayote, *Sechium edule*
Also known as chayotl, sou-sou, vegetable pear, choke
Perennial vine producing a tuber, not cold hardy
Native to Central America

Value as an edible	6
Value as an ornamental	2
Multi-purpose	yes
Continuous harvest	yes
Ease of culture	9
Overall rating	****

This is one of the best kept secrets of the vegetable kingdom. The pear shaped fruit has so many uses and it keeps so well that it ought to be a featured item in every produce department. They can be eaten raw as a snack, added to a salad, sliced and deep-fried to produce food similar to French-fries in taste. They can be pickled, stir-fried, sauteed, baked, boiled, steamed, stuffed, grated, creamed, added to soups and stews, made into puddings, pies fritters or almost any other food you can think of. The flavor is neither sweet nor tart, it is simply pleasant, with a crunchy almost radish like consistency. You can use the young leaves, stems and tendrils as a potherb. The stems can be cooked like asparagus or added to a mixed vegetable dish. One source insists that the steamed shoots and stems are great with a cheddar cheese sauce. The fleshy tuber is known in some regions as *chinta* or *chinchayote* and it is baked, roasted, fried, boiled, smothered with honey or cane syrup, or grated and used as a source of starch. It can be grated, dried and stored for months.

The fruit is a palm sized fruit containing a single seed. To start new plants you can plant the entire fruit so that about half of the dimpled end is uncovered. Often you can see the vine starting to grow if they have been left on the windowsill too long. They enjoy a compost rich soil that is evenly moist but well-drained. They will climb tall trees and leap over large buildings with little or no encouragement. The tuber is best harvested after one or two years. After that it becomes woody and less valuable as a food source.

Chayote

Cucuzzi, *Lagenaria Siceraria 'Longissima'*
Also known as Italian edible gourd, New Guinea bean, New Guinea butter vine
Vigorous annual vine

Value as an edible	8
Value as an ornamental	4
Multi-purpose	yes
Continuous harvest	yes
Ease of culture	9
Overall rating	****

'Longissima' is a variety that really deserves its place in the sun. What a versatile plant this is. It produces fruit up to 4' in length with a flavor and texture of green beans. They are best harvested before they reach 2 feet, because after that

they tend to become too tough and fibrous. Once harvested these delicious fruits can be steamed, sauteed (with mushrooms it is a gourmet's dream), baked, pan fried, stir-fried with other vegetables, stuffed and baked, batter dipped and deep-fried or added to soups, stews and mixed vegetable dishes. Sliced and baked with cheese and tomatoes it makes a better eggplant Parmesan than does the eggplant. The young shoots are also great as a steamed vegetable or cooked as a potherb. The white flowers can also be dipped in egg batter and fried.

This is a vigorous vine that is best grown on a trellis to be most productive. They thrive in a sunny location with compost enriched, well-drained soil and regular watering.

Egusi, *Citrullus lanatus* ssp. *Colocynthoides*
Also known as wild watermelon, ibara, egusi-ibara or tsama
West African native

Value as a food source	6
Value as an ornamental	4
Multi-purpose	no
Continuous harvest	no
Ease of culture	8
Overall rating	***

This is a first cousin of the common old watermelon that produces a fast growing vine. It's traditionally inter-planted with other crops like cassava or grains. Each vine will produce many fruits that look like small watermelon, but the flavor of the fruit is anything but a treat. It's grown for the seeds, which are flavorful and serve as a daily vitamin supplement. They can be eaten raw but are usually dried, hulled and roasted. The seeds are a rich source of nutrition and a high quality vegetable oil. After hulling these seeds can be roasted and eaten like pumpkin seeds. In some locales they are mixed with ground pepper corns, then pressed into cakes and sold as a popular food in the marketplace. They can also be ground into *ose-oji*, a nutritious peanut butter type spread that can also be added to soups, stews, or thinned with water and sweetened with honey to make a healthy food for infants. These seeds contain amino acids, vitamins, calcium, potassium, iron and many other minerals and compounds that are good for you. These de-hulled seeds can be pressed for the oil, and in the process a pasty meal is left behind. This can be pressed into cakes and fried, or added to soups and stews. There are some reports that they can be made into meatless hamburgers. This meal can also be dried and powdered for future use in baking or as a thickening agent.

The vines cover the soil surface around the cassava or corn. This helps to conserve soil moisture and control the weeds. The young leaves and stem tips can be harvested and cooked as a potherb.

This is a vigorous vine that will thrive under a wide range of conditions. They can tolerate heat, humidity and heavy rains, but will also tolerate drought during the growing season. In fact the productivity is increased if it is dry during the ripening season. They will begin to flower in about a month from sowing and fruit are ready for harvest in 4 to 5 months. They do best in a compost rich, well-drained soil with full sun. The large pale seeds can be planted as you would pumpkin or watermelon seeds in hills about 1 m (3 ft) apart. The fruits can be harvested when growth has stopped and the rind begins to pale. They will store for several months, but the system worked out by the native populations is easy and effective. They go into the field and break open the melons with a club. The pieces are spread on the ground in the field and left until the flesh has decayed and dried. Then the seeds are collected, washed and de-hulled.

Figleaf gourd, *Cucurbita ficifolia*
Also known as Malabar gourd, chilacoyote and zamba
Perennial vigorous vine
Central American native

Value as a food source	6
Value as an ornamental	4
Multi-purpose	yes
Continuous harvest	yes
Ease of culture	9
Overall rating	***

The young fruit can be used like zucchini or cucumbers. They are best boiled, baked or added to a stir-fry, soup or stew. The ripe fruit can be scooped from the rind and cooked with milk and cinnamon and honey or cane syrup. This is sometimes used as the base for a fermented beverage. The small seeds have a tasty nutty flavor when shelled, and can be eaten raw or roasted like peanuts. These seeds also yield a high quality, long lasting vegetable oil. One type, *Alcayota*, has a flesh that separates into sweet, white noodle-like strands. These can be eaten in a salad or added to the typical stew, soup or stir-fry.

When fully mature the fruit has a hard shell that can be used as a container after the flesh has been consumed. They are sometimes made into as rattles or maracas. The hard shell also gives the fruit tremendous keeping qualities. The will last for months if kept cool and dry.

This is a vigorous vine that will thrive in frost-free areas. It accepts poor soils, poor drainage and sun or light shade. It doesn't take drought well, but when kept evenly moist, or even soggy, it can grow over 20 m (60 ft) in its first year. They will scramble up trees and over fences. In temperate climes that can be treated as an annual that will produce well in the first season.

Fluted gourd, *Telfairia occidentalis*
Also known as fluted pumpkin
Frost sensitive perennial vine
Native to Tropical West Africa

Value as a food source	6
Value as an ornamental	4
Multi-purpose	yes
Continuous harvest	yes
Ease of culture	8
Overall rating	** Can become seriously invasive

This is a rugged, drought tolerant vine that produces large, but inedible, gourd-like fruit. The food value isn't in the flesh of this fruit, but in the seeds that are rich in oil and contain about 30% protein. These seeds are much enjoyed because of their almond like flavor. They can be boiled or roasted and eaten as a snack or dried then ground into a meal that can be added to soups, stews, and sometimes breads. These seeds can also be fermented for several days in the hot sun to produce a pasty liquid called *ogiri-nwan* that is considered quite good. This seed yields a good, versatile cooking oil. The tender leaves and vine tips can be used as a potherb, added to soups, stews and vegetable dishes. A close relative, *Telfairia pedata*, often called oysternut, is another drought tolerant perennial vine that produces large edible seeds. This one is native to Central and East Africa and is used in much the same way as *T. Occidentalis*.

The fluted gourd is easily grown from seed. It will accept a wide range of soils, but doesn't like wet feet. It is most productive when trained on a trellis or other support. This is a perennial vine that will take a year or more to produce fruit, but during that time it can be a source of cooked greens. This vine has done well in tropical areas beyond its African homeland and may well be a valuable subsistence vegetable in many areas such as Haiti. This plant isn't recommended for frost free areas not considered arid because it will become dangerously invasive.

Ivy gourd, *Coccinia grandis*
Also known as scarlet gourd or scarlet fruited gourd
Perennial vine, considered very invasive in many areas of the tropics
Native to East Africa

Value as an edible	7
Value as an ornamental	2
Multi-purpose	yes
Continuous harvest	yes
Ease of culture	10
Overall rating	*

The fruit, when ripe is bright red and sweet and is locally popular as a fresh fruit or snack. The unripe fruit, while still green is sliced raw in salads or cooked in a number of ways. It can be boiled, steamed, added to soups, curries, stews or fermented for use in cooking. The young leaves and stem tips are used as a potherb or added to soups and stews. Both the unripe fruits and leaves are added to many rice dishes.

We might conclude that a vegetable this productive, offering multi-purpose and continuous harvest potential ought to be grown throughout the topics. Wrong. This is vine is so invasive that it makes kudzu look like a botanical wimp. In many areas of the Pacific it has been so prolific that it literally destroys everything in its path. The tuberous roots spread faster than herbicides can catch them, the vines root at leaf nodes that come in contact with the soil, and birds carry the seeds to new sites. This gourd is dioecious (male and female flowers are on separate plants), but even if only one plant is introduced, as happened in Guam, it can still run amuck. Because it spreads so vigorously asexually it has become a major ecological threat to native plants and animals. In its African home there are insects and fungi that help to keep it in check. In other areas of the tropics these checks and balances don't exist, or, in some cases they come along with the plant and then attack other melons and cucurbits as well as papayas. Because this plant is so easily propagated and so difficult to control it isn't recommended for experimentation or cultivation. The seeds germinate readily, it starts from pieces of stem or tubers. It will grow in any soil and is the schoolyard bully of the tropics. It is unfortunate that a nutritional and versatile plant like this is so anti-social.

Luffa gourd, angled luffa, *Luffa acutangula*
Also known as silk gourd, towel gourd, ribbed loofah & long okra
Annual climber
Native to India

Value as a food source	6, fruit only
Value as an ornamental	4
Multi-purpose	yes, fruit and sponges
Continuous harvest	yes
Ease of culture	9
Overall rating	***

This is a gourd with ten ridges running lengthwise so that very young fruit resemble okra. It should be noted that this fruit is only edible when young because as they age they become more and more bitter. The immature fruit are often called Chinese okra. The mature fruit we call a sponge. This is one of the gourds grown commercially for the bath sponge or dishcloth inside. The angled luffa fruit will grow to almost a meter (30 to 35 inches) in length, but is usually harvested for the dinner table when less than half that size. The immature seeds can be eaten in soups where they add a nutty flavor or they can be roasted and eaten as a snack. The young fruit can be washed and sliced like cucumbers before cooking. Some locales soak the sliced fruits in saltwater to release some of the bitterness. They can be cut lengthwise and stuffed with rice, meats or fish then baked. They are then added to soups, stews, meat dishes, stir-fries, boiled, baked, roasted or batter fried. The flavor is not bad but rather bland without seasoning. Very young fruit can be pickled. In many regions the flesh is sliced and dried as a means of storing it for future use. The fruit is an excellent source of vitamins A & C as well as a blend of minerals and carbohydrates. Young leaves , flower buds and stem tips can be eaten raw as an addition to a fresh salad, the flavor is on the bitter side, but it works well as a flavor accent. They can also be steamed, boiled or used as a potherb.

This is a vegetable for hot humid summers. The hotter the weather the more female flowers are formed, thus the greater the yield. Each plant will yield 12 to 24 fruit, sometimes more. The highest quality and productivity requires trellis cultivation. This also affords the greatest productivity with limited land use and water resources. These vines will make a vigorous groundcover but the fruit tend to be smaller, misshapen and fewer in number.

They are easily started from seed sown where they are to grow or in 4 or 6 inch pots on a windowsill or greenhouse. They require about four months of warm weather to produce a crop of sponges, but the harvest of edible fruit can begin in 8 to 10 weeks. They are adaptable to a wide variety of soils, from sandy to clay, but do best in a compost rich site with good drainage and full sun.

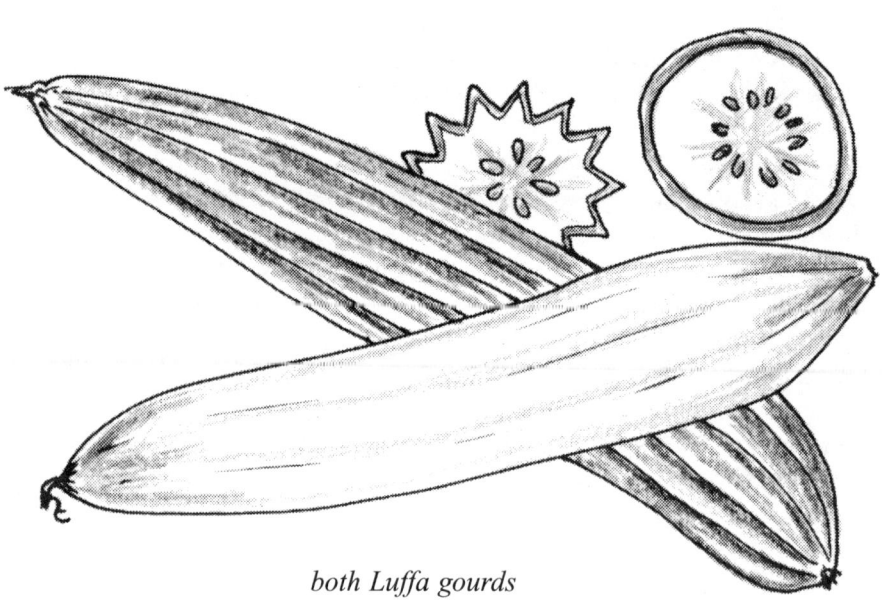

both Luffa gourds

Luffa gourd, smooth luffa, *Luffa aegyptiaca* or *L. Cylindrica*
Also known as smooth luffa, vegetable sponge, dish-cloth gourd, hechima, vine okra, dhundhul, loofa and loofah
Annual vine
Native to India

Value as a food source	6
Value as an ornamental	4
Multi-purpose	yes
Continuous harvest	yes
Ease of culture	9
Overall rating	***

  This luffa is as much fun as the one above. The fruit are less bitter than the angled luffa and the young gourds are great sliced raw in a salad. They can be pickled, or sliced and dried for easy storage. They are also excellent steamed, boiled, baked, or added to soups, stews, stir-fries, curries and rice dishes. The young leaves, stem tips, flower buds and flowers are delicious steamed with rice or cooked as a potherb. The flowers and fingerling fruit are also great batter fried. The seeds can be roasted and served as a snack. In many areas the seeds are a source of a high quality vegetable oil used in cooking and food preservation. The seeds can be mashed and fermented into a tofu look alike with a mildly nutty flavor.

  The mature fruit are also a source of vegetable sponge, same as the angled luffa. Cultivation is the same.

Narra melon, *Acanthosicyos horridus*
Perennial shrub reaching 1.5 m (4 to 5 ft) in height with a much broader width
Native to Namibia and deserts of Southern Africa

Value as a food source	6
Value as an ornamental	7
Multi-purpose	no
Continuous harvest	no
Ease of culture	4
Overall rating	***

  For gardeners who like weird plants it doesn't get any better than this. We have to respect a completely leafless bush that literally grows sand dunes, tangles of thorns worse than a briar patch and sweet orange fruit covered with stubby spines. This isn't your average garden variety melon. The palm sized fruit are interesting in that when ripe the flesh tends to separate from the rind. This flesh is orange and pleasantly sweet when ripe, but the spiny outside remains green. Before the melon is ready for harvest this pulp is extremely bitter, but this is the stage when the jackals seem to prefer it. Purdue University has been researching ways that this and other potential new crops can be utilized. While the Knung and other Bushmen have traditionally boiled the fruit into a thick syrup then dried it in strips for later use, the scientists have suggested that it be used to make ice cream, or dried and covered with chocolate. In my personal lifelong research I have concluded that ice cream and chocolate are two of the most important food groups. I must applaud the work being done at Purdue.

The fruits can be eaten raw, cooked into a sweet sauce, used as a flavoring and preserved as jams and jellies. The seeds are sometimes referred to as *butter pits*, because they contain a soft kernel that is a source of quality vegetable oil, but it's also about 30% protein. They are a shear delight when roasted, although locally they are more often boiled. The flesh is used in some areas as a rennet for curdling milk in cheese production.

There are male plants and there are female plants, and to produce fruit they need to be growing in close proximity to each other. It has no leaves but does produce green stems and branches along with the green fruit. What it doesn't give us in leaves it more than makes up for with its roots. Seeds germinate quickly with a rare Namibian rain and send roots deep into the ground, seeking subterranean water. The twigs and branches are designed to absorb the moisture from morning dew. They form colonies that trap sand in the branches, thus they are constantly growing to keep above the growing dunes. In this way they create micro-habitats for a wide variety of plants and animals as they help to stabilize the soil. This is a plant that may have some value in arid climates where frost is as infrequent as the rains.

Narra melon

Oyster nut, *Telfairia pedata* See **Fluted gourd**
Also known as Zanzibar oil vine, fluted pumpkin

Red bone vine, *Thladiantha dubia*
Also listed as red hailstone vine
Locally known as wang kua or t'u kua
Perennial vine
Chinese native

Value as an edible	3
Value as an ornamental	3
Multi-purpose	yes
Continuous harvest	no
Ease of culture	8
Overall rating	**

This is a vigorous perennial vine that produces an abundance of juicy small, pickle-shaped, fuzzy orange-red fruit in late summer and autumn. The flesh is sweet and is sometimes eaten out of hand. They also make a refreshing juice from these cousins to the zucchini but they aren't a staple in the native diet. It's grown for the young shoots and leaves, particularly spring growth, are both flavorful and nutritious prepared a number of ways, as a potherb, in soups, stews and as a side dish. It also produces a white carrot-like root that sometimes appears on the dinner table, but more often is processed into a valuable starch with many uses. The roots, fruit and seeds are also used extensively in folk medicine.

This is an easy plant to grow in northern climates. It is adaptable to a wide variety of soils and will clamber over weeds that get in its way. If you want the fruit you will have to plant both male and female plants. They are started from seed in much the same way you would grow cucumbers, except that when they are planted out, they are there to stay. Remember they are perennials and even if you did the roots for culinary use, you will never get them all. This is one that may have the potential to become invasive.

Snake gourd, *Tricosanthes cucumerina*
Also known as club gourd, snake tomato, padval and chichinda
Annual vine
Native to India

Value as a food source	6
Value as an ornamental	4
Multi-purpose	yes
Continuous harvest	yes
Ease of culture	9
Overall rating	***

The long thin fruit frequently exceed a meter (3 feet) in length. This gourd has a tendency to twist and curl into unusual shapes, hence the name, snake gourd. In some areas the gardeners will tie a stone to the end of the fruit to make it grow straight. This is a gourd with an interesting flavor and a wealth of ways it can be prepared. The young fruit can be peeled and sliced, then added to soups, stews, stir-fries, curries, or baked, boiled, batter fried or steamed. When the fruit mature the seeds are surrounded by a bright red pulp. This tomato-like flesh is used in cooking to add flavor and color. The young leaves and vine tips are often boiled, steamed or added to stir-fries; although the flavor is sometimes quite bitter.

This is a vigorous vine that will thrive in the hot summers of the tropical and temperate zones. For most efficient use of space and greatest productivity they should be grown on wires, trellis, fence or other support. They grow rapidly and the first fruit may be ready for harvesting in less than two months. They thrive in a sunny location with almost any compost enriched soil, but good drainage is required for best results. As with most squash and melons, they are easily started from seed.

The Japanese snake gourd, *Trichosanthes cucumeroides*, (also known as Karasu-uri) produces a thin fruit that is harvested when very young and pickled with salt or miso. It also produces a starchy tuber with an interesting flavor.

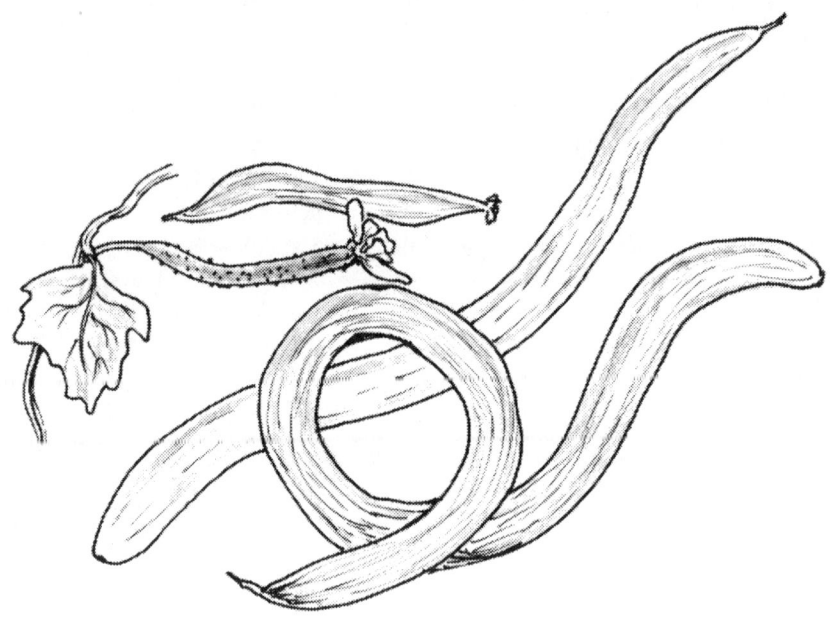

Snake gourd

Sweet tea vine, *Gynostemma pentaphyllum*
Also known as Southern ginseng, Jiaogulan
Perennial in frost free areas, treated as an annual elsewhere
Native to China & Southeast Asia

Value as an edible	2
Value as an ornamental	6
Multi-purpose	no
Continuous harvest	yes
Ease of culture	7
Overall rating	**

While the leaves and tender stem tips are cooked as a potherb, and are used as a natural sweetener for rice dishes and numerous snacks and desserts, this cucurbit is listed for its beverage value. Hot drinks can be made by steeping either the fresh or dried leaves. A bottled tonic water is also made from the boiled leaves and stems. These leaves have a sweet flavor, and are used as a tea throughout the Orient where it is valued as a stress relaxant and rejuvenator. This is one of the plants that is being intensively researched for its medicinal potential in controlling cholesterol levels, high blood pressure and possibly diabetes. There does seem to be some evidence that it strengthens the immune system, improves circulation and reduces blood sugar levels. In traditional medicine it has been used for everything from stress and exhaustion to asthma and cancer. While this may well be the only plant on the face of the earth that someone hasn't listed as a coffee substitute, it is regarded by many as an aphrodisiac. Extracts are also used extensively in the cosmetics industry.

This is a dioecious plant, that is there are male plants and there are female plants; if you want to harvest the seed you will have to grow both. To harvest the leaves you only need one plant. They require a long hot summer to do their best. They thrive in a greenhouse in cold climates, or outdoors to USDA zone 8. It enjoys almost any soil that is both well-drained and compost enriched, as long as it gets full sun and can be kept evenly moist. Since they climb with tendrils it is best to grow them on a trellis or other support. Once they are growing well the leaves can be harvested continuously for fresh use, or dried to be used as needed. One source claims that the leaves are sweetest in late summer. They are started from seeds soaked in warm water overnight, then sown in a quality potting soil 2 to 4 seeds per 4 or 6 inch pot. These seeds usually germinate in 2 to 3 weeks. Thin to two plants per pot after they germinate. This is an attractive vine that can make a fine background for flowering plants, grown in containers or trained on an arbor, fence or railing.

Wax gourd, *Benincasa hispida*
Also known as winter gourd, white gourd, Chinese watermelon, tallow gourd, tung-qua (China), petha (India)
Annual vine
Native to Southeast Asia and Indochina, now pan-tropic

Value as a food source	7
Value as an ornamental	4
Multi-purpose	yes
Continuous harvest	yes
Ease of culture	7
Overall rating	***

This rugged and vigorous vine is grown mainly for the white wax coated fruit with large seeds and light colored flesh. The wax helps the harvested fruit keep for as long as half a year or more stacked on shelves or hung from the ceiling in sacks. The wax also helps to control insect pests but it is so thick that it can be used for candles. The mature fruit can be eaten raw, or baked, fried, added to soups, stews and curries, pickled and used like citron. They are frequently cut in half, the seeds removed then the cavity is stuffed with meat, seafood or vegetables or, as the Native Americans did with the pumpkin, they fill the cavity with a mixture of fruits, nuts and honey. This stuffed fruit can then be steamed or baked using the shell of the gourd as the cooking pot. By itself the flavor is rather pleasant but bland. When added to soups, stews or baked with other foods it provides valuable nutrition. They are sometimes cut into strips and boiled in a sweetened sauce. The immature fruit can be peeled and cooked like zucchini or used in soups, stews, and stir-fries. The seeds are enjoyed roasted or fried and are often added to other dishes as a flavoring. The young leaves, flowers and flower buds can be steamed, fried or added to soups and stews.

There are several named varieties and *Small* is one of the most productive for temperate climates. The 5 pound fruits are fine textured and great for stuffing. *Large round* is a variety producing fruit weighing up to 20 pounds. It is very prolific, with fine white flesh. This is the most popular variety in Japan.

This is a plant that thrives in the summer heat of temperate climates, but will suffer from high humidity. They enjoy a compost enriched well-drained site in full sun. They are moderately drought tolerant and little irrigation is needed if a good mulch is used. While the vines can be left to scramble over the ground, in areas where space is limited they can be trained on trellises, wire or fences. In areas where flat roofed buildings are the norm they can be trellised to the roof where they will spread, providing insulation and a good crop protected from hungry wildlife. They start easily from seed the same as we would grow squash and melons. It will take about four months for fruit to mature, but the immature fruit, flowers and young leaves can be harvested throughout the growing season.

Weeds and Wild Things

Many of the wild plants we call weeds produce beautiful flowers, form a part of the magnificent coat of many colors that Mother Nature wears in all her glory. Many of these we think of as weeds because they are so common. Yet, as we discussed earlier, most of what we consider important food resources today were once weeds that thrived in disturbed spaces, grew with ease and speed, tolerated diversity. We curse the dandelion, yet it is nutritious in leave and flower, provides a tasty wine from the flowers, an acceptable coffee substitute from the roots and great natural toys for our children. Yet we spend billions to kill this beautiful plant. Kudzu, that most despised plant of the American Southeast is good grazing for livestock, produces a delicious tuber and may play a key role in the treatment of alcoholism. The following are a few of the wild plants and flowers that we can serve on the dinner table.

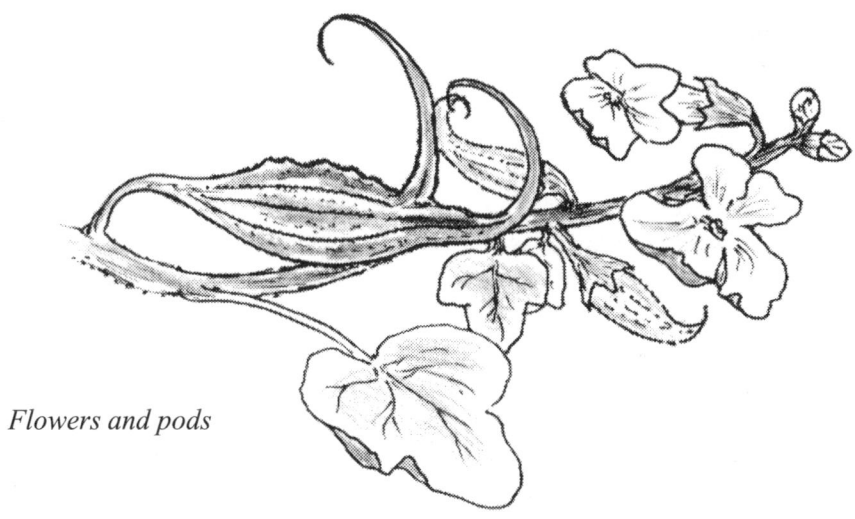

Flowers and pods

Unicorn Plant, *Martynia proboscidea louisianica*
Martynia family, *Martyniaceae*
Also known as devil's claw & elephant's tusks
Annual semi-vine Native to the American Southwest and Mexico

Value as a food source	3
Value as an ornamental	8
Multi-purpose	yes
Continuous harvest	yes
Ease of culture	7
Overall rating	**

Ok, so we're talking about eating something that the Native Americans have used for thousands of years as a needle for sewing, weaving, etc. This is a fruit with long sharp curved spines, Mother Nature's version of Velcro. But the immature fruits are not bad tasting if roasted or pickled as you might prepare cucumbers. Of course, if you research this plant you will find that you can roast the seeds inside and use them as a coffee substitute. Many texts will describe the fruit as almost inedible, to be considered only as a famine food. This is a fruit much like okra in that the younger the fruit harvested, the better it tastes. The very young pods can be boiled, stir-fried, batter dipped and deep-fried, added to soups or stews, or roasted with other vegetables. They are an interesting addition to a veggie bar-b-que with such companions as onions, summer squash, carrots, peppers (both sweet and hot), celery, bok choy, and jicama. The immature seeds are highly nutritious, rich in protein and edible vegetable oils. The seeds can be eaten raw, or roasted. One variety, *Tohono O'odham*, produces large (15 inch) pods with seed that are used as a snack, just like sunflower seeds.

The plant produces beautiful flowers in yellow, purple or spotted patterns. This makes it a valuable addition to the landscape. The mature and dried pods can be used in floral arrangements. Butterflies and hummingbirds also seem to enjoy these flowers.

Martynia is easily grown from seed. It likes hot weather and we have grown it well as a colorful companion to okra. It needs full sun and a well-drained site. It does best in a compost rich, sandy soil but will grow in much less. If you continuously harvest the immature pods before they exceed 2 inches in length the plants will continue to bloom and bear until cool weather.

The Milkweeds, *Asclepias*

This is an intriguing mystery. Native populations have known and enjoyed many members of the milkweed, *Asclepiadaceae* family, but it has never become a part of the everyday table fare. The flavor is good, they are easy to grow, easy to harvest and are quite productive. Yet, the primary reason we grow these beautiful plants today is to feed Monarch butterfly infants and toddlers.

This is a global family with some interesting members like the bunga siam (*Telosma cordata*) that produces a fleshy root that is much enjoyed as a sweetmeat in Java, while in Thailand the leaves and flowers appear on the dinner table. In India leshwe, (*Pergularia daemia*) produces edible leaves, flowers, flower buds and stems that are prepared in a variety of ways. The large tubers of Kambro (*Fockea edulis*), are enjoyed as an alternative to watermelon in the deserts of South Africa. The common milkweed, (*Asclepias syriaca*) from North America is delightful cooked in a great variety of ways.

This is a diverse family with some members adapted to swamp habitats while others are at home in deserts all over the globe. Some of our common ornamental plants like the hoyas and butterfly-weed and many others are also members of this family. It is advised that members of this family always be cooked because some species do contain toxins. It should also be noted that some are edible but not palatable, while others are absolutely delicious. Sometimes the suitability for your dinner table is dictated by the season and the state of maturity or the parts harvested. The following are a few of the good ones for the global dinner table from North America. There are many others, and each has a following with favorite ways of preparing and serving them.

Butterfly weed, *Asclepias tuberosa*
Also known as pleurisy root
Perennial
Native to North America
Value as a food source	6
Value as an ornamental	8
Multi-purpose	yes
Continuous harvest	yes
Ease of culture	9
Overall rating	**

The tender shoots can be harvested and cooked as we would asparagus. The flavor is nothing like asparagus but it does have a pleasant, almost sweet taste that is a great addition to a stir-fry. Both the flower buds and the flowers can be eaten, but they should be cooked first. The Sioux even made a sweetener from the flowers. The leaves, at least the young ones, can be used as a potherb or steamed. Mature leaves are too bitter. This plant also produces a tuber that has been used in herbal medicine for centuries to treat asthma, pleurisy and congestion. Some sources claim this tuber is edible when cooked, others insist that it is toxic. No part of this plant should be eaten without cooking it first.

This is one of the favorite larval foods of the Monarch butterfly, and a multitude of other butterflies and hummingbirds will visit the bright orange blossoms. This makes it a valuable addition to your informal, wildflower or butterfly garden. This perennial will thrive in a wide variety of soils ranging from sandy to clay, as long as the site is well drained. It also needs full sun to do well. Once established it will handle drought with ease but it doesn't handle transplanting well. Butterfly weed is easily started from seeds sown in a 4 or 6 inch pot and grown there for the first season. Then they can be carefully transplanted to their permanent home. Don't hesitate to enjoy the tender new shoots and flowers as a cooked vegetable. The baby Monarchs will share with you.

Common milkweed, *Asclepias syriaca*
Perennial
Native to North America
Value as a food source	6
Value as an ornamental	8
Multi-purpose	yes
Continuous harvest	yes
Ease of culture	9
Overall rating	***

What a versatile vegetable, and it's so often overlooked because it's a 'weed.' In the spring the tender new shoots can be cooked like asparagus, steamed, boiled, stir-fried, or roasted. They are great sauteed with mushrooms and chives. The immature leaves can be cooked as a potherb or added to soups and stews. But it gets better. The clusters of flower buds can be cooked as you would broccoli. They have a flavor not unlike garden peas, and are great steamed then served with a cheese sauce. The open flowers can be added to soups, stews, cream sauces and stir-fries. If you pick the young seed pods when they are about an inch in length they can be boiled first to remove any bitterness then prepared like okra. These pods are great deep fried, added to soups, stews, stir-fries or pickled. Immature silk and seeds can be eaten raw and have a flavor similar to garden peas. Even the mature seeds can be sprouted and eaten in salads or added to a stir-fry, rice, corn or pasta dish.

This and most other milkweeds are easy to start from seed sown in 4 or 6 inch pots or where they are to grow. All are at their best in full sun, some are extremely drought tolerant while others are at home in swamp conditions.

Swamp milkweed, *Asclepias incarnata*
Perennial growing over a meter tall (sometimes exceeding 4 ft)
Native to North America
Value as a food source	6
Value as an ornamental	8
Multi-purpose	yes
Continuous harvest	yes
Ease of culture	9
Overall rating	***

The Native Americans used the unopened buds in soups and stews, and often added them to corn meal dishes. The young pods were also eaten in soups and stews or baked. The early settlers used this and the variety above as both survival food and common fare. We have a recipe from 1756 for making milkweed potpie that calls for two cups of unopened buds and pods no longer than 1 inch.

All of these milkweeds are a great addition to the meal, but they are truly multi-purpose in that their stems produce fibers that can be made into twine, cord or cloth. The floss of the mature seed pods was gathered by children all over the United

States during the Second World War as a warm kapok-like stuffing for flight jackets and winter wear. Today it is still used for life jackets and candle wicks. The sap of the growing plants is a latex that can produce a reasonably high quality rubber that at one time was used in chewing gums. It was also said to remove warts.

Australian bush banana, *Leichhadtia australis*
Poinsettia family, *Euphorbiaceae*
Also known as native pear and doubah
Perennial evergreen climber reaching 1-3 m (3 to 9 ft) in height and spread
Native to Australia

Value as a food source	5
Value as an ornamental	3
Multi-purpose	yes
Continuous harvest	yes
Ease of culture	5
Overall rating	***

Spring heralds clusters of fragrant, cream colored flowers that are so sweet they're picked and eaten by the handful by Australians who know their bush foods. The secret to the sweetness is that each flower is filled with nectar. The flowering continues over a period of months as pear shaped fruit begin to develop. The immature fruit are a flavorful source of thiamine and other vitamins. These young fruit are enjoyed by the Aboriginal population either raw or cooked . The flavor is somewhere between green peas and squash. They can be roasted, boiled, stir-fried or added to soups and stews. When they become slightly more mature they can be cut open to expose the seed cluster which can again be eaten raw or cooked. The skin is too tough to be of value. The leaves are also edible cooked as a potherb and the fleshy roots are roasted or baked as a vegetable.

This sprawling shrub thrives in the more inhospitable regions of Australia and will do quite well with 12 to 20 inches of rainfall a year. It doesn't like wet feet or high humidity, but a frost is not a problem. It responds well to a trellis in the full sun and an occasional feeding with a light balanced fertilizer. It can be started from seeds sown much as we would squash or cucumbers. They will germinate in 10 to 30 days in a sandy soil mix kept lightly moist. Too much water and they will fall victim to fungus diseases. They can also be started from cuttings taken in the spring or summer.

Hottentot fig, *Carpobrotus edulis* and
Sweet Hottentot-fig, *C. Deliciosus*
Sea fig family, *Mesembryanthemaceae*
Also known as fig marigold
Native to South Africa
Perennial spreading as a groundcover
Value as a food source   4
Value as an ornamental   7
Multi-purpose   yes
Continuous harvest   yes
Ease of culture   8
Overall rating   ***

    The succulent slightly salty flavored leaves are used in salads, as a snack or pickled. The daisy-like yellow or white flowers are followed by a fleshy fruit that is somewhat reminiscent of a tart strawberry. The fruits can be rolled in a piece of bread dough and baked. The resulting fruit roll is dipped in honey to become a delightful dessert. These fruits can also be eaten raw, boiled, baked, dried or made into jams or preserves. The leaves can also be consumed as with the cousin mentioned below, ice plant.

    This is an easy plant to grow from seeds or cuttings and will thrive in salt spray, arid conditions and many other harsh regions. It works well in hanging baskets, window boxes and as an edging in flower borders. Because this is a rugged independent survivor it will often outgrow native plants and can become invasive, although it has been used in erosion control in many parts of the world, including California.

    A related plant, *C. Aequilaterus*, is commonly called pig's face or sea fig. The fruit of this South African native are eaten raw or cooked and the leaves can be enjoyed baked or stir-fried

Ice plant, *Mesembryanthemum crystallinum*
Sea fig family, *Mesembryanthemaceae*
Also known as frost plant or dew plant
Native to the Mediterranean region
Perennial ground cover, often grown as an annual
Value as a food source   4
Value as an ornamental   7
Multi-purpose   no
Continuous harvest   yes
Ease of culture   8
Overall rating   ***

    This is one of those arid climate plants that are often used in the landscape, but for many people in the global garden this is a food resource that can be grown where little else will survive. The name, ice plant, is a reference to the silvery dots that cover the leaves. These fleshy leaves are acid and somewhat salty to the taste. Raw they make a valuable addition to a salad or can be eaten as a snack, but they can also be boiled as a potherb, added to soups and stews or pickled like small cucumbers.

Ice plants are easy to start from seed sown lightly and barely covered in a site that gets lots of sun and is well drained. They are not fussy about soil type, is slat tolerant and delights in a drought. They are so adaptable that in some areas they are considered a dangerous invasive plant that is overtaking native species. It works well as a border or windowbox plant where the leaves can be harvested as needed for use as a garnish, snack or salad green.

Watermelon berry, *Streptopus amplexifolius*
Lily family, *Liliaceae*
Also known as wild cucumber, twisted-stalk, liver berry, clasping twisted-stalk
Perennial reaching about 1 m (3 feet) in height
Native to North America

Value as a food source	4
Value as an ornamental	3
Multi-purpose	yes
Continuous harvest	yes
Ease of culture	8
Overall rating	**

Another of those multi-purpose but often over-looked plants of the North American woodlands. The small, oval shaped fruit average less than an inch in length and have a decidedly cucumber-like flavor when eaten raw. The make a good snack or addition to a salad. They can also be cooked in soups or stews. The leaves and shoots also have a refreshing cucumber flavor and can be eaten raw in salads. The tender stems can also be boiled, baked or steamed as we would asparagus. The root can be harvested any time of the year and added to a salad or eaten as a crispy cucumber flavored snack.

This is one of those plants that is almost carefree. It thrives in dense shade in a moist woodland setting. It isn't particular as to soil type, as long as it's constantly moist.

They are best started from divisions or small roots planted where you want them to grow. This vegetable can be started from seed but it takes two years before any harvest is possible.

Chapter Nine
Wetlands and Coastal Gardens

Bogs, Puddles & Ponds

We think of a garden as a series of neat rows of produce on the hoof in the back yard, a patch of ground tilled and forced into our perception of a mini-agricultural habitat. But in many places in this world the back yard is under water, in some places fish are a part of the garden's yield. In other locales the garden is a swamp, bog, marsh, or frequently flooded lowland. While the village of gardeners can possibly build dams, drainage systems, raised beds or fields so that they can grow the popular vegetables of commerce or expand their production of traditional upland crops this is expensive and labor intensive.

It is also a fact that for many people the resources to convert the environment to their liking are simply not available. But there is a wealth of nutrition that can be found growing in these bog gardens and wetland farms, often cultivated in partnership with the natural forces rather than mortal combat. Some of these plants are multi-purpose like the cattail on the North American wetlands. There are aquatic plants like the lotus, *Nelumbo nucifera* that have religious symbolism as well as food value. In many parts of the world a true ecosystem for plants, fish and fowl can be achieved. At ECHO in Fort Myers, Florida they are growing ducks, tilapia (Nile perch) and vetevier grass together. This system can be expanded to include local edible aquatic plants and have a highly efficient system where frequent harvests can sustain an entire community.

We are familiar with a number of aquatic gastronomic delights like Chinese water chestnuts, cranberries, some mints, watercress, elderberry and rice. The following are a few other aquatic plants that supply nutrition in our global community. Note that many of these are multi-purpose plants.

Arrowhead, *Sagittaria latifolia*
Arrowhead family, *Alismataceae*
Also known as duck potato and wapatoo
Cold hardy perennial
Native to North America

Value as a food source	4
Value as an ornamental	6
Multi-purpose	no
Continuous harvest	no
Ease of culture	8
Overall rating	***

So often, those of us who live in North America neglect our native resources. The arrowhead is a good example. The Native Americans and the European settlers both used this as a staple food source, unfortunately we lost our taste for it through the years. The tubers are about the size of a potato with a starchy flesh and flavor very similar to potatoes. It shouldn't be eaten raw. The original Americans boiled these tubers then strung them on cord to dry for storage and later use. The European adventurers boiled, baked, roasted, fried and creamed these easily harvested roots as they had the turnips of Europe. This was a valuable addition to the diet because of a high protein level, 4 to 6%.

They can be started from the seeds planted as soon as possible after maturing. They can be placed in 4 or 6 inch pots filled with a compost rich sandy soil, or pond muck. They can then be immersed in water so that the pot is completely submerged or kept in a watering tray so that the soil remains soggy. Germination can occur in 2 to 6 weeks and growth will be rapid. In a month or two they can be planted where you want them to grow. They need a soggy soil if not about 15 cm (6 inches) of standing water. Full sun is also a part of the equation. The plant grows and produces a large tuber along with a number of tuberettes that can be removed at the time of harvest and replanted for the next crop.

The Chinese arrowhead, *Sagittaria sinensis*, is cultivated and enjoyed in many parts of Asia. They also cook and enjoy the young shoots.

www.globalgardening.info

Cape asparagus, *Aponogeton distachyus*
Aponogetonaceae family
Also known as Cape pondweed, water onion and water hawthorn
Perennial, frost hardy, but suffers in a severe freeze
South African native

Value as a food source	5
Value as an ornamental	8
Multi-purpose	yes
Continuous harvest	yes
Ease of culture	7
Overall rating	***

    Beautiful spikes of fragrant white flowers grace this semi-aquatic plant for most of the growing season. Not only are these flowers beautiful, they taste good too. In Africa the flower spikes are boiled, fried, roasted or pickled. The open flowers are used as a garnish and a seasoning. The young shoots are delicious when cooked as we do asparagus, or boiled as a potherb. Even the fleshy tubers are boiled, baked, roasted or added to a stir-fry. They are rich in starch and considered gourmet food.

    This is a plant that is at its best when wading in a shallow pool. It grows well in water from 15 to 60 cm deep (6 to 24 inches). The richer the soil the better it grows, but it will accept a wide range of soil types. To perform well it must be in full sun. When growing these from seed it is best to plant two or three ripe seeds as soon as possible after harvest in a pot of soil submerged in water. The water should just cover the rim of this pot. Germination will occur in one or two months. Protect from frosts the first year. They can also be propagated from divisions.

Cattails, *Typha latifolia*
Cattail family, *Typhaceae*
Also known as bulrush, great reedmace and gama
Perennial often exceeding 2 m (6 feet)
Found pan-global

Value as a food source	9
Value as an ornamental	7
Multi-purpose	yes
Continuous harvest	yes
Ease of culture	10
Overall rating	*****

    To the Native American this plant was the "supermarket of the swamp." Few plants are more versatile that the common cattail. The tender new spring shoots can be eaten raw or cooked. The flavor is similar to cucumbers. The immature flower heads can be eaten raw or roasted and eaten like a corndog on a stick. In fact the flavor is similar to sweet corn. The green flower spikes can be scraped into a stew, soup or baked like a casserole. Even the pollen can be gathered and added to flour as a source of vitamins and proteins. The pollen is also eaten raw sprinkled over other foods, or added to soups sauces and porridges as a thickening agent. The young shoots and hearts of the stems are, in some regions, referred to as Cossack asparagus. These tasty treats are enjoyed either raw or cooked in a variety of ways. The fleshy rootstocks are dried and ground into a flour that is about 80% carbohydrate and 6 to 8% protein. This flour has a pleasant, almost nutty, taste. The tender roots are pickled in some areas as well. The yield per square foot far exceeds potatoes.

The Native Americans did a lot more than serve cattails for dinner though. The pollen was used as a hair conditioner, was placed on wounds to control bleeding. The pollen is so flammable that it has been used in the manufacturing of fireworks. The sticky sap from fresh cut leaves and stems was used as an antiseptic and pain control for bites and wounds. The down from the female flower heads was used as tinder, and also as a dressing for burns, injuries and diaper rash. The dried flower stalks can be dipped in grease or animal fats to make an effective torch. The stalks were used as arrow shafts and the leaves were made into baskets, cordage, thatching, dolls and toys. Today this could be considered a valuable biomass resource. The fiber from the leaves can also be used to make a low-grade paper or cardboard.

This is an easy plant to cultivate in a moist location. It thrives in full sun, but will exist in light shade. It also provides erosion control and wildlife habitat. It is best propagated from cuttings but can be started from seed sown on the surface of pots or in trays that are kept soggy, or sown in the bog garden site. Plant in their permanent site as soon as they are 4 to 6 inches high. They grow quickly and need little maintenance.

There are many varieties found growing throughout the world. In tropical Asia a variety called Elephant grass, *Typha elephantina*. In India the pollen is gathered and used to make a bread called booree. The young leaves are also eaten. This is an aggressive plant that will take over when presented with the opportunity. It is considered an invasive plant and a noxious weed in Australia and some parts of the United States.

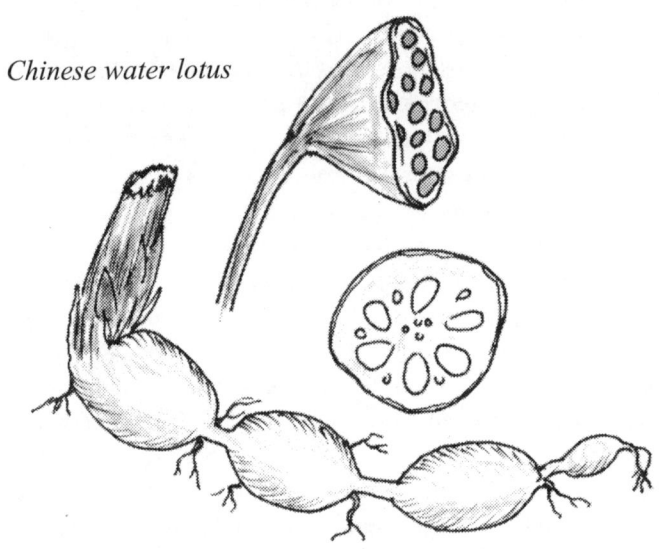

Chinese water lotus

Chinese water lotus, *Nelumbo nucifera*
Lotus family, *Nelumbonaceae*
Also known as Sacred lotus of India, pink lotus, lotus bean, lien hua
Perennial aquatic plant
Native to Tropical Asia and Australia

Value as a food source	9
Value as an ornamental	9
Multi-purpose	yes
Continuous harvest	yes
Ease of culture	8
Overall rating	*****

What a plant to have in the garden. Beautiful pink or white flowers and the graceful charm of circular leaves floating or rising on stalks from the pool or pond. The flowers produce an enticing fragrance that is said to calm and soothe the troubled soul and stressed psyche. So powerful were these fragrances that both Ancient Egyptians and Chinese used lotus pools as a part of the treatment for the mentally ill.

But this isn't a book about fragrance as much as it is about food. This is considered a sacred plant for more than its overwhelming beauty, it is a dynamic food source as well. Let's start with the root, technically a rhizome. It can be boiled, baked, stir-fried, tempura fried, pickled or sugared. It's also a source for a popular Chinese starch called *nagau fan*. The flesh of these roots has a crisp texture and a mild pleasant flavor. They are great combined with other vegetables or added to soups and stews. The stems are a special treat in India. When peeled and cooked they have a flavor somewhat like beets only sweeter. The immature leaves are tender and fleshy with a pleasant flavor and aroma when eaten raw or in a salad with sesame oil. The leaves are frequently used in many parts of the world as a wrap for foods when cooking, baking or roasting.

The flower petals are used as a garnish on both the main course and desserts, floated in soups or drinks. The stamens are used to add both flavor and fragrance to teas, cold drinks and alcoholic beverages. Even the pollen is used for both flavor and perfumes. The seeds have a delightful subtle flavor when eaten raw or roasted. They can even be popped like popcorn, or puffed then used to make sweet treats. The seeds are also ground into a flour and used in baking, as a soup thickener and added to puddings. The seeds contain over 15% protein and about 70% carbohydrates. They can even be roasted and used to make a coffee-like beverage.

There is a multitude of medicinal benefits reportedly derived from this plant too. Various parts are used for everything from sunstroke to bleeding ulcers, hypertension to insomnia, dysentery to nose bleed. Current research has isolated several compounds that seem to demonstrate anti-cancer potential.

The flowers are so beautiful, and the value to humanity so great that this is considered a sacred plant to Buddhists, Hindus and the people of Egypt over two thousand years ago. Cleopatra used lotus blossoms to perfume her bath water. Buddha, as a newborn baby, was given a wreath of lotus flowers. There are reports of lotus seeds germinating after hundreds of year of dormancy. Throughout the world it is cultivated for its aesthetic value, but in many regions it is a matter of life and death. It is an efficient food to grow in water where other crops are difficult to cultivate.

While this is a plant that thrives when growing in water at depths ranging from 30 cm to 2 m (1 to 6 ft) most varieties aren't reliably cold hardy and can only survive north to USDA zone 8 without protection. They need full sun and a growing season at least five months long. They are easily propagated from seeds scarified (carefully filed across the center to break through the extremely hard seed coat) then placed in a small container of warm, not hot, water. Change the water daily until the seeds begin to sprout. This may take a week or as long as a month. Once germination is underway plant each seed in an individual clay pot filled with a rich, sandy soil. Submerge the pot in a tub of water so that the top of the pot is just below the water surface. Increase the dept of the water as the first leaves grow. Once you have several leaves they are ready to place in their permanent home. They can either be planted in the soil of a pond bottom or in larger containers submerged in the pool. The rhizomes can also be divided just before the spring growing season begins. It should be noted that some varieties don't handle root disturbance well.

Common reed, *Phragmites australis,* or *P. Communis*
Grass family, *Poaceae*
Perennial grass
Occurs globally

Value as a food source	6
Value as an ornamental	4
Multi-purpose	yes
Continuous harvest	yes
Ease of culture	9
Overall rating	***

The common reed is an extremely versatile plant. On the dinner table the young stems are used like bamboo shoots. All over the world native peoples have used the creeping rhizomes as a vegetable. It could be considered the global potato. It has been fried, baked, boiled, creamed, steamed, pickled, fermented, sliced, grated, dried and powdered. These shoots can be used raw, boiled, baked, roasted, stir-fried or pickled. Native Americans dried these fleshy stems and made a marshmallow-like treat from them. The nutritious young leaves can be dried and powdered, then added to flour for baking, and cooking. When a mature stem is cut it bleeds a sweet sap that can be rolled into natural candy or used as a sweetener. Even the seeds, while difficult to hull, are nutritious. There are also a multitude of other uses including woven mats, pulp for paper, erosion control, water purification and biomass production.

This is a plant for shallow water along the banks of ponds, lakes and drainage ditches. It needs soggy soil but isn't otherwise fussy about type or acidity. A place where it can bask in the sun is all it asks. It ranges naturally from north temperate to tropical zones.

The common reed, and many of its kin are easy to grow from rhizomes planted in shallow water. They can also be started from the seeds, either sown at the water's edge or in pots of soil kept soggy.

Houttuynia, *Houttuynia cordata*
Lizard tail family, *Saururaceae*
Creeping perennial
Native to temperate woodlands of Eastern Asia

Value as a food source	4
Value as an ornamental	8
Multi-purpose	no
Continuous harvest	yes
Ease of culture	7
Overall rating	**

This is a member of a small and primitive family of plants and is sometimes referred to as a living fossil. There are only three other species known. Houttuynia are sometimes grown as a shade loving ornamental, particularly the variegated form with its red, white and green foliage. All are edible. Young leaves and tender shoots are harvested for use raw in salads, with the best flavor being in the spring. Leaves can be cooked as a potherb or added to soups, stews , meat and fish The mature heart-shaped leaves can be harvested any time and cooked as you would any potherb.

They will thrive in a moist, semi-shady woodland setting, even in shallow bog situations. They will form an edible groundcover with little effort on your part. Easily grown from cuttings.

Houttuynia

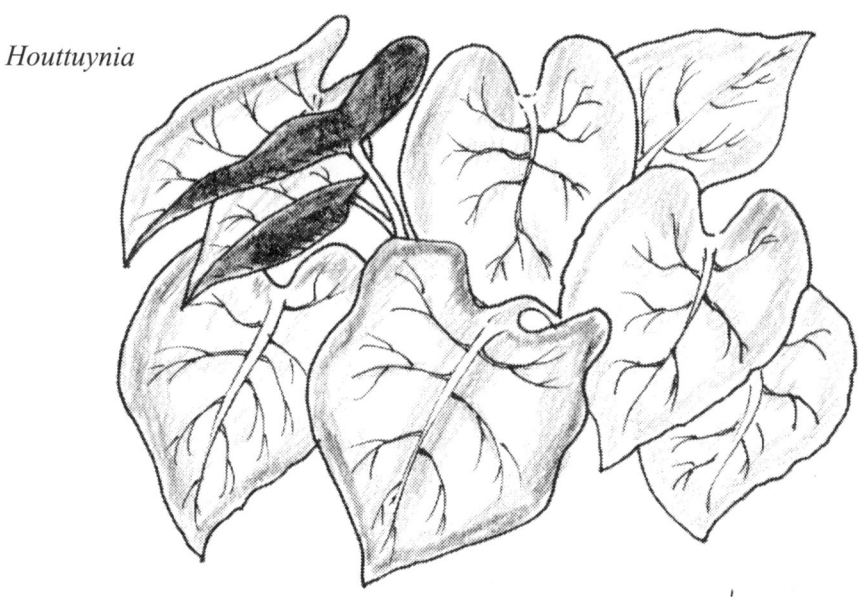

Ixeris dentata
Daisy family, *Asteracea, (Compositae)*
Perennial reaching about .5 m (15-18 inches) in height
Native to Eastern Asia

Value as a food source	5
Value as an ornamental	5
Multi-purpose	yes
Continuous harvest	yes
Ease of culture	8
Overall rating	**

Here we have a rugged, cold hardy plant that resembles the common dandelion in leaf form and a yellow daisy in flower. The tender young leaves are a slightly bitter addition to a salad while the more mature leaves are best used as a potherb. One source suggests bringing the leaves and flower stems to a boil, discarding that water and boiling a second time to eliminate the bitterness and make it possible to appreciate the real flavor of these nutritious greens. This individual also suggests that they are great sauteed with mushrooms. The root can also be boiled, baked, fried or diced in a soup or stew.

This perennial thrives in full sun but will accept light shade. It will also accept a wide range of soils, doing best in a compost rich, almost mucky earth. It demands even moisture and seems to be happiest with wet feet. The flowers are informally attractive and can be used in arrangements. The leaves can be harvested throughout the growing season, although spring leaves are the least bitter. It will form a clump that can easily be divided in spring or autumn. This Japanese favorite is also easily propagated from seed sown in seeding trays or in the garden. Germination can begin in a week and continue for over a month.

Sweet flag, *Acorus calamus*
Calla lily family, *Araceae*
Also known as Calamus, sweet sedge, myrtle sedge, sweet root & sweet rush
Hardy perennial reaching 1 m (3 ft) or more in height
Native to Asia, now temperate global

Value as a food source	5
Value as an ornamental	7
Multi-purpose	yes
Continuous harvest	yes
Ease of culture	8
Overall rating	**

The leaves and roots have a cinnamon scent and have been used to repel insects. The root, or rhizome, is listed as poisonous in some texts while others provide recipes for eating it raw. This spicy root can be candied and used as a treat, baked, boiled, roasted or added to stir-fries, soups, stews and rice dishes. It can be used as a ginger substitute, and an oil extracted from the roots is used as a flavoring in everything from ice cream to fine liqueurs. This rhizome can also be dried and grated for use as we do cinnamon and nutmeg. The young leaves have a flavor similar to vanilla once cooked and are used to flavor rices, puddings and custards. The immature stems can be added to a salad and the young flower spike is eaten as a sweet treat.

There is also a wealth of traditional medicinal value in this plant. It has been used as a stimulant and a sedative, a tonic and treatment for rheumatism. Some report hallucinations when large amounts are consumed, while others warn of a possible carcinogenic danger.

This is a rather easy plant to grow in shallow water or soggy soil. A sunny location is best. They can be started from seed, but the most common way to propagate them is from divisions that can be taken at any time during the growing season.

Wasabi, *Wasabia japonica* or *Eutrema wasabi*
Cabbage family, *Brassicaceae (Cruciferae)*
Perennial reaching about 40 cm (8 inches) in height
Native to East Asia
Value as a food source   2
Value as an ornamental   4
Multi-purpose   yes
Continuous harvest   no
Ease of culture   5
Overall rating   **

    This is the source for the green horseradish flavored paste that goes so well with sushi and raw fish. The fleshy rhizomes are harvested fresh and grated into a fine paste that is then mixed with soy. The leaves, stems and flowers can also be eaten as a seasoning in salads or used in cooking.

    It grows in cool fresh water in temperate zones, producing creeping rhizomes and toothed, almost kidney shaped leaves on an elongated stem. White flowers form in clusters on a stalk that rises above the leaves. This is a vegetable that is best when grown in light shade, but it will tolerate full sun. Wasabi is easily started from seed sown on the surface of a pot filled with sandy loam and kept soggy. The seeds can also be sown in shallow pools. Root divisions can also be used to propagate more plants.

Water chestnut, *Eleocharis dulcis*
Sedge family, *Cyperaceae*
Also known as Chinese water chestnut and matai
Perennial
Native to Asia, but now global
Value as a food source   6
Value as an ornamental   2
Multi-purpose   no
Continuous harvest   no
Ease of culture   7
Overall rating   **

    This aquatic vegetable has a sweet, nutty flavor and can be eaten raw, cooked in stir fries, roasted, boiled, baked and added to many Oriental dishes. The corms can be dried and ground into a starchy flour that is used to thicken sauces and a batter for fried foods.

    The plant thrives in bog-like conditions where it looks like a sedge with the stalks growing out of the water. The corms form in the mud after a growing season of at least 110 days. It's easy to propagate from the small corms. Dr. Martin Price, director of ECHO, suggested this. "A convenient way to grow it is as a child's wading pool. Start the corms in Styrofoam cups. Fill a wading pool tightly with pine needles. Add fertilizer with micro-nutrients and dolomite for calcium and magnesium. Plant among the pine needles and add water. After the reeds die down at the end of the growing season pull up the mass of pine needles. All the water chestnuts will be on the very bottom of the root mass and can be picked like berries."

Water chestnuts

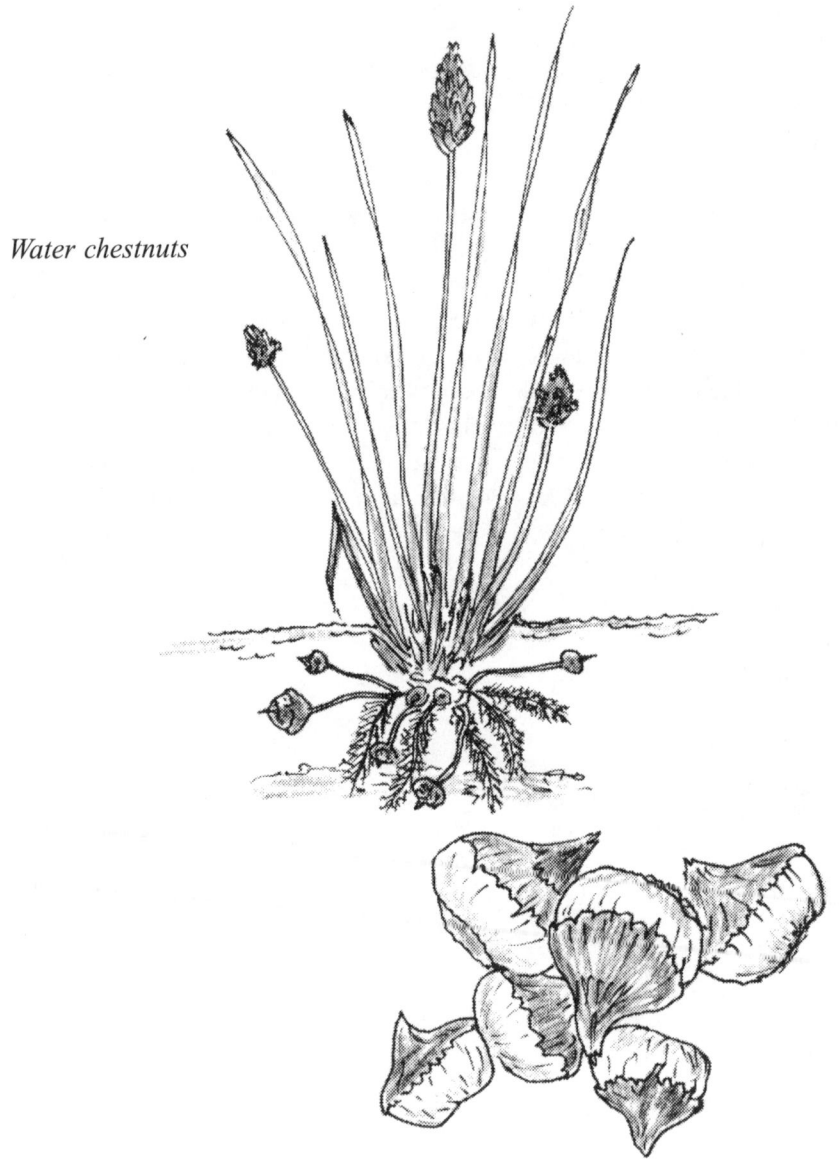

Water Caltrop, *Trapa natans*
Trapaceae family
Also known as Jesuit nut, water chestnut and lingchio
Perennial invasive weed
Eurasian native now global
Value as a food source		4
Value as an ornamental		3
Multi-purpose			no
Continuous harvest		no
Ease of culture			10, invasive danger
Overall rating			*

This floating weed produces underwater seeds that look like a bull's head. The sweet meat of these nuts is delicious raw, roasted, boiled, fried, candied or prepared almost any other way you can imagine. The problem is that they are so aggressive they make water hyacinths and kudzu vines look like wimps. Their value as a food source is so overshadowed by their potential as an environmental disaster that many areas forbid their cultivation, and all over the world millions of dollars are spent in their eradication. We only list it here to illustrate an edible disaster. There is considerable potential for harm when aggressive plants are introduced without understanding their role in the ecosystem. We don't need more global weeds.

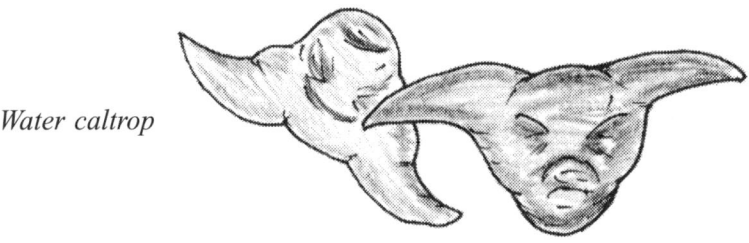

Water caltrop

Water cress, *Nasturtium officinale*
Cabbage family, *Brassicaceae (Cruciferae)*
Annual aquatic and semi-aquatic trailing plant growing 30 to 45 cm (4 to 6 inches) tall.
Native to Eurasia
Value as a food source		5
Value as an ornamental		7
Multi-purpose			no
Continuous harvest		yes
Ease of culture			8
Overall rating			***

This is a semi-aquatic vegetable that thrives in irrigation ditches, slow moving water of shallow streams and low-laying areas where there is constant moisture. It has creeping stems that readily root at the leaf nodes, and will form mats along waterways. This is a temperate zone vegetable crop that will grow in a wide variety of conditions. It is so popular that it can be found on dinner tables all over the world.

Throughout history this has been used both as a food and a medicinal plant. It was valued as a food that could prevent scurvy and other diseases resulting from a poor diet. The fresh leaves are rich in vitamins A, B and C as well as iron and calcium. In Europe and North America we tend to use it raw as a salad green. In China the succulent leaves and stems are stir-fried with a dash of wine or a sprinkling of sugar. In many parts of Asia watercress is used raw or cooked with sesame dressing. This popular spring vegetable is a flavorful addition to soups, stews and purees. It makes a great seasoning for potatoes, mushrooms, artichoke hearts, Chinese cabbage, green beans and almost any other vegetable that might be found on our dinner plate. There are delightful recipes for water cress pasta sauces, salad dressing, vegetable juices, flavored breads, butters, cheeses and yogurt.

Watercress can be harvested daily as needed or kept for a week or more in the refrigerator in a glass of water. This is one those fresh vegetables that we can grow indoors with an amazing lack of effort. Purchase some fresh cress at the supermarket and select a few sprigs that still have sections of the creeping stem attached. Place a few of these leaves and stems in a glass of water on your windowsill, and wait patiently for a few days. As soon as roots form on these stem cuttings you can plant them in a pot of soil and keep the pot in a saucer of water. You now have a source of fresh watercress for months.

Watercress is easy to start from seed and grow as a spring green, so easy in fact, that many gather it from the wild rather than grow it as a garden vegetable. It doesn't have to be growing in water but a shallow stream or the edge of a freshwater pond grows the most succulent leaves. If you want to grow it in standard garden soil it must be kept moist. We have a friend who grows it as a container plant, allowing the creeping stems to drape over the edge of the large pots that sit in a saucer of water. It can be grown in full sun or light shade, with the tenderest leaves being produced in the partial shade. The harvesting can begin in less than four weeks from sowing the seed and can continue for months. Growing it in the shade will prolong the harvest season.

The plant will begin to produce stalks of white flowers in late spring. For many this signals the end of the harvest season, for others this is a second crop. The white flowers and immature seed pods can be used as a seasoning for almost any vegetable or meat dish. The young seedpods can also be used to make flavored vinegars and oils or produce a delightful salad dressing. The spicy-peppery flavor makes it a good salt substitute.

Water lily, *Nymphaea odorata*
Water lily family, *Nymphaeaceae*
Also known as Fragrant water lily
Perennial hardy to USDA zone 5
Native to North America from Newfoundland to Mexico

Value as a food source	8
Value as an ornamental	9
Multi-purpose	yes
Continuous harvest	yes
Ease of culture	8
Overall rating	****

This is another of those amazingly versatile vegetables we don't think of as edible. Perhaps we can't envision such a beautiful flower with such a haunting fragrance on the dinner table. Yet to many cultures this is a supermarket worth wading to. The fleshy roots are boiled or roasted, baked, grated, fried, added to soups and stews. The young leaves can be used raw in salads or cooked in soups and stews, or used as a potherb. The leaves are also used to wrap fish and meat in, much as we might use a tortilla, before baking. The flower buds are used as a cooked vegetable, preserved in oil or pickled in vinegar. The young flowers are used raw as a salad vegetable while individual petals are added to drinks for the taste and fragrance. The ripe seeds are cooked and eaten like peanuts or ground into a protein rich meal. The flower is also used as a source of fragrant oils used in perfumes.

They are easy to grow in standing or slowly moving water that is at least 30 cm (12 in) deep. Water lilies come in two types, 'crawlers' and 'clumpers.' Crawlers have roots that spread out horizontally and send up new plants in sufficient quantity to fill a pond solid. Clumpers have roots that grow more vertically and form offsets around a central crown. Either type enjoys a soil that is slightly alkaline and not too nutrient rich. Full sun is best. They can be easily grown from seed sown in a pot of sandy soil submerged so that the rim is covered by at least 1 inch of water. As the seeds germinate the water level can gradually increase by several inches. Germination can be hastened by nicking the seed coat with a file before planting. Water lilies can also be started from divisions with at least one eye. Plants started this way can become established quite quickly.

Waterlily

Water plantain

Water plantain, *Alisma plantago-aquatica*
Arrowhead family, *Alismataceae*
Also known as mad dog weed, water baby's breath and swamp plantain
Hardy perennial for temperate regions often reaching .6 m (2 ft) in height
Native to much of northern hemisphere

Value as a food source	4
Value as an ornamental	5
Multi-purpose	yes
Continuous harvest	yes
Ease of culture	8
Overall rating	**

    The fleshy swollen stem (tuber) can be harvested any time during the growing season, but in many areas they are dug and dried for winter use. The fresh tubers are quite bitter and somewhat toxic. This drying process reduces both the toxicity and the bitter taste as well as facilitating storage. They can also be soaked or boiled in salt water to make them more palatable. Some sources recommend bringing them to a boil in salt water then discarding the first water and boiling until tender. These tubers can be roasted, fried, or added to soups or stews. They are somewhat richer in protein than are many other tubers. The leaves and petioles (leaf stems) are also used as a potherb. They must be thoroughly cooked to make them safe and palatable. They have a somewhat salty flavor that enhances other greens and can add to a soup.

    The entire plant has been used by herbalists for thousands of years. An oil extracted from this plant was used as a diuretic and as a treatment for dysentery and epilepsy. The roots were considered a cure for rabies, hence the common name, mad-dog weed. In North America it was valued as a treatment for rattlesnake bites. Even the powdered seeds were valued as an antiseptic that helped the blood to clot in sword wounds. It should be noted that some people will develop a rash from handling the raw leaves.

This is an easy aquatic plant to grow in almost any pond or drainage ditch that is usually soggy. They are grown easily from seed or divisions and are a popular plant for water gardens.

Water shield, *Brasenia schreberi*
Cabomaceae family
Cold tolerant Perennial, to zone 6
Native to North America, very popular in the Orient
Value as a food source   6
Value as an ornamental   5
Multi-purpose   yes
Continuous harvest   yes
Ease of culture   8
Overall rating   ***

The young leaves have a transparent liquid on their surfaces, sometimes thick and sticky. This disappears as the leaves mature. These unfurling leaves are valued as a salad green usually served with a dash of vinegar or soy sauce. In Japan they sometimes use sake as a dressing for these leaves and shoots. Mature leaves are added to soups as a flavoring and thickener. In summer the flavor becomes harsh and astringent. The summer leaves are used medicinally as a dressing for rashes, infections, and abrasions. The seeds have been used in the treatment of several illnesses, and the plant is being researched currently as a treatment for cancer.

The roots are peeled and boiled used much like potatoes or carrots. In some locales the roots are sliced and dried for later use in soups and stews.

This is a semi-aquatic plant found at the edge of ponds and slow moving water. It grows naturally floating in fresh water, but is often grown in lightly acid, moist to wet soils. It's not particular as to soil type and will thrive in sandy, loam or clay. It needs full sun to grow productively. It is slow to get started from seed, but divisions taken in spring tend to establish themselves with little effort.

Sea Coasts and Salt Marshes

Much of the earth's land surface is so near the oceans and salt seas or lakes that the land and even the air itself is laden with salt. Most of the plants that we as humans choose to dine upon are reluctant to grow in soils thus polluted. It was a Roman tactic to salt the soil of vanquished nations to destroy their ability to produce food. In other regions entire populations were literally driven to the unproductive salt marshes and shores of oceans or inland seas where survival was difficult and agriculture almost impossible. In areas like Ethiopia and Eritria the choice is between arid deserts of the interior or barren sea coast. Inventive and creative peoples have, through centuries and millenniums, explored their environment and experimented with potential indigenous resources. There are palms and many other trees that thrive on the beaches of the tropical world. However, no matter how hard we try we cannot live on coconuts alone.

In some areas great efforts have been made to remove the salt from the sea water, create dikes, levees and channels, or redirect interior water resources to put fresh water into coastal plains. All this effort is aimed at changing the environment so that the familiar cash crops can be commercially cultivated. Certainly there is overall economic value in doing all this but there are environmental impacts that will include altering the salinity of the coastal seas and marshes, depleting fresh water resources and consuming energy reserves that could be used in other ways.

We often think of the coast as beachfront property, the high rent district, but this is not always the case. Most coastal property is non-productive, difficult soil, drought prone or brackish, not an ideal place to farm and garden. These marginally productive areas often become the only refuge for the poor, for the victims of war, refugees from both military and economic conflict. For those who are left with no place else to live than the coastal barrens all the grand schemes and lofty ideals, research budgets and manmade farmland are solutions that come too late. They will not fill the empty belly or pay for the burial of the children who have fallen to starvation.

Throughout our history on this earth we have attacked many problems in many ways. As a society, as a culture, we seek solutions to the big problems with energy and religious zeal. But, often the problem is so large that it must be solved one person, one family at a time. Hunger is one of those problems for which solutions are held in the hands of each of us. For most of the challenges we face today, there is a precedent. As a teenager assumes that he or she is the first to ever face the stresses of growing into adulthood and feels isolated and alone, so does each age assume that its problems are unique, and that the solutions can come from only the unknown and insecure future. Yet, we can always build on the wisdom of those who have walked this trail before us.

Ancient peoples gathered, or harvested, plants and fish, learned how to use the coastal resources. Let's take a look at some of the plants that have been a part of those diets. Plants that can tolerate sea spray or thrive in salt laden soils are referred to as halophytes. If the *Salicornia* of Ethiopia and Eritria can be developed into a commercial crop, if the home gardener in Mexico can cultivate *Atriplex canescens* (saltbush), if those living on the shores of temperate salt lakes grow sea kale and *Eryngium maritimum*, or island nations cultivate the Australian native, *Apium prostratum* then health can improve and survival becomes easier. We can sustain life with a diet based on plants that naturally thrive in this environment.

These plants can be grown commercially and literally irrigated with sea water. Scientists are working now in many parts of the world with the plants and the people in these marshes, coastal and island environments. They are striving to develop stronger, more productive varieties, create the market potential for new crops, and work together with the indigenous peoples. The following are some of the halophytic plants that have serious potential for both the family garden and the farmer seeking a cash crop.

Australian Celery, *Apium prostratum*
Carrot family, *Apiaceae (Umbeliferae)*
Perennial
Native of Australia
Value as a food source   6
Value as an ornamental   4
Multi-purpose   yes
Continuous harvest   yes
Ease of culture   4
Overall rating   **

It's related to parsley, looks like and smells like parsley too. In fact, it's sometimes called sea parsley. The leaves are pleasantly salty to the palate but some sources describe it as bitter and strong flavored. The leaves and stems are used as a rich green garnish, breath freshener and seasoning in soups and stews, but they can also be added to cooked greens. The stems can be blanched like celery but tend to be quite small. The roots can be peeled and cooked as we would carrots. They can be boiled, roasted, baked and stir-fried. They are also sliced or grated and added to soups, stews and rice dishes. The seeds taste much like celery seed and can be used as a seasoning.

This is a vegetable that tolerates a wide range of soils, as long as they are kept moist, but it doesn't take drought well. Light shade produces the most succulent growth and saline conditions aren't a problem. This can make an attractive border or edging plant in the landscape. They can be started from seed sown lightly and barely covered. Germination usually occurs in 2 to 4 weeks and the seedlings are ready to transplant when they have 4 to 8 leaves. Since this is a perennial that readily forms a clump, it can also be propagated from divisions in the spring or autumn.

Glasswort, *Salicornia europaea*
Beet family, *Chenopodiaceae*
Also known as marsh samphire, sea saltwort, jointed glasswort, common glasswort and sea asparagus
Annual rarely exceeding .3 m (12 in.) in height
Native to British Isles and Europe

Value as a food source	5
Value as an ornamental	3
Multi-use	yes
Continuous harvest	yes
Ease of culture	8
Overall rating	***

This plant is striking when growing enmass in a salt marsh. The leaves and stalks turn deep red in autumn and the appearance is like a field of seaweed reaching for the sun. While valued on the dinner table for thousands of years it was traditionally used throughout much of Europe in glass making, hence the common name, glasswort. Tons of mature plants would be gathered into great piles and then burned to produce a fine ash that was key to the manufacturing of fine glass.

This plant produces an abundance of succulent stems with a salty flavor that can be harvested when about six inches long and prepared in a number of ways. There is a woody core that is easily removed, then the stems can be eaten raw as a snack, used in salads, or briefly boiled or steamed as a potherb or added to soups and stews. In many regions sections of stem are brine or vinegar pickled. The leaves are a popular vegetable both raw and cooked in many areas. The seeds are added to soups as a thickener and flavoring. They are also added to breads as a nutritious seasoning because they are rich in protein. These small seeds can also be pressed for a high quality vegetable oil.

The ash obtained when the plants are burned is high in potassium. This potash continues to be used today in some areas in glass production, but it's also used in soap making. Because this plant will tolerate extreme salinity it is being researched as a cash crop in struggling countries such as Eritria, and areas where salt marsh extends inland such as the Pacific coast of Mexico. There are many varieties and most are easily started from fresh seed sown where they are to grow. They thrive in a compost rich soil that is in full sun. Once the roots are established it will take a good deal of drought, but occasional wet feet aren't a problem. There are many other varieties growing in many coastal regions of the world.

Golden samphire, *Inula crithemoides*
Daisy family, *Asteracea (Compositae)*
Perennial reaching 1 m (3 ft) in height
Native to British Isles and European coastal areas
Value as a food source   4
Value as an ornamental   5
Multi-purpose   no
Continuous harvest   yes
Ease of culture   6
Overall rating   **

    Many view this as a condiment or culinary herb rather than a vegetable. It's often used as a flavoring both raw and cooked. The fleshy leaves and immature shoots are used in salads or to make sauces and relishes. They also make a tolerable potherb, best when combined with other greens. These leaves are sometimes bitter, but always nutritious.

    This is a rather cold hardy plant that accepts saline soils and salt spray. The plant itself is informally attractive and thrives in a wide variety of soil types as long as the drainage is good. It's at its best when the soil is kept evenly moist but can tolerate some drought conditions. It also thrives in light shade or full sun. The plants are easily started from seed sown where they are to grow, or in seedling trays in a greenhouse.

Gray sage brush, *Atriplex canescens*
Beet family, *Chenopodiaceae*
Also known as four-winged saltbush, chamisa, chamiso blanco
Evergreen shrub maturing at 2 m (6 ft) or less, very cold hardy
Native to Western North America from Dakotas to Mexico
Value as a food source   8
Value as an ornamental   10
Multi-purpose   yes
Continuous harvest   yes
Ease of culture   9
Overall rating   *****

    This is one of the best halophytes we can grow. The leaves and tender young shoots are delightful raw or cooked. The salty taste is a pleasant addition to a salad, or we can eat them as a fresh snack right from the bush. They can also be cooked as a potherb, combined with other greens or added to soups and stews. These leaves can be used as a shampoo because they will produce a pleasant scented lather. The leaves also yield a yellow dye. It has long been a Hopi tradition to mix the ash from burnt leaves and stems with the blue corn meal when baking or cooking. This enhances the blue coloring and serves as a light seasoning. This nutrient rich ash can also be used as we would baking soda.

The seeds are ground and added to flour to impart a color and flavor. The ground seed can also be used to make a refreshing drink. Some add the crushed seed to soups and stews as a seasoning and thickening agent.

Because this plant is so salt tolerant it's valuable as an erosion control and a low maintenance hedge, but it has one other advantage. It doesn't burn well, thus it can be a valuable part of a fire-resistant landscape and used to produce a green buffer zone.

These ruggedly attractive, cold hardy shrubs will thrive in almost any sunny, well-drained site, but they don't respond well to wet or humid climates. This is one of the premier arid lands and coastal plants. It handles extreme drought and high heat without a whimper. It can be propagated from seed sown in 4 inch pots and kept lightly moist. Germination usually occurs between 1 and 3 weeks. Allow to grow into a bushy little plant before planting in its permanent site. They can also be propagated from cuttings of half-ripe wood placed in a sandy mix in mid summer. They will root in about 2 to 4 weeks and are ready to pot up or plant out in a couple months. As they mature they resent transplanting because of the deep roots.

Four-winged saltbush

Rock samphire, *Crithmum maritimum*
Carrot family, *Apiaceae (Umbelliferae)*
Also known as sea fennel, hinojo marino, sanpetra
Perennial reaching about .3 m (12 in) in height, cold tolerant
Native to most of Europe

Value as a food source	3
Value as an ornamental	5
Multi-purpose	yes
Continuous harvest	yes
Ease of culture	7
Overall rating	**

This is one of those plants that may not be the most glamorous, nor is it the most delicious, but it will grow where many others cannot. The leaves can be used raw in salads. The flavor is more like celery than fennel, but there is a salty bitterness to it that some find offensive. One source describes it as tasting similar to turpentine, another calls it "brackish" while another says it is refreshingly tart. As an addition to mixed greens, soups, stews and rice dishes it serves as a flavorful addition to what might otherwise be rather bland fare. Regardless of how one views the flavor, there is agreement that the leaves are rich in vitamin C. The seeds are also used as a seasoning, much as we use celery seed. They add flavor to soups, stews, meat dishes and baked goods.

In folk medicine the leaves have long been used as a digestive aid, and several sources consider rock samphire useful in weight control programs and claim it can improve overall vigor. The plant is currently grown commercially for an essential oil that is used in the fragrance industry.

The plants thrive in a sandy or rocky site with good drainage and full sun. While it does quite well in areas where the soil is poor and saline, it is difficult to grow successfully in compost-rich garden beds. It seems that adversity brings out the best in rock samphire. In temperate areas it can be grown as a container plant. They can be propagated from seed sown in 4 inch pots of coarse sand and lightly covered. Germination occurs in about a month and growth is slow for the first year. They can also be grown from divisions of the root mass in early spring.

Saltwort, *Salsola kali*
Beet family, *Chenopodiaceae*
Also known as glasswort, spiny saltwort, marsh samphire, pickleweed, sea bean and a number of other local names.
Annual growing to .5 m (1 ° feet)
Native to the beaches of Europe and the British Isles

Value as a food source	5
Value as an ornamental	4
Multi-purpose	yes
Continuous harvest	yes
Ease of culture	8
Overall rating	**

The young leaves and stems have a pleasant salty taste that makes them a nutritious and flavorful addition to salad and a more than acceptable garnish.

Immature stems and older leaves can be cooked as a potherb, added to soups and stews. The tender stems are delightfully preserved by cooking in salt water then pickling in spiced oil or vinegars. The protein rich seeds are produced in great quantities and were traditionally ground into a meal and used as a porridge or a thickener in soups, gravies and other dishes. The meal is also added to flour and used to make a dark, hearty breakfast bread. These seeds can be pressed to produce a valuable culinary oil.

Saltwort has an interesting history of non-food uses. The common name glasswort refers to its onetime popularity in the art of glass making. The plants were collected and burned to produce tons of ash for use in the British glass making industry. It was also used throughout medieval Europe in soap making. Even today the ashes are frequently used as a versatile and effective household and clothing cleanser.

This is a salt tolerant plant with some potential for coastal gardens. All it asks is full sun and a well drained site, preferably sandy loam. It's an easy plant to grow in temperate regions from zone 3 through 8. Saltwort will stoically accept drought although a better harvest can be had with good soil and regular watering. The seeds should be sown where the plants are to be grown after danger of frost is past. It grows with such enthusiasm that it is considered a noxious weed in several states, including Hawaii.

Sea blite, *Suaeda maritima*
Beet family, *Chenopodiaceae*
Also known as seepweed
Annual rarely exceeding .3 m (12 in) in height.
Native to Europe

Value as a food source	6
Value as an ornamental	5
Multi-purpose	yes
Continuous harvest	yes
Ease of culture	6
Overall rating	***

The leaves and tender stems have a pleasant lightly salty taste that adds much to a salad. The young shoots are a healthy snack food when eaten raw, but they are also frequently soaked in vinegar or pickled and used as a condiment. The leaves and shoots also make a great potherb, either by themselves or mixed with other greens. Some find the taste too salty and bring the leaves to a boil, discard this first water then bring them to a boil a second time. These leaves and shoots can also be added to soups and stews while the seeds can be used raw or cooked. Added to soups the seeds serve as a thickening and flavoring agent.

This is a great coastal plant for alkaline soils. It thrives in full sun in a sandy soil with regular watering. With it's botanical cousins, the *Salicornea*, this plant has the potential to improve diets in many temperate coastal areas. Like the glassworts, it was burned for the soda ash that was valuable in glass making and soap production. This is a vegetable that can be easily started from seed,, best sown where they are to grow. Harvesting can begin in 4 to 6 weeks and continue until frost.

Sea holly, *Eryngium maritimum*
Carrot family, *Apiaceae (Umbeliferae)*
Also known as cardo, eryngo & sea hulver
Perennial evergreen forming a mound about .5 m (18 in) in diameter
Cold tolerant to USDA zone 5
Native to Europe

Value as a food source	5
Value as an ornamental	7
Multi-purpose	yes
Continuous harvest	yes
Ease of culture	8
Overall rating	***

    A fragrant edible landscape plant and valuable erosion control all wrapped into one. The new shoots can be blanched by hilling up soil, straw or yesterday's newspaper up around them. The tender, succulent growth that results can be used as we would asparagus. This is considered gourmet food in some circles. The flavor is somewhat similar to mild celery. These shoots and young leaves can also be cooked with other greens or added to soups and stews. The roots are somewhat like a long white carrot. They have a sweet taste and when boiled, baked or roasted the flavor is somewhere between chestnuts and parsnips. These roots were sliced and candied in Shakespeare's time and called *eringoes*. In the lusty days of Elizabethan England sea holly roots were valued as. an aphrodisiac and a tonic. The fresh leaves, roots and flower umbels were used as a room freshener. Slices of root (called wafers or lozenges) were set out in smoking rooms. Today we value the flowers because they attract bees and butterflies. The roots grow several feet deep and spread to form extensive mats that control beach and soil erosion. Since it has such a deep root system it doesn't transplant well. While they thrive in saline soils and enjoy the salt spray in the air, they will tolerate inland gardens quite well, although the flavor of the shoots and roots is somewhat different. It will accept most soils but does better in alkaline sandy conditions. They will do well in hot drought prone areas.

    This versatile vegetable can be started from seed sown in sandy soil filled 4 inch pots and kept lightly moist. Germination is erratic, ranging from 5 days to 3 months or more. They can also be propagated root cuttings taken in the dormant seasons, or carefully removing new shoots for the clump in early spring.

Seakale

Seakale, *Crambe maritima*
Cabbage family, *Brassicaceae (Cruciferae)*
Long lived perennial
European coastal native
Value as a food source   5
Value as an ornamental   5
Multi-purpose   yes
Continuous harvest   yes
Ease of culture   7
Overall rating   **

    This is one of those salt tolerant plants that thrives in a north temperate setting. The traditional way to use this plant is to take root cuttings and force (grow in a season when the plant would not normally be growing, or under artificial growing conditions) in a warm dark room for tender winter greens. In the wild it forms a nice mound of grey-green foliage from spring through early autumn but goes completely dormant in the winter. The young leaves and flower stalks can be harvested and eaten as a salad green or cooked throughout the growing season. The best flavor is in the spring, with the young leaves having a pleasant taste. They can be started from seed or root divisions and once established are relatively care free. Away from the coastal salt spray slugs and snails can be a problem, but they can be controlled with a light sprinkling of chili powder or table salt. In some locales the leaves and stalks have been pickled for later use.

Sea Orach, *Atriplex halimus*
Beet family, *Chenopodiaceae*
Evergreen shrub reaching about 1 to 2 m (3 to 6 ft) in height
Native to Mediterranean basin, North Africa and Eurasian coasts

Value as a food source	9
Value as an ornamental	8
Multi-purpose	yes
Continuous harvest	yes
Ease of culture	9
Overall rating	****

    Not only does this interesting plant grow in poor soils along sea coasts where few edible plants are willing to set up housekeeping, it even tastes good. The fresh leaves, similar in size and flavor to lambs ears, have a spicy, salty flavor that adds much to a salad. They can also be eaten as a snack and serve well as a potherb. When briefly steamed in a microwave the flavor is delicious and a pleasant crispness is retained. The leaves can also be added to soups and stews. The plant exudes a thick sap from wounds on the stems. This *manna* can be collected and used in cooking, baking or eaten out of hand. The seeds can be added to soups as a flavoring and thickening agent. Often the seeds are ground and added to flour for baked goods or breakfast cereals and porridge. Ash obtained from burning these bushes was traditionally used in soap production.

    Because this is such a rugged shrub, able to withstand drought, coastal winds, saline soils and is hardy north to USDA zone 8, it's an ideal plant for erosion control. It makes an attractive hedge that responds well to pruning and serves well as an edible landscape plant. It has the ability to draw salts out of the soil and has been used to desalinate contaminated areas.

    Sea orach is comfortable in a wide range of sandy, rocky and loamy soils, and enjoys the adversity of drought and poor soil. It does demand good drainage and full sun. It doesn't respond well to wet climates and high humidity. It's most often propagated from cuttings, either soft wood or hardwood. Seeds can be sown in four inch pots of a sandy soil mix and lightly covered. They will germinate in 1 to 4 weeks and will be ready to set out after they fill the pot. They don't take transplanting well after they become established because of their deep and extensive roots.

Sea purslane, *Halimione portulacoides*
Beet family, *Chenopodiaceae*
Perennial evergreen shrub reaching .75 m (28 - 30 inches) in height
Native to Eurasia and Mediterranean coasts

Value as a food source	7
Value as an ornamental	5
Multi-purpose	no
Continuous harvest	yes
Ease of culture	8
Overall rating	***

This shrub produces leaves that are thick and succulent with a pleasantly salty flavor. Raw they make a nutritious and tasty addition to a salad. They can also be cooked as a potherb, or added to soups, stews, meat and vegetable dishes. This is a 12 month salad on a shrub that may be a valuable food resource in wet coastal areas where traditional vegetables are difficult to grow.

Sea purslane thrives in a wide range of poor soils and is at home in highly alkaline sites and salt marsh areas. It does require constantly moist soils and can even handle tidal inundations. It's at its best in full sun but will tolerate light shade. As with many halophytes, it will grow in soils that aren't saline as well as the coastal sites.

It can easily be started from seed collected as soon as ripe and planted in the autumn. We prefer starting the seed in 4 inch pots filled with sandy soil. The seeds germinate erratically, even during the cooler months. They can also be started from cuttings taken in mid-summer and by division in the spring.

Seashore Mallow, *Kostelectzkya virginica*
Hibiscus family, *Malvaceae*
Perennial reaching 1.5 to 2 m (4 to 6 ft)
Native to Caribbean area and eastern North America

Value as a food source	5
Value as an ornamental	5
Multi-purpose	no
Continuous harvest	no
Ease of culture	8
Overall rating	**

While both the flowers and leaves are listed as a famine food this isn't the greatest asset of this plant. It produces large quantities of valuable seed that has the potential to be a salt plains grain source. The hulled seed resembles millet and contains over 30% protein and at least 20% useful vegetable oil. The seed can be used in cooking as we would rice, barley and corn. It can be ground into a flour and used in baking.

This mallow thrives in poor to moderate soils and accepts the salt levels found in many coastal areas. This is a potential perennial crop for sea water irrigation in areas with full sun. Once the fields are established the seed can be harvested, the stalks used for paper pulp, compost or bio-mass energy production.

It's an easy crop to grow from seed planted as we would any other field grain, but it can also be efficiently propagated from cuttings.

Sea rocket, *Cakile maritima*
Cabbage family, *Brassicaceae (Cruciferae)*
Annual reaching .3 to .6 m (1 to 2 feet) in height
Native to Eurasia and North Africa
There is also a North American native, *C. Edentula*

Value as a food source	3
Value as an ornamental	5
Multi-purpose	yes
Continuous harvest	yes
Ease of culture	9
Overall rating	**

The pink or white flowers are fragrant and attractive, but they are also edible. In fact the flower buds, stems and succulent leaves have a hot, almost horseradish flavor that adds zest to a salad or a sandwich. The unripe seed pods are great as a seasoning in soups, stews and vegetable dishes.

This is one of those weeds that are the first green wave in natures's reclamation of disturbed areas along sea coasts. They are so salt tolerant that they will literally grow right up to the tide line. This is an annual for temperate and tropical areas, but it is sometimes considered invasive and will crowd out desirable plants, although it does help to hold soil and provide cover for wildlife. Seed scattered where it's to grow will germinate within a week and the plants will be blooming in less than two months.

Chapter Ten
Hunger is the Symptom; Poverty is the Disease

"Make us worthy, Lord, to serve those through out the world who live and die in poverty or hunger. Give them, through our hands, this day their daily bread; and by our understanding love, give peace and joy. Amen"
                    Mother Teresa of Calcutta

The rest of this book goes beyond the garden. In no way do we wish to inflict guilt, as is so often the case with television programs and magazine articles that focus on pictures of starving children. Rather our goal is to help the reader to understand both the causes and effects of hunger, then arm you with the knowledge that we can all be a part of the solution. There is hope. We invite you to read on, then give yourself a role in the solution stories that follow. You are the hope of your neighbors.

Part I: Poverty of the Land

We can view poverty as a disease much like cancer. With both we can identify a multitude of causes, a multitude of manifestations and must seek a multitude of cures. The greatest tool we have at our disposal is the innate human ability to work together. The simple fact is that the luxury of conflict and competition no longer exists in the new millennium. We have no choice but to employ the wisdom of all people and all ages.

Each cause of hunger has a number of possible solutions. What will work in one area might not be the appropriate solution somewhere else. As each problem is a reflection of unique climatic, geographic, societal and religious conditions, so must each solution be a special response to the same factors. In many situations the best solution may not be financially feasible. As an example, water is in short supply in many areas. Drought, declining water tables and desertification may be the result of deforestation, poor agricultural practices, global warming, or overuse. In Florida the cultural traditions of swimming pools, lawn sprinklers, even personal cleanliness use far more water than is necessary for comfortable survival. Still most residents are linked to their cultural water use practices and are reluctant to give up the useless lawn, the long shower, the inefficient dishwasher. So the water table continues to drop, salinated water creeps further and further into the aquifers, and tapwater is often no longer potable or safe.

The ecosystems are raped and plundered, often out of ignorance, sometimes with the best of intentions. Regardless, the effects are the same. Poor soil makes the people poor as well. When the earth is hungry, so are its people.

Let's take a look at some of the causes of hunger in various parts of the world and a menu of their potential solutions.

Water Shortages

Water is dynamic. It is the essence of all life. The power in a drop of water is awesome. An earthen jar filled with it sustains life. A river is a living thing capable of giving life to a community, or taking it away. We exist because there is water. As gardeners we can grow nothing without water, yet much of this globe is faced with a profoundly limited supply.

This is a problem that can manifest itself in a number of different ways. In Senegal and many other places on this globe, there is an incredibly dry season that makes traditional farming and gardening difficult from four to six months of the year. In desert areas of the horn of Africa Eritria and Ethiopia face a chronic water shortage. On many islands of the Pacific Atolls there is an unlimited supply of salt water, but little fresh water for human consumption or traditional gardening.

One of the most common solutions is to dig irrigation ditches and bring water from a river, lake or other source to the fields and gardens. This is simply using gravity to carry the water. Other peoples are limited to the water they can carry on their shoulders. For others there is simply no water available, other than dew and fog.

Indigenous cultures in areas of seasonal drought have had centuries worth of experience living with the seasonal transitions, growing traditional crops and using food storage techniques that make survival possible. With the agricultural research being done throughout the world new varieties with higher yield, improved resistance to drought and greater nutritional value are all very real possibilities. This makes it possible for native populations to enjoy, and in some instances rediscover, their traditional foods while coping with the limited supply of water.

In other areas it is often necessary to conserve water, and this may mean modifying the way we live, the way we garden, the plants that we grow and the harvest cycle. Water can be conserved by reducing the overall use, by reclaiming and reusing, by using intensive gardening techniques and planting drought tolerant crops. Using surface mulches, cover crops and rugged legume intercropping can increase yield while limiting water demand. Bare soil loses far more water to evaporation than do green plants growing on it. A cover crop helps to reduce the soil temperature and this decreases evaporation while improving root systems. Intensive water efficient growing techniques like the Cellugro system developed by ACF Environmental, or raised beds, hydroponic systems and large container cultivation are all potential answers.

In many desert areas dew can be harvested, and this provides sufficient moisture to sustain both the garden and the gardener. In other areas keeping water supplies underground or covered to limit evaporation is the answer. For still others recycling isn't a choice, it's a survival tactic. Sprinkler systems are incredibly wasteful, yet large scale agriculture depends on it in many areas. In the backyard garden drip irrigation is a solution that works. Timing the application of irrigation and sprinkler systems to minimize evaporation can save thousands of gallons of water in a family garden over a year's time.

By rediscovering and improving the plants native to a given area, or similar area elsewhere, that are xeroscopic in nature, mature quicker, or naturally use less water in their growth cycle, we can grow more productive gardens and farm crops with the limited water supply. Jojoba and agave are two good examples of this type of cash crop that thrive in desert conditions. There are numerous root and fruiting crops that can answer the hunger needs of a population even if they don't have great value as a market crop.

The Hopi in the American Southwest planted in a gardening tradition called waffle gardening. This was simply the creating of little wells around each planting to hold any available water in place until it has been absorbed by the soil and roots of the plants growing there. This is much the same principle as the Cellugro system discussed earlier. The goal is to make every drop of this precious liquid count.

In coastal areas where salt water is abundant productive gardens and crops are limited. There are two directions researchers can explore. Scientists are doing extensive research right now on salt tolerant plants that can serve as either forage for livestock or food on the dinner table. Salicornia is only one of these halophytes that may well answer the food needs of millions of people living on islands and salt water marshes. Plants growing in salt water can also provide numerous economic harvests for the nearby peoples, including fibers, dyes, building materials and fuels.

The other approach is to remove the salt from the water. Desalinization is an expensive and questionable solution that can be used to provide drinking water, but the question remains about the disposition of the extracted salts and the effects of the seas on the resulting changes in salinity.

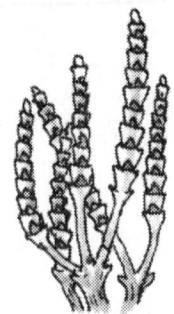

*Known as Salicornia,
Pickleweed, and Samphire*

Desertification is a problem being addressed by several organizations such as SEPASAL (Survey of Economic Plants for Arid and Semi-Arid Lands) of Kew Gardens. This is simply the advancing of desert conditions into areas where gardening and agriculture used to be possible. This can be the result of depleted aquifers, dammed and altered river courses, deforestation, over grazing and changes in climate as we experience the effects of global warming. To successfully counter this environmental degradation requires rethinking the ways we live. The unfortunate factor is however, that the people most seriously affected by desertification aren't the ones that were instrumental in causing it. Desertification can be halted in many areas by the appropriate use of plants and growing techniques. We can restrict the use of available water by growing plant material suitable for arid conditions. We can use mulch, even moisture retaining fabrics, intercrop with soil enriching legumes, permit cattle and goat grazing to control weeds and provide nutrient, avoid the soil trauma of seasonal tilling, accept the value of multi-level cropping.

Too Much Water

We think of drought and deserts whenever the term "water problems" enters the conversation, but there are many places on our planet where the problem is one of excess, sometimes violent excess. This can be a problem in areas where monsoons relentlessly deluge the fields and gardens. Flooding drowns many crops and washes away others along with buildings and livestock. Agricultural, logging, mining and building activities often compound the effects of heavy rain. When the natural cover of trees and undergrowth is removed from a hillside to plant fruit trees or to harvest the timber, rain water carries the soil downhill with it as it rushes to the seas. These mudslides can be far more devastating than an avalanche, with catastrophic changes to the landscape that effect generations. The thin layer of topsoil is gone, the aquatic eco-systems of streams, rivers and the sea coast are severely damaged.

In the last century the way hillsides were tilled encouraged erosion and resulted in the great dust bowl in the American Midwest. Some resources argue that the solution to our present soil depletion lies in no-till agriculture, the extended use of perennial crops and cover crops. Weeds get a bad rap, but they are a natural erosion control and can even be used to advantage by the wise gardener. In some areas raised beds and terraced gardening can provide some stability, but the cost of creating such structures can be prohibitive. Intensive gardening can help to overcome some of these problems.

Terracing is great in areas where there is no shortage of rocks and stones or even recycled concrete. The use of plants like vetiver grass *(Vetiveria zizanioides)* make ideal living terrace walls and boundaries around the banks of ponds. These living walls literally grow to match the natural geological principle of downhill creep. That means that the layer of soil that cloaks a hillside can be viewed as a thick liquid that ever so slowly oozes downhill, driven by the force of gravity. Roots growing in this soil layer, and the organic matter on top of it, help to slow the process and replace the soil weather claims.

In some areas the seasonal flooding of river banks creates the broad flood plains that encouraged the first agricultural efforts. This annual flooding spread a layer of nutrients over the area making the cultivation of crops easy and success a sure thing. When we dam the rivers to prevent this, we deplete the soil because the natural cycle of renewal is destroyed. In flood plains where we plant villages and cities, instead of trees and grasses, problems are bound to arise. Along the Rio Grande in the American Southwest this natural flood cycle has been prevented by dams and the use of the water upstream for irrigation. The natural flooding watered the sprouting of cottonwood seeds. Now the seed falls on dry soil and young trees are no longer growing up among the grandfather trees so that the ecosystems along the river banks are literally dying of old age.

Irrigation systems, with their canals, pumps and ditches can be viewed as artificial and controlled flooding. Since their early efforts at agriculture, humanity has changed the course of rivers and drawn water from lakes to make possible the crop production that was vital to sustain the life of the village, community, city or state. Modifying nature is not a twentieth century phenomenon; it is a part of our universal human survival.

The Nile River is the most dynamic historical example of flood plain agriculture, but the Amazon also floods annually, and will continue to because irrigation isn't necessary and damming the river is impractical. This inundation provides nutrition, controls pests and makes possible a multitude of plants that can grow only in these narrow bands along the rivers. Again the key to these great flood plains is usually the trees, and as we begin to implement the principles of sound agro-forestry and gain an understanding of the value of the forest in climate and erosion control we can improve the quality of life for peoples throughout the global community. Agroforestry is the best answer we have to survival in flood prone areas. Dams aren't always a practical solution and may only create other problems, often those we can't even imagine yet. By planting trees we can hold the soil in place, provide eco-sound cash crops and help to feed the people living in the area.

There are also indigenous crops that match the seasons and permit harvest before the rains come, or can withstand the rains and provide fresh food during the rainy season. In the tropics many of the "greens" come from trees such as bauhinia, sesbania, chaya, moringa and katuk. These can provide a continuous nutritious harvest. Many of the trees that can be grown for their fruit, fibers, medicines, construction and fuel. The forest can be cultivated and the cultivator can be a partner in the life of the flood prone forest, together all can survive.

Soil Fertility

Soil isn't always healthy enough or sufficiently nutrient laden to support the plants we would like to grow. In harsh deserts where rainfall is recorded in inches per decade and years may pass without measurable rainfall, there are still plants that survive. Yet, in areas where moisture isn't a problem the soil may be used up, worn out, worked to death, or poisoned.

Soil is a living organism teaming with life. We think of soil in terms of the nutrients it contains. We are convinced by advertising campaigns that if only we feed with the best brands, we can grow perfect plants. While nutrition is important for plants, as it is for people, and while it is true that our gardens suffer from deficiency diseases just as we do, it is also important for us to remember that the garden isn't a series of plants living in a vitamin jar. The plants we are cultivating are only a part of an unimaginably complex community of plant and animal life plus some organisms that fit neatly into neither of these two classifications of living matter. There are symbiotic relationships between bacteria and legumes, fungi and trees, insects, beneficial nematodes, earthworms, other plants and small vertebrates. Many of these organisms have the job of breaking down the discarded leaves and dead roots, turning them into compost. Other organisms affect seed coats to initiate germination, surround roots to help absorb moisture and nutrients, defend against harmful organisms, convert the nutrients we apply into chemical compounds that our chosen plants can use.

What happens when we pour fungicides, herbicides, nematocides, insecticides, mulloskocides, rodentocides and all the other chemicals designed to kill living organisms? These are all killers and the effects often go far beyond the intended target. We often condemn the farmer, but in reality in the United States it's the homeowner and the golf course that are often the greatest risk to the overall environment. The soil is poisoned, the aquifers, waterways, lakes and coastal estuaries become poison laden kettles of a witch's's brew, while advertising campaigns provide the chants and incantations.

In the farming industry in many parts of the world, the crop depends on the use of these defensive chemicals. The responsible farmer uses these wisely, as a tool, and with a full understanding of their nature and lateral effects. Still the excesses continue. Pesticides like DDT continue to be produced and used in Asia and Latin America even though the dangers are well known and their use is forbidden in most of the industrialized world. Other chemicals are used in concentrations that far exceed the allowable or recommended rates. In some cases the soil and water are so effected that the essential organisms, this subterranean web of life, are destroyed and the soil is dead.

The unfortunate fact is, however, that for most of the globe's impoverished, for the hungry and mal-nourished all over the world, the cost of chemical pesticides makes this an impossible means of pest control. Even the concept of fertilizer is an expensive dream in regions where every twig is used as fuel rather than compost. All soils are not created equal, but each soil type has plants that will grow in it. Unfortunately, the human tendency for thousands of years has been to use the soil up, deplete it, exhaust it, then move on. We have the romantic notion that this is true only of the industrialized cultures of today, but slash and burn agriculture is nothing new. The way we do it is however. When we deny our natural harmony with the soil and the life that it supports, we also deny not only our past but our future.

Soil, being a living organism, is capable of healing, strengthening or replenishing itself. This is the whole principle behind the rhythm of fallow fields. But in areas where starvation is the monster lurking in the empty closet, it's impossible to leave any spot of land unused for a season or a year. There are uncounted reasons why humanity has found itself in such a precarious position today. Some argue that it is because we have been too successful, we have multiplied beyond what the earth can support. Too often we seek to cast blame, rather than seek solutions.

For the past several millennia we have engaged in terrible wars to claim the lands and labors of our neighbors. When we found ourselves at the top of the food chain we began to devour each other in the form of warfare and slavery. Where disease failed to limit our numbers we employed the sword and the gun, but now war can no longer be considered as a noble, wise or appropriate use of human life. War is no longer economically profitable nor is it morally appropriate. If we can join together to feed each other, as the micro-organisms in the soil do, perhaps we can weave a most beautiful fabric of life. But it begins with the soil. All life is from the dust under our feet and the water in the stream. Great civilizations and quiet populations were born where the flesh of the earth meets the life blood we call water. Whether we choose to admit it or not, the fact remains that we are a part of this great system. We are all kin.

In many farming cultures of the past there was a stable relationship with the land. The farmers were in harmony with this ecosystem and they were very much a part of it. But for others the pressures of population, the concept of personal ownership of the land, the competition within the community cost these agricultural and pastoral communities their place in the web of life. They ceased to be contributing members and became consumers only. We are partners with the soil and we have it within our power to strengthen, enrich and preserve this valuable resource. But, we must move beyond ideologies, politics and belief systems and focus on hands and minds working together.

Depleted soils can be rebuilt with time. The chickens in the garden is a prime example of how we can utilize limited space efficiently. Chickens are a source of eggs and meat, but they also devour insects and weed seeds. They engage in "scratch tilling" as is showcased at ECHO in Fort Myers, Florida: by dividing the garden into three sections, one section newly planted, the second being harvested, and the third used as a chicken run. By rotating these so that as the garden is harvested, the chickens clean and fertilize the soil, that area is soon ready to plant.

Productive shrubs and trees can serve as fence posts and fuel sources, natural insecticides and food.

Soil can be enriched with periodic applications of mulch that will decompose and filter down into the soil gradually. This is again a no-till technique that works well in hillside farms and gardens where to plow is to create erosion and mudslides. It also works well in the average backyard.

The soil also contains some organisms that are hostile to the crops and produce we are trying to cultivate. Nematodes are among the worst offenders. Even here though we must remember that in the over all scheme of things, there are beneficial nematodes as well as villains. An efficient way to achieve an acceptable number of these organisms in the soil is to increase the organic material. Compost is a great nematode control, but more than that, it makes the soil a better home for plant roots, holds moisture better, retains soil nutrients better, encourages the earthworms, insects, fungi and bacteria that make this living soil so remarkable and keep it healthy.

We can apply packaged fertilizers to enrich soil, and this is done in most farming and gardening endeavors in the industrialized nations. Americans spend more feeding their non-productive lawns than the entire continent of Africa can afford to raise their life-sustaining food. While these specially formulated chemical compounds are maligned by the agro-fundamentalists, the fact remains that this is what makes feeding billions of people possible. This is definitely a part of the answer for agro-business, and for the small gardener where such nutrients are obtainable and affordable. Unfortunately, in many parts of the world this isn't an option. What does a mother with three children whose husband has been lost to political conflict do with no income, a goat, half a dozen chickens and a small plot where she needs to raise the food for her family's survival? In such situations we can't even think about school for the children, or health care, or even new clothes. This is a family that gathers twigs and dried cattle dung for fuel and carries water from a polluted well for all their needs. How do they even think about buying a bag of plant food? How do they find hope in the soil that is also suffering from starvation, just as they are?

The only way to break this cycle is through global cooperation. Not only donations of emergency food relief, but the development of family gardens where the first step is planned, together hope is planted and a future is cultivated. And, this must begin with the soil. First we must feed the soil. It is difficult to sacrifice the organic waste, the fallen leaves, twigs and even manure to the garden, but this is the meal the soil craves. It may require the introduction of legumes to work with their microzia to feed the hungry soil, leaf crops that can be tilled into the soil, mulches that can be allowed to become soil. Gray water from washing clothes, dishes and bodies can also be used to slowly rebuild hungry soils.

If we can increase the diversity of plant material grown rather than focusing on vast expanses of single crops, there is less damage to the soil and a decreased opportunity for disaster if a crop fails. The key to success in the fields, gardens and communities is in diversity. The very existence of humanity relies upon our diversity as well.

www.globalgardening.info

Part of the problem comes from the crops we try to raise in areas where the nutrients are wrong or the water supply insufficient, or the climate inappropriate. We can rediscover the indigenous fruits, vegetables and grains. We can support research that develops improved varieties with a shorter growing season, pest and disease resistance or drought tolerance. We can explore growing techniques that make gardening on a micro-scale productive.

Part of the solution to empty soil might lie in incremental building. By starting with a small plot that can sustain the family, making it healthy and productive, then gradually expanding to a garden large enough to grow a surplus that can be marketed. Perhaps the residents of communities can work together to care for each other and answer one another's needs.

We make donations of seed as an expression of generosity and concern, but if we fail to involve those who are receiving this gift in the decision making process, we limit the success of the program. Without the input, understanding and support of the population, the donor nations are continuing the colonial tradition. Often times the aid and assistance reflects the interests of the economic powers more than it does the needs of the starving population. Part of this is because of ethnocentrism, part of it is a manifestation of profit motive, part of it is the need to be in control. ECHO in Ft Myers engages in active research, seeking answers from those who are facing the daily crisis of food production and hunger. It's not only the recipients who need training, so do the scientists, the agro-industries, and those of us all over the world who are disturbed when any one goes hungry.

When every backyard gardener in the United States is "Planting a Row for the Hungry," we can gain an empathy that goes beyond contributing money to someone else's solution to someone else's problems. When gardeners all over the world are growing fruits and vegetables that aren't a part of their traditional garden plot we can begin to be partners in the "global garden." When adults and children have access to displays of experimental crops and techniques at local botanical gardens, agricultural extension services and school grounds, we can begin to understand something of the diversity of both the problems and the solutions, perhaps then we can grow an end to hunger, malnutrition and death by starvation.

Soil Type and Climate

Soil doesn't just happen. It's a reflection of the mountains and hillsides, the lakes and seas, the ever changing expression of geologic processes that have been going on for millions of years. The forces of nature are sometimes violent, moving great quantities of soil in minutes. Flash floods move acres worth of soil, sand storms carry dust and seeds miles, mudslides strip the hills and mountains of their cloak of life sustaining soil. Sometimes the geologic changes are as slow and as painstakingly gradual as drops of rain dissolving sandstone or the alternate freezing and thawing that turn granite into sand. Rocks tumbled smooth in a stream produce dissolved minerals and larger particles that enrich silt downstream. Glaciers move inches a year, moving soil and boulders with them, but they also carry with them the dust and airborne particles drawn to the surface with the snowflakes. Nature not only builds the Andes and the Himalayas or digs the Grand Canyon, it is also the great leveler, washing the Appalachians away as the lakes are filled with rich silt. Great volcanoes produce lava and ash as the makeup of the soil is changed overnight. In the daily drama of the earth's crust we as humans were for most of our existence more spectator than participant. Today we dam the rivers, chemically alter the soils with both fertilizers and pollutants, alter the air we breath, level forests, create deserts and damage the protective ozone layer of our atmosphere. Weather is both the builder and destroyer of soil.

www.globalgardening.info

In the midst of this never-ending climatic change we plant gardens, raise crops, feed our children, build our lives and cling to survival. We think of the problems of hunger and malnutrition occurring in the equatorial regions of our globe, but people starve in the mountains of China, South America, India and the Near East. Hunger exists in both the cities and the countryside of virtually every nation on earth. In both the tropics and the mountains, the problem of food production is compounded by an uncooperative climate. Even when the soil is rich, if the temperatures are too high or too low to support the growth of edible plants, nutritional needs aren't going to be met. This means that crops that have a short growing season and can be efficiently stored are a part of the solution. While there may be indigenous fruits, vegetables and grains, survival of communities may depend on the introduction of foods from similar climatic regions elsewhere in the global garden. The potato was carried from the Andes to the British Isles and the Steppes of Russia and the sometimes harsh climates of Maine and Idaho. There may be other of the Andes root crops that have value to other temperate and mountainous regions.

Our great grains, wheat and corn, were carried around the planet along with cabbages, tomatoes, peppers, cassava, breadfruit, watermelons, millet and so many other staples of human existence. This principle of carrying our foods with us is a human trait. Every people have their "Canoe Plants" that accompany them in their travels. Corn was a good idea whose time had come. Native Americans carried it with them in their settlement of two continents. The cassava has saved millions of lives in Africa, the moringa tree will save millions more in many regions of the world. The goal is not to just grow native plants and attempt subsistence in much the same way as our hunter-gatherer ancestors. What we need to do is accept the diversity of food sources, rejoice in the potential and share with one another.

There are scientists working all over the planet to produce more productive strains, discover better growing techniques, find new potential crops, create more efficient harvesting and preservation systems. These people are true heroes and we need to understand what it is they are doing. Science doesn't just happen in a sterile laboratory hidden away in the bowels of some agro-industrial complex. The scientists are in the field, sweating, swatting mosquitoes, sharing their knowledge and acquiring the wisdom of village and rural populations, with urban peoples who can raise their own fresh produce and farmers all over the world.

Sometimes the crop failure in field and garden is not the result of improper techniques, the wrong plants or ignorance. When an unseasonal freeze destroys the tender young plants or the harvest before it is ripe, when flood, drought, sand storms, hail or ash clouds turn hope into despair, we need a system of emergency relief. For long term survival we need to pool our collective resources and wisdom, not to battle or defeat the climate and the forces of nature, but to understand how to use these dynamics, how to work with them, how to be a partner with nature.

We need to keep in mind the positives of harsh climate. The cold weather keeps both insects and weeds in check, slows the spread of disease. The heat and humidity of summer encourage the rapid growth of our chosen crops. We can continuously harvest when we use successive cropping. We can learn to use intensive gardening, heat generation to lengthen the growing season in cold climate, alley cropping and living fences to protect against wind.

In harsh climates the use of cold frames, plastic sheets to create makeshift greenhouses, fresh manures and compost to generate heat are all traditional techniques to extend the season even a few weeks. Using the harvested hay for destined to be livestock as a deep protective mulch until it is consumed is another way to help less hardy crops survive and also a way to raise the soil temperature even a few degrees. Growing perennial, shrub and tree crops that can handle the extremes of temperate and subarctic regions can feed the mountain villages. Home gardeners all over the United States can be a part of the informal exploration and experimentation with uncommon fruits and vegetables. There are citrus that will grow and bear fruit in regions where the temperatures drop well below freezing. Can this be part of the solution to vitamin deficiency in areas where importing fresh fruit is cost prohibitive?

Weeds

In my backyard garden, and yours as well, we plant cabbages, carrots and tomatoes and turnips. But we also grow sedges and pigweed, dollarweed and lambs quarters. Invading vines slither over fences and through the flowerbeds. This happens to other gardeners and farmers all over the world. Weeds can be a serious competition. We think of them as seizing the nutrients and moisture from the defenseless roots of our chosen crops. We struggle to keep them from overshadowing the crops and stealing the sunlight. There is a real and present danger to the crops from the weeds when we employ cultivation methods that are not in harmony with the systems nature has put in place. Sometimes we simply cannot beat the weeds at their own game. Sometimes the answer is mulch, weed block or something as drastic as chemical weed controls. Sometimes the answer lies in changing our techniques and employing intercropping, intensive gardening and no-till cultivation. The weeds may be more adaptable and more vigorous than the crops we are trying to coax into production, sometimes they have been designed by nature to grow where we are trying to grow something else. But, before we accept the demonization of weeds so common on our TV commercials let's step back and give them a fair assessment.

We are programed by our traditions to view weeds as the enemy, a dark force of nature dedicated to overtaking our farms, gardens and lawns. We are so conditioned to this adversarial posturing that we often overlook the benefits that can be ours if we judiciously cooperate with some of these weeds. As Kim Wilkinson and Craig Elevitch have explained in their AgroForester article, *If You Can't Eat Them, Succeed Them! Working with Weeds in the Tropics* (copyright 1998) weeds have a number of roles to play.

Nature doesn't grow weeds as such, but there is the danger that we can create a world where plants that do not support a diversity of life can dominate, at least for a time significant regions of the earth we call home. In the Disney movie, *The Lion King*, we are presented with a dramatic glimpse of a world that can be the result of short-sightedness and greed. A world of deserts and leafless thorn bushes. These were the only resources the earth had left to defend herself. Nature doesn't grow weeds, but she does cultivate diversity and sometimes we don't appreciate or enjoy these survivors, like poison ivy or ragweed.

Weeds are scorned because they aren't what we want growing there. Many of the crops we grow today were once used by nature as weeds, and some of what we call weeds still have value as famine foods in times of crisis. Weeds are defined differently by different people. Some call any plant not growing where they want it to grow a weed. Others will tell you weeds are all those invasive non-indigenous species like kudzu and loosestrife in the United States, or cactus in Australia. Thus pineapples are weeds in Hawaii, tomatoes are weeds in Minnesota, corn is a weed in Russia and cassava is a weed in Africa. We cannot be isolationists and grow the global garden that will feed a hungry world. But we can all be wise gardeners and farmers, using these global resources with wisdom and caution.

In fact, the more specialized a natural, or garden, plant community is the easier it is for a general practitioner at life to take over. We become very concerned about defending the "native" plants of a region, but generally, what we mean when we say "native" we are referring to plants that arrived before the people did. Nature colonizes with the wind and ocean currents, stream beds and even the fur of animals and the wings of birds, or more properly, the bowels of these animals. Nature knows the value of diversity in her communities.

Many of the plants we call weeds, like dandelions and water hyacinths are colonists from somewhere else. In Hawaii buddleja (butterfly bush), grape ivy and blackberries are considered noxious weeds while in most of the world they are desirable ornamental plants or a food source. Other weed pests are native plants just doing their job. Nature abhors a vacuum and will go to great lengths to cover as much surface as possible. When we till the soil nature views this as a wound, a potential site for erosion. When we clear forest land seed germinates that has lain, patiently waiting for perhaps decades, until it was needed. A forest fire releases the life forces in some seeds, making the first stage of nature's reclamation possible. Even acres of volcanic ash won't stop the "weeds" from doing their job. Mount St. Helen was sporting green almost as soon as the dust settled. We build a road and then refer to the roadside weeds, or wildflowers if we think they are pretty, that spring up with the first rain. We have asters, chicory, ragweed, wild morning glories, daisies, goldenrod, briars, and the list could fill volumes.

Weeds are nature's first line of defense against erosion. They form a living mulch that helps to maintain a more even soil temperature and conserve moisture. Meanwhile their roots, like millions of mini-hands, holds the precious soil in place. Then, in the natural cycle of life, the roots, leaves, stems and even the fruit become the life sustaining soil from whence they grew. But more is involved than the process of turning once living plants into compost. The diversity of organisms in the soil increases as the organic matter increases. These microscopic plants and animals, the fungi, the insects, even the burrowing mammals all play a part in turning dirt into soil, and they all depend on the tough, ugly weeds, these botanical pioneers, to get it started.

Weeds are the nursery of wildlife and their supermarket as well. Insects, butterflies, birds, reptiles, amphibians and even small mammals make their homes there. We think of insects as the enemy, as we do weeds, but the fact is most of our crops wouldn't grow without them. Nature has this system that involves bees, flies and other insects as pollinators, uses the birds as population control and works diligently to establish and maintain a balance, a harmony within the system. The weeds are the part of the natural community that serves as an insurance policy as they encourage diversity. In some areas "weeds" are being planted along the edges of fields to attract the insect pests and keep them away from the main crops. Collards are planted beside cabbage fields in Florida because the insects that feed on cabbage like collards better. This lures them away from the cash crop and reduces the need for pesticides.

When growing up on the family farm we did much of the weeding in the garden with the ducks and geese, they were also on patrol against the bugs. In many areas of the world the weeds are providing a valuable food source for the livestock. At ECHO in Fort Myers, Florida they are showcasing scratch tilling as a part of the gardening program. Beyond the value as dinner for the livestock is the potential for some of these weeds to land on the dinner table of the gardener or farmer. We talk of the wild harvest of dandelions, pokeweed, burdock and a list could continue until we filled a heavy book. It might be that we are not as far removed from our hunter-gatherer ancestors as we would like to think. There is a certain joy in finding wild food, and wild beauty. The fact is that for much of the earth's population the gathering of wild fruits, leaves and roots isn't only a matter of spiritual connection with the earth, it is a matter of survival. Many people depend on the "weeds." Beyond the weeds that might appear on the dinner table are the ones that are traditional sources of dyes, medications, cosmetics, preservatives, building material, fuel and many other commodities.

Sometimes there is a symbiotic relationship between the weeds providing a living mulch or shade and the plants we wish to grow. The weeds are a part of the ever changing and never ending parade of life. What we can do is observe the weed and its role in the ecosystem we are striving to either influence or be a part of. Understanding what the weed is doing there gives us clues as to how we should respond. Are the weeds providing immediate cover, erosion control and soil building functions? Do I need to interfere with this process or am I better off cooperating with it? The garden, the landscape and the farm are always engaged in an evolutionary process, always striving for tomorrow, so is the natural world.

When we wound the soil with roadcuts, mining, overgrazing or relentless assault with the plow the earth brings forth its first line of defense and we ask, "Where did all these weeds come from?" If we grow more perennial food crops there is less opportunity for weeds to become invasive. No-till and limited tilling are cost efficient and labor wise but they also help to build a healthier soil. We can learn a great deal from weeds. They grow in diversity, they follow a series of stages in rebuilding the environment, they enrich the soil, conserve moisture then become mulch. If we are willing to follow this example we can be a part of the cycle of the seasons and the evolution of the land we occupy.

As backyard gardeners we should never pull the weeds, stuff them in plastic bags and send them off to the landfill. The weeds we pull from our flowerbeds and gardens are a valuable resource. They make great compost, or at least a serviceable surface mulch. The trimmings from our "chosen" plants can have the same destiny. When we ply the shovel, roto-tiller or plow we are encouraging the germination of more weed seed. There are multitudes of seeds in that soil, just waiting for the right conditions for sprouting. Bare soil, warmed by the sun watered by our irrigation system are all a part of the perfect conditions for these seeds to become seedlings. When we don't till we slow this process, we wound the earth less and decrease the need for weeds to grow.

Pests

We view every bug, every creepy crawly thing that wanders through our micro-environment as a detested intruder, an enemy to be vanquished, no destroyed. Truth is the commercial growers all over the world are faced with the same problem. Corn borers, cabbage loopers, locusts and the plagues are legion. It sometimes seems that if it isn't the drought or the floods or the winds it's the swarms of insects. This wasn't a problem to our ancestral hunter-gatherers because they didn't have vast fields of foods set like a banquet for the appropriate insect with an appetite for that meal and the ability to produce generations of offspring in a season or two. We made it easy for them by creating agriculture on a large scale.

Even in areas of the world that have been turned into deserts we have pest populations struggling to make ends meet, trying desperately to find their next meal, just like the human population of these regions. One of the greatest problems for the human population in these impoverished and marginal areas is the insect population that feeds on them. It isn't only the crops, the gardens and the livestock that are a meal waiting to be served. We, as human beings are the life-blood of mosquitoes, tse-tse flies, fleas, and so many others; some with ghastly and debilitating consequences that further weaken the farmer and her family as they shorten life spans and fill the cemeteries. Again there are teams of dedicated scientists struggling to research and understand the life cycles of these minute bearers of disease, enervation, frailty and death. Clean water, improved sanitation, healthier diet and pesticides are all prescribed as the way to halt many of these diseases of poverty, but when a population is forced to the brink of starvation, weakened by disease, dulled by poor nutrition few of the tools of survival remain. It is the great sin of the industrialized nations that they either close their eyes to the manifestations of poverty or condemn the victims rather than work together as a community to solve the problems. If we spent as much on water purification and improved sanitation as we spend advertising MacDonalds hamburgers millions of lives would be saved and these people could be productive responsible members of the global community

Throughout Africa and Asia AIDS is dealing death and destruction to villages, cities and rural families. This is a plague far worse than the black death of Medieval Europe. We live in the middle of this and some say "it isn't my problem," or "it's nature's way of enforcing population control." How do we teach these people good nutrition and modern farming practices when they are too weak to hold a spade and won't live to see the harvest? This isn't someone else's problem. This is pandemic and affects every neighborhood in our global village. This is solvable if we face it as we would approach a military threat, if we all accept responsibility for our neighbors.

The insects, parasites and the diseases that affect the people should be a major focus of our efforts, our research and our budgets. Then we can focus on the pests affecting the crops. Although, with the crops many of the pests are hand picked and can become chicken feed. Sometimes the wild birds and fowl harvest their own dinner from the field as they dine on the insects. Unfortunately chemical pesticides are also frequently employed and often these are pesticides that have been banned in the United States and other industrialized nations. Why is it so difficult for us to comprehend that what is done in the remotest places on earth affects us all eventually. There is no escaping the fact that we are a global community.

There are organic pest controls and insecticides like those derived from the neem tree that are quite effective at controlling many of the pests that challenge the gardener and farmer. As we learn more about how to use natural insect repellents and natural predators we can gain some measure of crop security. The greatest problem, however, isn't pests while the crops are growing, it's the destruction of produce and grains after the harvest. In some areas pest damage and loss can be as high as thirty percent.

Environmental Degradation

When all the talents and resources the human animal can marshal are directed, either intentionally or unintentionally, at the ecosystem we are part of, we can expect the land to suffer. We see the dangers and the consequences of strip mining, irresponsible logging, slash and burn agriculture, urban sprawl, landfills, misplaced dams and industrial pollution of the land, waterways and atmosphere. We decry the industrial pollution and destruction of environments by these highly visible forces as we climb into our automobiles and drive around the corner to the discount store with its chemical arsenal and purchase our weekly fix for our chemically dependent landscape and the garden where we raise the food we hope to eat. In the process we complain about the lack of songbirds and how we miss the frogs and toads that were once a part of the garden. We are all guilty. We are all the problem. We can all be the solution.

Let's leave our comfortable suburban home and all the trappings of the "good life" and visit a family in Haiti or Nigeria or Kenya or North Korea, or parts of Russia. There the environmental degradation goes on as well. The mechanics may be different but similar results occur. Desperate to feed a hungry family, crops are grown and harvested in soil where nutrients have already been depleted. The leaves are fodder for the starving livestock, the stems, twigs and branches are fuel for the cook stove. The dung from the cattle is fuel as well. How do you enrich such soil where mulch is a luxury, where there are no fertilizers? How can we condemn these people for harvesting for today when to wait until the crop is full and ripe the children will be dead? The real question is "How do we break this cycle, this downward spiral?"

In areas where colonial markets were satisfied with imported crops grown to the exclusion of native produce and the water tables were depleted to raise those crops, now we have deserts and people who live daily with desperation. In other regions forests were destroyed, grasslands grazed and fields cropped into dust bowls. Deserts dominate these lives too. The indigenous economics have been shattered, families broken, disease runs rampant and the pleasantries of our world aren't even a distant dream.

The poor in all nations are pushed to the marginal areas. Those are the regions where the soil is the poorest as well, where the water is a rare or seasonal commodity, where gardens, farms, livestock and families are the most difficult to nurture. Yet these people have all the emotional tools to build a good life, what they lack is the opportunity. We can't solve their problems with temporary infusions of surplus and unfamiliar foods. They know and understand the land, they possess the wisdom of generations. If we can all join together we can empower them. Together we can slowly build soil and gradually renew forests, but water will be the greatest challenge. For many of the problems that took several centuries to create it will also take years to resolve. Scientists are working hard to develop new crops and new techniques. They are also working with the indigenous populations to learn the traditions that allowed harmony with the land, the ancestral crops and the potential for new economies. The best we can do currently for many of these people is sow the seeds of hope. The reality is that we have much to learn from them, and the keys to a better future for the poorest nations and the wealthiest lies in learning from each other.

Can we, in our backyard gardens experiment with the little known and uncommon foods, try intensive growing techniques, conservation practices, pest controls and sustainable techniques that will help to bring the poorest of us back from the edge, while we learn how to live within our ecosystems as a partner not as an outsider? Our collective futures may well depend on the diversity of foods and the wisdom we can share with each other.

Part II: Poverty of the People

"Recent research shows that many children who do not have enough to eat wind up with diminished capacity to understand and learn. Children don't have to be starving for this to happen. Even mild under nutrition - the kind most common among poor people in America - can do it."

Carl Sagan

Nutrition is a Part of the Poverty Spiral

It's so difficult for a society that throws away enough food daily to sustain life for a family of four, or individuals who live on over 4000 or 5000 calories a day, to empathize with a people forced to exist on a diet that may be limited to 300 calories a day. In the nations considered prosperous in the post industrial age, we spend more to visit weight control gyms per month than the income of the average worker in the undeveloped and developing regions. Yet it is obvious that money doesn't buy a good diet; it simply makes it possible for us to afford to make the mistakes.

Starvation is brutal, debilitating, cruel, and insidious. Starvation is a slow death, a slow and horrible death. Yet most of the deaths that occur in hungry villages, refugee camps, disaster areas are the indirect result of a lack of food. When we don't get sufficient caloric intake, or an unbalanced diet our system is weakened, our resistances are lowered and the door is open to those natural forces that engage in population control. Diseases relentlessly attack, but a healthy body resists, fights back with an immune system. In areas where the dietary problem is one of excess we have heart disease, diabetes, cancer and a host of other diseases that prey on that weakness of plenty and excess. When the diet is meager, and sound nutrition is an impossible and unfamiliar dream, other diseases strike.

Malnutrition in early childhood seriously affects mental development just as it affects the child's physical growth. "Each day in the developing world, 30,500 children die from preventable diseases such as diarrhea, acute respiratory infections or malaria . . ." (UNICEF, World Health Organization). This doesn't include the blindness, rickets, poor bone and muscle development, internal parasites or fatalities from simple childhood diseases, even the common cold. In the past fifty years, according to statistics from Bread For The World, hunger and poverty have killed almost 400,000,000 people, that's far more than the population of the United States. This is three times the number killed in all the wars we have fought in the 20th century. In developing nations one child in ten dies before his or her first birthday. Most of these children came from the 32% of the world's population that lives on less than $1.00 a day. The poorest 20% of our neighbors consume less than 1% of our earth's resources, while the richest 20% over 80%. This doesn't have to be. We can all be a part of the solution.

When the available food is barely sufficient to sustain life, and the variety is seriously limited, we see the mental capacity of the infants and young children affected for life, vision difficulties leading to blindness can be the result of a serious nutritional problem. Studies are being done that indicate that inclusion of something as simple as sweet potatoes in the tropical diet can prevent much of this childhood blindness. When the diet is drastically limited, many of those affected lack the energy to farm or tend gardens, divert water for crops, care for farm animals, or hold a job if one were available. When a family is trapped in this devastating poverty spiral, it's difficult to climb out. It isn't because these people have chosen to be stupid, or lazy that they are trapped in poverty. Poverty is not for the faint of spirit. It takes every ounce of courage to face the next morning when you know your children are dying, you lack the means to care for family members, you don't have the opportunity to drink clean water, pay for a doctor, or even possess a new shirt. Poverty is itself a debilitating disease that destroys the spirit as it weakens the body and limits the mind.

What is the cost of hope? How do we reach out? What do we do? No one on the face of this earth should starve, or even know hunger. There are sufficient resources, a surplus of food, a wealth of skill and knowledge; yet we let it happen. Starvation is ugly, so we don't like to look at it. It's easier to blame the victims, than try to understand them. In a society that glories in a good fight, we can be a part of the solution. Not only can starvation be eliminated, but it is also possible for us all to work together and universally improve the nutrition of all peoples, and be a responsible part of the economy and environment as well.

Nutrition is a problem for the poor because a good diet costs money, and in the developed nations junk food, empty calories and high fat content are more affordable than fresh fruits and vegetables, are easier to prepare and easier to store. In the United States we have urban poor who don't even have fresh produce available, rural poor, elderly and small children who can't afford to eat right, let alone eat well. It isn't only in the undeveloped regions of the world that people go to bed hungry, that poverty traps people in its ugly grasp. We can all be a part of the solution to a problem that is truly global, but can be found in our own neighborhoods.

A diet that includes fresh greens, fruits and root crops is possible through community gardens, rooftop gardens, raised bed and intensive gardening programs for the elderly poor. It is possible to enrich the diet during an extended growing season with an intensive garden as small as 4 x 4' with the proper crops and techniques. The author was fortunate to have been involved in some research on the Cellugro Gardening system that involves a growing bed divided into cells and a specially designed drainage system that uses about 20% of the water and about 50% of the nutrients required by a conventional garden. This means that with less than ° hour per day spent in the garden a steady supply of produce can be available and little cost. This research has culminated in the Abundant Harvest Gardens System, a small solution to a major problem. See Chapter 12.

Part of the nutrition shortage is eliminated by growing multi-use crops such as beets and radishes that mature quickly and produce edible leaves while the roots are developing, sweet potatoes that produce edible leaves all season before the harvest of tubers, and many of the cole crops and Oriental leaf vegetables that can provide a continuous harvest rather than waiting several months for a single harvest. Leaf lettuce is more efficient than head lettuce to grow and harvest, collards and Chinese cabbages are more efficient to grow and can be gathered one leaf at a time.

Many of the vegetables discussed and explored in this text have these twin advantages of multi-use and continuous harvest. For the commercial grower this isn't practical, but it makes sense in the family garden, anywhere in the world.

The problems that the poorest of peoples of this earth encounter work against easy success. They don't have garden space because they have consistently been pushed to the most marginal and least productive land, or crowded together so that space isn't available. They can't afford the best and most productive seeds and plants, not can they pay for fertilizers and pest controls. They have to defend their gardens against theft, weather, and pollution. To be successful in many parts of the world requires a community effort, and the cooperation of the global community. But, the key also lies in working together, combining the traditional wisdom, and blending the past with the benefits of modern science to produce a positive future.

These aren't problems that can be eliminated in a few years, it will take generations to overcome the cycles of poverty and the diseases it generates. Each region of the world has indigenous edible plants that are designed by nature to survive and thrive in a given environment. These are a valuable resource to be explored, tested and evaluated. There are also widely adaptable food crops that may prove valuable in many areas, filling in the seasonal gaps and answering nutritional and environmental needs. To solve global hunger will take a global view. Retreating to the foods that were the mainstay of a diet 500, or 1000, or 5000 years ago isn't the answer. Depending on space-age technology isn't the answer either. The answer is a compromise between these approaches to food production, gathering and storing.

Not all of the techniques and plants that our grandparents used were the best, nor all the new ideas and products of genetic engineering the only answer. As humans we are caught in the dynamic dichotomy of the need for the comfort of tradition and the need to go beyond where we have ever gone before. The human animal insists on being a creature with our roots in the past while we reach with open arms for tomorrow. Our nomadic hunter-gatherer instincts drive us to be seekers of what lies beyond the mountain, across the river and after today. The questing scientist and the vagabond share the same heritage that calls us beyond where we are to someplace yet unknown.

Conflicts, Civil Wars and Religious Wars Cause Poverty

It is a basic element of human nature that we don't always get along with each other. We are naturally cooperative, but we are also instinctively competitive. Some behaviorists claim that we enjoy sports as a surrogate battle, but when we study the activities of so called "primitive" societies it may well be that both sport and battle are hormonal and psychological expressions of what we are. Consider further that both the army unit and the football team depend on cooperative effort to succeed as much as they do individual brute force. We are by our instinctive nature social animals.

Often the conflict is an expression of individual, or group greed. Could it be that greed is an expression of insecurity, or an instinctive need to assure survival by setting aside more than we can use? Or, could it be an acquired trait from the times 10,000 years ago when we became farmers and faced famine, epidemics, slavery and warfare on a scale unimaginable to our hunter-gatherer ancestors?

Unfortunately, in many corners of the globe the artificial boundaries of the colonial powers have created nations that have neither geographic rationale nor a common people to bind them together. This lack of cohesiveness all too often results in civil wars and tribal conflict, even among those we might not consider tribes. We see this throughout Africa, in the Middle East and what was once the Soviet Union. This isn't to say that a nation must be ethnically pure to be successful or survive. In fact, the most successful cultures are those that encourage diversity and glory in the variety of their people and their traditions. Diversity is a valuable resource for nations, because for each problem there are many possible solutions derived from the variety of perspectives. Still the instinctive need to belong to a tribe, or at least a gang, is a powerful psychological need. We think of our tribal ancestors as forming tribal units as a means of defense, but they spent far more time making pottery, singing songs, telling stories and expressing themselves with art than they did preparing for, or engaging in battle. Could it be that we became social animals, formed communities so that we could share our thoughts ?

Religion has been used as a means of setting a people apart, giving them a divine purpose and unquestioned righteousness. So determined are we that there can only be one way to view God, one code of laws, one pathway to the hereafter. Religious disputes have been the cause of some of the most horrible of conflicts. Yet, universal among all faiths are compassion, the drive for peace, mutual caring and a hopeful future. Much of the hunger relief and efforts toward food security aren't the inspiration of governments, but the hard work of people living their faith. Faith gives us unified answers to collective and individual questions of why and how we function. When we seek understanding through faith we work together, we cooperate in our spiritual quests, and our conviction to love one another. This universal desire to live a life of caring and sharing makes the religious institutions all over the world a most powerful force to eliminate hunger and poverty.

Misguided Governments Can Cause Poverty

Often the efforts of governments are well intentioned but misguided or shortsighted. Efforts to dam rivers to control floods, clear lands for agriculture, permit urban sprawl and industrial pollution in the name of progress are all the result of a desire to do good things for the people. Often the consequences of our efforts aren't known until a generation or more afterward.

Sometimes governments are controlled by one group that feels that, to hold or expand their power, they must disenfranchise other groups. In governments where democracy is little more than a mockery, where power rules, the needs of the poor and the powerless are often ignored. As Cardinal Bernardine said, "We love to hate the poor." Yet the poor are often those with disabilities both mental and physical, the uneducated and the children of hunger. They are trapped in a spiral that many governments refuse to understand, so we blame the victims and condemn their children to the never ending hunger of mind and body. Even in our richest cities we condemn the homeless and perpetuate the myth of laziness and drug addition as the cause when, in fact it is the society that cast out its mentally ill and closed the doors of progress to those who lacked understanding. Local governments pass ordinances to make certain that the social elite don't have to see those of us whom society failed. It isn't only children living on the edges of society in some third world country, it's women and children living in cardboard boxes behind our investment banks and rummaging through the dumpsters of our grocery stores. The poor and the hungry walk among us everywhere and they are invisible to us. One in five children in America experiences malnutrition, as does one in five of our senior citizens. This doesn't need to be. This should not be. All parts of our societies must work together, the religious community, the governing bodies, the businesses and each of us as individuals. We can find it in our hearts to care and to act. We can use our minds and bodies to build a future for our neighbors. Let's join hands and do it!

We are at one of those pivotal points in time where technology is putting in our hands the solution to so many of these critical problems like hunger and poverty, ignorance and disease. Will we seize the opportunity to make this a better and safer world for our children and grandchildren, for all the children and grandchildren, or will we use the technology to control each other, exploit the earth's resources and lay waste the futures of generations to come?

For communities, religious groups, governments at all levels, businesses and industries the inclination is to control. The real question is whether or not we can climb beyond the insecure drive for control and reach the pinnacle of human expression where we find hands extended in friendship, diversity honored and respected, and cooperation the universal ideal.

Gender, the Garden and the Gardener

If you educate women, you have educated a population.
Burundian proverb

"The problem," this research scientist from India told us, "is that the subsistence garden has traditionally been the responsibility of the women in the village. Men don't garden, they farm, or go off to the city to work for a living."

"No," the gentleman from Senegal argued, "it's because we have devoted all our energy to the economies of the neo-colonial powers. We are still paying the price. The men have to be where the work is and it's the economy that . . ."

"Stupid, senseless warfare," the nutrition specialist from Nigeria interrupted with despair in her voice. "We go about killing and mutilating our parents and children." There were tears in her eyes. It was obvious that she spoke from personal experience.

"Yes." the Indian researcher added. "Yes, but it goes far deeper. In so many of the areas where hunger and starvation claim so many of our children, it is because the society doesn't value its women as political or economic equals of men. We are considered intellectually inferior and little more than possessions. How can we enter a new millennium continuing to waste half of our human resources this way?"

The discussion was getting heated, but the issues were all valid. For whatever reason, many cultures do display a serious gender gap. Women are undervalued as individuals, and their potential to produce ideas, hold positions of responsibility, and be equal players in many of the developing nations is culturally limited. Because of disease, warfare, economics and a number of other reasons, all over the world we see mothers struggling to provide for a fatherless family. They try to garden, tend a few animals, perhaps even raise a few crops for sale. Many of the world's women can't even dream of a new dress, will never experience a bouquet of roses, a candlelight dinner, air conditioning, or even clean drinking water. They will experience the weakness of hunger, the exploitation of their society, the death of their infants and children, and the chronic prospect of abuse and rape. They face all this and still try to raise and gather enough food to keep their children alive. For so many of the earth's people simply surviving is the goal.

A struggling mother of five doesn't have the time, strength or resources to cultivate a farm, but can start with a family garden and perhaps a tree nursery. The assistance that we provide cannot just be dumped at an airstrip then we return to our comfortable office and pat ourselves on the back. We need to work with each other, we need to help these women establish their gardens and begin their farms. We need to work with the communities, sharing knowledge, not being judgmental, not condemning, not trying to make them look like us. There is much we can learn from each other. The Hunger Project has devoted much energy to improving the legal status of women in Africa. They have worked to create systems for education, micro-loans, property ownership, developing markets and so much more. Still throughout the continent, 80% of the family's food is produced by the women, who own 1% of the land. We owe these women a tremendous amount of respect.

Future Harvest states, "Women are vital in nourishing the world. They produce 60 to 80 percent of the food in most developing countries, and their role in farming continues to grow. In 1950 women performed almost 40 percent of agricultural work; today they perform close to half globally, and they are the primary food producers in many parts of the world. As the ancient African proverb wisely states, 'Without women we all go hungry.'"

On International Women's Day 2001 Future Harvest launched a new web page dedicated to women farmers, foresters, fishers and herders, highlighting how women overcome long odds to feed their families, promote peace and gain livelihoods in developing countries. To read more see www.futureharvest.org

Colonial Legacy Continues the Poverty Cycle

Over much of the globe a legacy of oppression, exploitation and the destruction of diversity is the disastrous gift of the colonial era. Entire indigenous populations were eliminated in a genocide we call today "ethnic cleansing." Other peoples were stripped of their honor, their culture, their past and forced, either physically or economically, into the service of the colonial powers. In the times when the Spanish were Christianizing the Americas, the British were 'civilizing' the Indian sub-continent, and the French and Belgians were dividing Africa, they honestly thought they were carrying the 'white man's burden.' The sad part of this colonial experience is the shattered sense of past, the cultures erased, the croplands and waterways destroyed. Even more unfortunate is the fact that the colonization continues.

Today it is more a matter of economic colonization by business and industry, with advertising dictating the tastes, defining the wants and needs of people all over the world. Each time a local beverage is replaced with Coca-Cola some diversity is lost. Each time a fast food restaurant replaces a family owned ethnic diner diversity is lost. Each time locally produced clothing is replaced with designer tee shirts diversity is lost. We are making the entire world a pale and imperfect reflection of a Western culture that becomes less and less diverse as it becomes bigger and bigger.

With this new economic colonialism the Money controls and small farms are forced out of existence, not only in the United States, but all over the world. The small farm isn't efficient in the short term, but the gigantic agro-business is a dinosaur waiting for the disaster that can result in hunger and starvation where it is least expected. The small farm, the permafarm, the family subsistence farm aren't anachronisms or living museums, they are humanity's insurance policy. By preserving the gene pool of heirloom and open pollinated species they are cradling the survival of the future.

It is vital to preserve as much diversity as possible. As we grow more and more of less and less, as the global economy focuses more and more on less and less diversity, we destroy the diversity that made humanity successful. We deny our intellectual instinct to learn the unknown, experience the exotic, discover what lies beyond our experience. We possess the instinct to seek and share cultural wisdom. This is the essential key to progress. All peoples dance, but they don't all dance to the same music.

Growing the Wrong Crops; Using the Wrong Foods

We discussed early in this book the origins of agriculture and how it may well have been the fatal mistake in our social evolution. Nutrition is a science that we should all pay more attention to, because it isn't a matter of how much we eat, but what we eat. We rely on a meat based diet, yet the beef and pork that form the bulk of this diet contain the elements of our own destruction when consumed in excess. Heart disease, obesity and cancer have all been linked to the animal fats in our diets. So we focus some media attention on this and turn to poultry and fish as the basic source of protein. Chickens and turkeys are much more efficient to raise than cattle, sheep or hogs. They take less space, mature sooner and cost less to feed. Fish in the sea, in the lakes and even the ponds of aqua-culture farms have an increasing role to play in our diet. But the raising of animals has both positive and negative impacts on the environment. On a small scale rabbits or poultry can provide both meat and fertilizer for a family garden or small farm. In mega-farms the potential for pollution of the soil and waterways is a real problem. Perhaps the answer lies in finding ways to process and utilize the waste products efficiently, effectively and safely.

We grow great fields of corn and potatoes, yet these aren't efficient in the yield per acre or the amount of energy required to plant, cultivate, harvest and process. We plant fields of tobacco beside the homes of mal-nourished children. We grow fields of lettuce with limited food value because it looks pretty in a salad and ignore so many of the more nutritious cole crops.

We ignore the food value of many trees and shrubs, and the perennial plants that require less energy for production and reduce environmental impact.

What if we, the family gardeners, grew the produce that is nutritious, and each season experimented with something different, then shared the experiences with each other. What if we tested new techniques and explored the rediscovered old ways? What if we shared the produce with a local food bank, church food pantry, homeless shelter, or, better yet, a neighbor in need. This is the principle behind the Garden Writers Association of America's "Plant a Row for the Hungry" program. What if we took this one step further and invited our children, our grandchildren, and the children of the neighborhood into our garden? What if we shared the labor, the joy and the harvest with them? After all isn't this the most important crop we could possibly raise in our own backyard?

Food production isn't as much a traditional routine as it is an ever changing evolutionary process. We can all learn from each other. In the research for this book the authors have had the opportunity to try foods we have never even heard of prepared in ways we didn't even know existed. What a wonderful experience it is to share with another tradition, experience another culture. In discussing food and gardening with people from all over the world we learned much of techniques, much of the problems encountered and the ways they can be overcome. Some may desire to cling tightly to the past, but even those of us most insecure about the future can't resist the exotic. With the ritual arrival of the spring seed catalogs immediately after Christmas, don't we all turn first to the page that says "New This Year" and study these never seen before offerings?

The garden is a living thing, and when we garden we are in a community of life. We are empowered with each germinating seed, every flower bud that bursts into bloom and every tomato that begins to blush red in the sunshine. We can't help but have hope for the future when we stand in the middle of our garden. Nor can we help but share in this experience. The gardener is the key to the problem of hunger. The gardening mother in Nigeria, the gardening orphans in Haiti, the rooftop gardeners in Japan, the backyard gardener in America. All are explorers, adventurers, gamblers. All plant, tend, and live with faith and hope. All see the beauty in tomorrow.

We are discussing hunger in this book not to inflict guilt, but to inspire hope. In the following pages are some examples of individuals and groups actively engaged in the effort to eliminate malnutrition, despair and starvation.

African village

Chapter Eleven
Solutions to Hunger

Hunger Is a Global Problem, but the Solutions are Local

For the hungry in our inner cities a community garden may be a part of the answer; family gardens and cooperative farms may be the solution in other areas. Hunger doesn't have one cause, nor does it have a single solution. To provide emergency relief in times of crisis the farmer always comes through with a desire to care and share that goes beyond generosity. Food distributors rally and do whatever is necessary to get food to wherever it is needed. Disaster tends to bring out the best in most people. But for many the disaster isn't an earthquake, hurricane, tidal wave or other natural event. Most often the disaster creeps slowly across the landscape like drought that is survived the first year, causes serious hardship the second, and starvation the third. Sometimes the disaster is generations in developing as in the case of desertification where the water is depleted and the soil gradually worn out by short-sighted use.

Often the hunger is a result of warfare as is the case in Chechyna, Ethiopia, Eritrea and many other regions of the world. It can be the effect of the political displacement of villages and peoples to make room for farms, mining and other economic endeavors as we see happening in Brazil. Sometimes it's the vicious ravages of disease that destroys the garden or the gardener. HIV/AIDS is as devastating to the production of food in Africa today as the blight was to the potato in Ireland in the 1840's.

The simple fact is that hunger, malnutrition and starvation are very personal problems that strike people one at a time. The solutions also need to be local. Communities must work together, families must work together. During America's Great Depression the owner of a local grocery in a small town in North Dakota would not stand by while his neighbors were unable to buy food for their families. He put his customers' purchases on credit, knowing full well they would never be able to repay the debt. This concern for one's community was echoed across the nation. These concerned people became true heroes, an example for us in later generations to live up to.

Our church had helped a Vietnamese couple settle in North Dakota and as I was going off to start seminary classes, Bay, the wife, came up to me at the airport with a twenty pound bag of rice and a rice cooker. As she handed it to me she said, "This rice for you. You no money, you no eat. I know what hungry feels like." Hunger is a very personal thing.

Active concern today can begin with the family garden and the community garden to raise sufficient produce to sustain life. Then gradually, working as a

www.globalgardening.info

community, projects can be started that provide goods for trade or commerce. In areas of serious food shortages the land is so marginalized that the soil must literally be grown before crops can be produced.

Urban Gardening

We think of food being produced on vast farms with fields of grain waving on to the horizon, and we think of the backyard garden so popular in rural and suburban America. Unfortunately, many of the world's poor live in cities, and villages surrounded by concrete, commerce and other hungry people, not open rural fields. Urban gardening is limited in space and resources so it must be efficient to be successful. At ECHO Dr. Price has grown food in gutters, old socks filled with soft drink cans, leisure suits, and old tires. In Tokyo, Japan rooftop gardens are now mandated as a means of insulating the home and reducing energy consumption. The fringe benefit is the oxygen the plants provide. Gardening on the rooftop is logical and efficient. This is one of the primary solutions to urban food production. Using the walls of the home or other building for vines is an application of vertical gardening that makes sense when we are faced with limited space. Composting and mulching use what would otherwise become landfill. This is recycling at its best. Composting can be done in a small space and soil for the urban garden can literally be grown from the garbage. One of the most efficient and long lasting systems for urban food production is the Abundant Harvest Garden by Cellugro.

Even the ability to personally provide part of the family's food from the garden is uplifting and empowering. As we feed the body from the garden we also feed the soul. Urban gardens and community gardens in the cities not only produce food, they provide responsible activity for youth, a way to circumvent the anger and frustration that is a part of the stress of poverty, and it provides beauty and vitality. Wouldn't it be great to see street gangs and drug dealers in our inner cities replaced with youthful teams of "Green Berets" that clean up vacant lots or help elderly neighbors plant a garden. Abandoned paved lots can become a series of raised beds with wheelchair access, so that a whole community can come togeher in the garden. Residents of senior care facilities can plant community gardens and not only grow some food for their own use, but supply a local food bank as well.

Positive vs Depletive Practices

We are exceedingly wasteful. In fact many of our problems come from our ability to waste resources beyond all reason. As our proud ancestors marched across the North American continent they cleared the land, tilled the soil, used it up and moved on. In other areas cultures used slash and burn agriculture. In many parts of the world overgrazing was such a common practice that deserts were created where grassland once was. Today there is simply no place to move on to, so we must explore ways to replenish where we are. Even in our suburban homes today we mow the grass, collect the clippings and pay to have them hauled way. Then we go to the nearest garden center and buy fertilizer and mulch.

In areas where the gardener is desperate, every twig, every cow patty is collected for the cook stove, leaves are feed for the animals and there is nothing to put back into the soil. These people can't afford chemical fertilizers and soil conditioners. Gray water and wood ashes are the only resources they have to replenish the land. If we can provide seeds or nursery stock in the form of legumes that will replenish the nitrogen in the soil, while providing either food, fodder or fuelwood resources, we can help them make soil. We think of agriculture as being vast fields of a single crop. This is the efficient way for the mechanized farmer to plant, cultivate and harvest. This may not be the best way for a subsistence farmer or family gardener to grow food. By planting moringa trees, then planting winged beans around them we have a trellis for the bean vines and the bean provides nitrogen for the moringa. Nature plants in diverse communities to ensure the survival of the community. Trees, vines, perennials and annuals from a great number of plant families all work together and help to support each other. Even the insects and grazing animals are a useful part of the system. We can be as well, when we work with nature, encourage rather than disrupt, plant as we harvest, become wise stewards and good neighbors.

The generation that has reached its mature years is a tremendously valuable resource. In many cultures the elders are respected as the source of wisdom and the ones responsible for the transfer of traditions from one generation to the next. We have wasted this resource. Yet in our nursing homes are people who know how to survive. They did survive a great global depression and a world war. Communities and schools could work with these people to learn ways of making do and putting by. This is a form of living history that could mean so much to the next generation.

Biodiversity in the Garden

In the last paragraph we spoke briefly about the inclination of nature to create diversity in every ecosystem. This is sometimes referred to as the "web of life" and sometimes as the "food chain." We think of the natural world, and our domesticated version of the untamed wilderness, our backyard, as a violent place filled with the constant battle for survival of the fittest. If we examine closely this phenomenon of life forms living with each other, we see a much different picture. We find an infinitely complex system of interdependence, where sharing of resources is the means of survival. What we, on the surface, might view as a vicious attack is actually pruning, the butterfly larvae devouring the leaves of the milkweed is also depositing on the soil nutrients that help the plant to form flower buds. The ants that dig in the soil as they farm aphids are in fact aerating the soil for the roots of their pasture plants and making it more efficient to get water to the roots when it rains. The birds that dine on the fruit are also planting the next generation. The fungus that fills the healthy soil is a part of a symbiotic relationship with the roots of trees and other plants. The insects we despise are busy breaking down the fallen leaves and discarded botanical bodies into the building blocks of a new generation. Plants follow as seasonal succession from spring flowers to autumn asters, and all along the way ground covers protect the feeder roots of the trees, and the roots hold the soil when the rains come. What a system of cooperation.

In our own backyard much the same diversity can exist if we can outgrow the sheep-like need to see green turf instead of the variety of life that a garden supports. We can use our landscape, our backyard, even our windowsill as a place to experiment. We can try different plants, different techniques for cultivation, different combinations. We can expand our vegetable gardens beyond tomatoes and zucchini. Use this book as a point of departure. Explore other's ideas and share your own. If we can work together in our own social ecosystem we can help to eliminate hunger for all the world's children.

At Peace with the Land

We have to abandon the old, outdated and romantic image of the farmer standing in his field prepared to battle the forces of nature. In reality the forces of nature are what we must engage in a partnership. It is possible to raise a farm, grow a garden, and sustain the land. We CAN be at peace with the land. Sustainable agriculture is simply wise use in a wasteful world. We can do this by rotating crops in the farm field and in the family garden. When we grow the same crops year after year in the same place two things happen. First the nutrients those plants use the most are depleted. Second, the insects and disease organisms that feed on those plants become well established. When we move the tomatoes and cucumbers we play a shell game with the bugs. When we learn more about the nature of the life around us we find that we have far more friends than enemies. In truth, Mother Nature rides the tractor across the prairie corn field with the farmer, and she tends the herb garden on the windowsill along with the school children.

There are so many ways we can replenish the soil, from composting, to mulching, from crop selection to wise watering, from limiting the use of chemical pesticides to cultivating diversity. Do we really need to assault the soil annually with the plow? No-till agriculture is being tried and used successfully in many areas of the world where to plow is to expose the soil to wind erosion, mudslides, water pollution and more. In a series of test plots with nutrient poor sandy soil, the land wasn't disturbed by tilling or cultivating. Instead, for several years layers of compost, mulch and wood ash from the cook stove were periodically applied to the surface while crops were being grown there. The results showed that the organic conditioners and nutrients from the decomposing compost naturally worked their way down into the root zone and that the beneficial organisms were more abundant than in tilled soils. This may not be the answer everywhere, but where wind and water carry the soil away when it's exposed it is worth considering. Another factor in no-till gardening and farming is that less energy is required, both human and mechanical.

Multi-cropping is also a way that we can be kind to the land. Planting beans with the corn and squash the way the Native Americans have traditionally farmed is not only good gardening, it's good for the soil. When we plant trees as wind breaks and shelter belts we help to protect the soil. In areas where the soil is so poor that crop production is limited, allees of *leucana* and other trees in the bean family are planted. First they add to the soil, second they provide compost to enrich the soil, they also yield forage for livestock, support for vines, and firewood for the cook stove. Cover crops such as sword bean and alfalfa can also be used to build or replenish the land.

It isn't only a matter of replacing what we take from the soil; it's also a matter of not poisoning it with what we add. The concentrations of salts, chemical fertilizers, pesticides, seepage from landfills and industrial waste all poison the land, all limit its productivity for tomorrow. This isn't to say that we shouldn't use chemical fertilizers. It is to say that we must use them wisely and efficiently. The same is true with the pesticides we employ. There are ways to apply, times to use and alternatives that are less harmful than others. Often the land is poisoned from the water that we polluted upstream. Most often this pollution isn't intentional, it is careless and thoughtless.

There are eco-farms all over the world that are doing actual field work in the development of a new perspective on living with the land and farming in a partnership with nature.

Perennial Crops

What would the impact on the land and the economy be if we grew perennial corn, wheat and other crops? Think of the cost efficiency for the farmer. Think of the environmental impact, because there would be less tilling, cultivating, planting. This all translates into lower fuel consumption and less air pollution. The ancestor to all corn, *Teosinte,* can be found in both annual and perennial forms. The agro-scientists in Mexico and the United States are currently working on the development of perennial forms that can withstand drought and produce a crop of fodder as well as a crop of ear corn each year. Meanwhile other scientists are exploring ways that this extra production of leaves, husks and cornstalks can be used as a raw material in the production of paper, building materials and crop blankets.

We think of the garden as something that is planted annually and somewhere between the harvest and the spring planting we bring out the Roto-tiller and then plant a new crop of seeds for our salad greens and fresh home grown vegetables. But in many parts of the world at least part of the garden is perennial, such as the shrubs and trees with edible foliage and fruit; for example, the moringa and the katuk. There are perennial cole crops such as the tree cabbage, and perennial gourds and eggplant. Plants such as the Okinawa spinach and Malabar spinach or some of the beans like Marama, winged bean and the lablab. Gardens in the European tradition also grow some perennial crops such as asparagus, rhubarb and horseradish. Many of the plants listed in this book are perennial, and there are thousands more that we can draw from for our global gardens and farms.

Preserving Our Human Diversity by Experiencing Diversity in the Garden

One of the goals in the writing of this book is to encourage the reader to pause and think. Each of us is born into a culture with its set of tastes and practices, customs, taboos, traditions and rules. All cultures have a grand and often detailed set of customs and rules about food. There is logic in this because food is the way the society sustains itself. Often a culture is best known to the rest of the world by its food customs. We think of Italian food and Mexican food. We delight in experiencing Indian cuisine, dining on a Moroccan meal, or savoring the efforts of a French chef. But this is only the beginning.

We tend to fear that which we don't know; other people, with other languages and other religions, other clothing and other foods. It's difficult to fear and hate those we know, and with whom we share experiences as we begin to understand each other's traditions. One of the most enjoyable aspects of growing a global garden is that we get to experience the culture, the foods and the beauty of so many other peoples. We share the dinner table with strangers who become friends through this dining experience. People half a world away now have something in common with you and your family. From your garden to your table you have come to know these peoples by the food they eat. You can explore deeper with visits to the local library, searches on the Internet, even communicating with these people in distant lands via the miracle of e-mail. We can become friends and neighbors, sharing thoughts, ideas and experiences. As we all till the garden together, share the wisdom of ages, old traditions and tomorrow's discoveries, we do truly become a global village, with a global garden.

Experimental Backyard Gardens

- You are conducting personal research, trying new plants and techniques. Expect some failures and partial successes. Not every plant is going to be happy with your accommodations. Remember, it's a learning experience.

- Be careful to control the plants you are growing. Escapees can become invasive weeds, challenging the native plants for their place in the sun.

- Containers often work well as a test site for new crops. This makes it easier for you to answer specific soil, water, light and temperature needs.

- You can keep notes and take photos of the progress of these experimental plants. This information can then be shared. It will be important to record the negatives as well as the positives.

- Schools, garden clubs, master gardeners, senior centers and individuals can make this exploration a part of their gardening experience. Each of us has an opportunity to add to the storehouse of knowledge, as we work together to solve the hunger problem.

- When we grow these uncommon foods we all have an opportunity to prepare meals and dine as do people in diverse cultures around the globe. This can help to create a greater understanding of others as we broaden our own horizons.

Marama Bean

Chapter Twelve
Everyday Solutions that Involve Real People

No one should go to bed hungry. That is uncalled for.
What can we do to prevent that?
Clara Saeni, Bread for the World

There are many causes of hunger. We have explored a few of them in this book. There are also many ways to halt and prevent this human tragedy. Dedicated scientists, government workers, missionaries and private individuals are working daily to make hunger and starvation a subject of history books, not the nightly news. ECHO, Educational Concerns for Hunger, in Fort Myers, Florida is one of those organizations that has accomplished so much. In the appendix to this text is a list of some of the most active groups and agencies. We encourage your support of these people and their work. In the following few pages is a brief outline of one idea that we have explored and are continuing to research, as it is being put in place in orphanages in Haiti and, hopefully, before this book is in print, many other places around the globe. Our research on this Abundant Harvest Garden has convinced us that we really do live in a global village and that all the earth is a global garden.

Part of the problem isn't that there is a shortage of food, but that surplus food doesn't get to where the hungry people are. Millions of pounds of fresh produce go to land fills or rot in the fields every year. This can be a matter of infrastructure, expense or manpower to move it. Another problem is that the poor can't afford to purchase their food needs and live on marginal, dry, infertile land or in urban areas where there is not space for a traditional garden. There are ways each and every one of us can play a part, get our hands dirty and feel good about it.

The Abundant Harvest Garden

Rennie DiLoreto of ACF Environmental has a sense of vision. He believes that hunger can be eliminated all over the world "One Family at a Time." Pursuing that dream, he has made possible the Abundant Harvest Garden, a unique intensive gardening system designed to create food security in some of the world's most difficult places.

Imagine a compact garden where a family can work together to raise a portion of the food needed for a healthy diet and sense of self-sufficiency. Imagine a program where families and even neighborhoods work together to not only grow fresh produce but cultivate a sense of community. Imagine a garden that can even be raised to a height convenient for wheelchair users, or those with arthritis or back injuries. Imagine a garden where hope and strengthened faith are among the greatest harvests, a garden that grows, not only food for the body, but food for the soul as well. That's what the Cellugro Abundant Harvest Garden is all about.

Part of what makes this all possible is the growing system. It enables a family to grow nutritious fresh produce in tropical and sub-tropical regions with a twelve month a year garden that can be established on a driveway, rooftop or corner of the yard. A family living on the edge of poverty, a family shattered by disease or warfare, a family living on the marginal lands of our earth where soil, water and labor are in short supply can grow fresh produce or start trees for fruit and fuel. They can grow hope and health.

This is a compact system that uses only 12 cu ft of growing medium such as soil, sand, or cocohusk mixes, for a 4' x 4' unit. This cellular growing system permits intensive gardening that requires about 20% of the water and 50% of the nutrients that a conventional garden demands. This is so much more than just a growing box because each plant grows in its own space, doesn't crowd its neighbors, can easily be replaced without disturbing other plants and serves as a great nursery for trees, shrubs and perennial crops.

The physical growing system is only part of the key to success with the Cellugro Abundant Harvest Garden, however. The principle of continuous harvest and the use of multi-purpose plants are other elements of the equation. While it's true that part of the secret lies in the plants we are growing in the system, and the techniques we use to plant, grow and harvest them, the real secret to success lies in the faith and vision of the gardener. This unique gardening system was designed to be easy to use, convenient for all, space intensive and environmentally efficient. It was designed for a mother trying to raise enough food to keep her children alive in a region ravaged by civil war and drought. For a family weakened by HIV/AIDS or other diseases, this makes food production easy and efficient. For a family living in inner city poverty this is a potential rooftop or dooryard source of sustenance. This system can improve nutrition for children, help to ease the threat of the diseases of hunger, promote self-sufficiency, perhaps even save lives. It offers a number of opportunities in regions where hunger is the constant visitor at the door and starvation is the face of the grim reaper.

This is a brief outline of the Abundant Harvest Garden. This isn't the answer for every place where there is hunger, malnutrition or starvation, but it is an answer for many. It does work in drought ridden regions, arid lands and those areas where desertification is the monster stalking the land. It is the answer for orphanages, refugee centers, impoverished elderly, the urban poor, those disabled by war or accident. It can serve as a continuous food source, but more than that it can serve as a nursery where moringa trees, tropical apples and other perennial food and reforestation plants can be grown. It can be the nursery where the seeds of peace are planted and hope for a better future can be cultivated. We have been honored with the opportunity to do some research and trials on this system and as this work continues, we become more convinced that this is a garden that can improve the quality of life and save lives by the thousands in some of the most difficult places people are living, and dying. For more information view the web site www.cellugro.com

ECHO's Global Village

Educational Concerns for Hunger Organization in North Ft Myers, Florida is a phenomenal place to visit. There they explore plants and techniques that can solve the problems of malnutrition, hunger and starvation. They also train agricultural missionaries, serve as a clearing house for information, produce and distribute seeds and support research all over the globe. There are many causes of hunger, many ways to grow crops, many climates, soil types, traditions and customs, many answers to many questions. For this reason ECHO is creating a Global Village that will showcase lifestyles in a variety of locations ranging from dry tropics to equatorial rainforest, from tropical highlands to urban living.

The purpose is to create a working model of these various neighborhoods in the global village. This will be a place where practical experience in farming and agriculture can be gained by interns and missionaries in training. It will be a community of ideas where the global knowledge can be shared. They will also be growing seeds for use all over the globe and teach crop knowledge, animal husbandry, construction and sound environmental practices.

Each showcase neighborhood in this Global Village will be between 1/3 and 1 acre in size with a homestead or farm including a typical residence and outbuildings. Tools, stoves, storage areas, latrines, wells, pumps, ovens, oil presses and other implements will be in use. This will also be an opportunity to test new ideas, new plants and animals, water use and irrigation methods, solar cookers, water purification systems and so much more.

This is an exciting project that I would encourage everyone to visit and support. See their web site at **www.echonet.org**

Gleaning, Food Recovery and Surplus

The American farmer is a gambling addict with overwhelming faith. This farmer borrows money to buy seed for a crop that he doesn't even know there will be a market for if it does survive drought, insects, disease, floods or other agro-disasters. If his fields produce well there may be a decrease in demand so prices are down, sometimes so low that it will cost more money to do the harvesting than can be recovered in the sale of the goods. Still these are among the most compassionate and generous people in the world. They willingly donate to local food pantries and hunger programs. In Florida, growers of everything from sweetcorn to watermelons have opened fields to volunteers willing to give their time to harvest food and transport it to those in need.

Barry Gilmore lives in Ocala, Florida. He is a 76 year old veteran with a passion for feeding the hungry. He has organized teams of gleaners to go into the fields after the commercial harvest to gather what is left behind. He has worked with farmers to rescue thousands of tons of cabbage, corn, potatoes, carrots, beans, watermelon, oranges, grapefruit and other produce that would have been otherwise wasted. Barry has taken veterans in wheelchairs into the orange groves, Boy Scouts into cornfields, and given meaning to the lives of some young people from a boot camp. The Society of St. Andrew is a national gleaning organization **www.endhunger.com** Founded by two Methodist ministers, Ray Buchanan and Ken Horne, in 1979. This organization now recovers millions of pounds of fresh produce every year.

They often bring a truckload (40,000 to 50,000 pounds) of potatoes or sweet potatoes to a community and stage a potato drop. One of the most memorable occurred in 1998 when a bulk load of sweet potatoes was shipped from North Carolina to the Westminster Care nursing home in Clermont, Florida. The residents spent two weeks preparing bags for the arrival. The community turned out in what became several hours of joyful chaos as people of all ages, from all faiths, schools, clubs, civic organizations, speaking at least three languages came together to bag and deliver the potatoes to homeless shelters, senior centers, food pantries, soup kitchens and other sites that provide for the poor, elderly, hungry and homeless. This event continues to be proof that a community can, and will, come together and get their hands dirty in an expression of sharing and love. The residents of the nursing home were an active part of this as they bagged potatoes, often from wheelchairs, provided water and cold drinks to the community and served as good hosts and hostesses. This is something that can be replicated all over the world. A few months later a hurricane devastated parts of North Carolina, and citrus growers and gleaners from Florida returned the favor by sending a truckload of fruit to the recovering communities.

Frito-Lay makes potato chips, but often truckloads of potatoes don't meet their standards for moisture or sugar content. These truckloads are rejected and often hauled to landfills. The Society of St. Andrew began working with local prisons to rescue and bag these potatoes for distribution to food banks. This is hard and difficult work, but the inmates willingly took on the task and often requested that we make certain that a church or agency in their home community got some of what they were bagging. They often provided the names and contact persons for local organizations that distributed food. These people had made mistakes, but that didn't alter the fact that they were getting their hands dirty in the quest to alleviate hunger for people they didn't even know. Theirs is an example we can all follow.

Food recovery is a matter of creating networks between the growers and the dedicated people who put the food in the hands of those who need it. This is a great way for churches to practice their faith in a tangible way, for youth groups to learn the meaning of sharing, and for senior groups to continue their value to the community. Gleaning and food recovery is a good thing to do, even if the gleaning is done in the grocery store and the recovered food is day old bread or produce beyond its prime.

Addendum:

"When you sit in council think not of yourselves, nor even your generation. Think of those yet unborn even unto the seventh generation, making all decisions with those generations in mind."
The Six Nations Iroquois Confederacy,
Circa 1000 AD

What We Can Do as Individuals and Families to Solve the Hunger Problem

Hunger seems like such a huge problem that it lies beyond the abilities of everyday people to overcome it. The fact is that it is only by each of us reaching out as individuals, families and communities can other individuals, families and communities know what it means to be healthy, gain an understanding of our commandment to love one another. An infant who experiences malnutrition is damaged for life, both mentally and physically. A woman with no rights, no way to maintain her health through pregnancy and the birth of her children cannot even dream of a better life for them. A man forced by conflict or poverty to leave his family and go to the cities or the army cannot provide for his family. The means to climb above this poverty, hunger and hopelessness is in our hands, as well as theirs. Together we are the solution. In so many ways the future of people we don't know, will never know, is in our hands, as our future is in theirs.

We can work in our own communities in a variety of ways. We can support organizations like the ones in the following list which provide emergency relief, long term recovery and research into the means to achieve food security and sustainability.

- As gardeners we can "Plant a Row for the Hungry" and take that produce to your local food pantry. This is a program that was started in 1995 by Jim Wilson and the Garden Writers Association of America. Millions of pounds of health giving fresh produce have been donated from America's backyard gardens, and the amount continues to grow every year. PAR has been endorsed by a number of corporations and national gardening associations.

- Encourage community gardens, school gardens and gardens in orphanages, senior communities and abuse shelters. If there isn't a community garden in your area, start one.

- Support your local homeless shelter, soup kitchen, abuse shelter, community or church food pantry with your time, your surplus food and your prayers as well as your money. Help them to organize a garden of their own.

www.globalgardening.info

- Grow the vegetables that are potential food resources for peoples in other parts of the world. Learn and share your knowledge. Have the courage to experiment, try something new and make discoveries.

- Become a community activist working to eliminate waste and hunger. Work with food retailers, restaurants and others in the business community to rescue surplus and unused foods and get them to food banks and soup kitchens.

- Support the work of the United Nations and its programs like UNICEF, FAO, UNIFEM and the World Food Program. Encourage our government to pay its fair share toward hunger relief and food security all over the world.

- Support and encourage the researchers who are working to develop the solutions to today's hunger while preserving the environment for future generations. Sustainable agriculture, appropriate technology, bio-diversity, and all the other terms we discussed in this book aren't something limited to laboratory applications. These are real solutions to the problems of real people.

- As a family, study the issues, explore the causes and solutions for hunger, malnutrition and poverty. Once we understand the problems, once we know the people trapped in the poverty spiral, we can quit blaming the victims and begin working together.

- Involve your church, your garden club, civic organization, youth and senior groups. Together we can create an awareness of the problems, and the confidence that they can be solved. This will require intellectual and physical effort as well as financial support.

- Join a gleaning team, or become a volunteer with the Society of St. Andrew. By recovering what is left in the fields, groves and orchards, by harvesting the under grade or the surplus and distributing it to the under-nourished we can be a part of the solution.

- As a family, or as a church or youth group, plan and serve a typical meal in sub-Saharan Africa, or Haiti, or Korea. This gives a small measure of understanding.

- Donate the cost of a fast food meal a week to the hunger relief organization of your choice. It's a small price to pay, but the result can be a life saved.

- Buy imported foods and products that have been produced by peoples involved in sustainable agro-forestry or eco-farming cooperatives Some of the best coffee in the world is grown by several of these co-ops in Africa, the Caribbean and Mexico. We will soon see rain-forest harvested fruits and nuts from both the Amazon basin and Africa in specialty shops and grocery stores.

- We can all use fewer pesticides and chemical fertilizers in our own gardens and landscapes. This can have an impact on the purity of the air, water and soil we leave as a life giving resource for our children and grandchildren. They depend on us.

- We can encourage energy conservation, and practice it. We can study, learn and share the information with family and friends. If each of us does a little bit, a whole lot gets accomplished.

- Explore the causes of poverty in our global village. Stereotypes are impressions and opinions held by those too lazy to learn the truth.

- There is a great diversity of people, the foods we eat, the ways we grow, preserve and prepare life sustaining meals. We can all enjoy this ethnicity, this uniqueness, this wonderful variety in the human experience. We can learn from our neighbors, share with each other and join hands to cultivate a truly global garden.

- We can join organizations that are involved in the preservation of heirloom species or work to prevent the extinction of both plants and animals. Our existence may well depend on the bio-diversity of our global village and the global garden.

- Devote some of your time to work in regions of the world where the problem is the most severe. It can be an enriching experience and lives can be saved. All the people in all the cultures of the earth have much to share with one another.

"Service to others is the rent you pay for your room here on earth."
Muhammad Ali

Organizations Working on Global Hunger and Food Security

The following are only a few of the organizations and agencies that are working to save lives, improve the quality of life and provide hope for the one in seven in this world that know hunger as the specter of the past and the ghost of the future. Most of these organizations have web sites that provide detailed information on the approach that they take. As hunger has many causes, so does it have many solutions. The first step for all of us is to increase our awareness, then we can reach out to our neighbors in the global garden and learn from each other.

For an up-to-date list of organizations, access our web site: **www.globalgardening.info**

Africa Faith & Justice Network, 3035 Fourth St NE, Washington, DC 20017, USA
Phone 202-832-3412   http://afjn.cua.edu

Alliance for National Renewal, 1319 F Street NW, #204, Washington, DC 20004, USA
Phone 202-783-2961   www.ncl.org

American Community Gardens Association, 325 Walnut St., Philadelphia, PA 19106, USA
http://communitygardens.org

American Jewish World Service, 989 Avenue of the Americas, New York, NY 10018, USA
Phone 800-889-7146   www.ajws.org

Bread for the World, 1100 Wayne Ave., Suite 1000, Silver Springs, MD 20910, USA
Phone 800-82-BREAD   www.bread.org

Carter Center, 453 Freedom Parkway, Atlanta, GA 30307, USA
Phone 404-331-3900   www.cartercenter.org

Catholic Relief Services, World Headquarters, 209 West Fayette St., Baltimore, MD 21201-3443
Phone 416-625-2220   www.catholicrelief.org

Church World Service, 28606 Phillips St., P.O. Box 968, Elkhart, IN 46515, USA
Phone 888-297-2767   www.churchworldservice.org

Congressional Hunger Center, 229 ° Pennsylvania Ave SE, Washington, DC 20003, USA
Phone 202-547-7022   www.ghn.org

ELCA World Hunger Appeal, Evangelical Lutheran Church in America, P.O. Box 71764, Chicago, IL 60694-1764. Phone 800-638-3522   www.elca.org/co/hunger

Food for the Hungry, 7729 East Greenway Road, Scottsdale, AZ 85260, USA
Phone 800-248-6437   www.fh.org

Freedom From Hunger, 1644 DaVinci Court, Davis, CA 95616, USA
Phone 800-708-2555   www.freefromhunger.org

Future Harvest, PMB 238, 2020 Pennsylvania Ave., NW, Washington, DC 20006-1846, USA
Phone 202-473-8110   www.futureharvest.org

NetAid, 336 East 45th St, 2nd Flood, New York, NY 10017, USA
Phone 212-906-6868   www.netaid.org

Oxfam America, 26 West St., Boston, MA 02111-1206, USA
Phone 800-77-OXFAM   www.oxfamamerica.org

Peace Corps, 1111 20th Street NW, Washington, DC 20526, USA
Phone 800-424-8580   www.peacecorps.gov

Presbyterian Hunger Program, 100 Witherspoon St. Louisville, KY 40202-1396
Phone 800-334-0434   www.pcusa.org/hunger

SOS, Share Our Strength, 733 15th St. NW, Ste 640, Washington, DC 20005
Phone 800-969-4767   www.strength.org

Stop Hunger Now, 2501 Clark Ave., Suite 301, Raleigh, NC 27607-7213, USA
Phone 888-501-8440   www.stophungernow.com

The Hunger Project, 15 East 26th St, New York, NY 10010, USA
www.thp.org

The Hunger Site   www.hungersite.com

USAID Humanitarian Response, U.S. Agency for International Development Information Center, Ronald Reagan Building, Washington, DC 20523-1000 USA. Phone 202-216-3524   www.usaid.gov

USDA Food Security, USDA, Room 536-A, 14th and Independence SW, Washington, DC 20250, USA. Phone 202-720-5746   www.usda.gov/foodsecurity/

UNICEF, United Nations Children's Fund.   www.unicef.org

UNIFEM, United Nations Development Fund for Women, 304 East 45th St, 15th Floor, New York, NY 10017, USA. Phone 212-906-6400   www.unifem.undp.org

WHY, World Hunger Year, 505 Eighth Ave., Suite 2100, New York, NY 10018, USA
Phone 212-629-8850   www.worldhungeryear.org

World Relief, International Office, PO Box WRC, Wheaton, IL 60189-8004, USA
Phone 630-665-0235   www.wr.org

Research Agencies

AgroForester, PO Box 428, Holualoa, HI 96725, USA
Phone 808-324-4427   www.agroforester.com

Australian New Crops Newsletter, School of Land & Food, University of Queensland, Gatton College, 4345, Australia. Phone 07-5460-1311   www.newcrops.uq.edu.au

CGIAR, Consultive Group on International Agricultural Research, World Bank   www.cgiar.org

ECHO, Eudcational Concerns for Hunger Organization, 17430 Durrance Road, North Fort Myers, FL 33917-2239, USA. Phone 941-543-3246 www.echonet.org

Eden Project, Badelva, St Austell, Cornwall, PL 24, 2SG, UK
Phone +44 (0) 1720-811911 www.eden-project.co.uk

FAO, the Food and Agricultural Organization of the United Nations www.fao.org

IALC, International Arid Lands Consortium, 1955 E 6th St., Tucson, AZ 85719-5224, USA
Phone 520-621-3024

IDRC, International Development Research Centre, PO Box 8500, Ottawa, Ontario, Canada.
Phone 613-236-6163 www.idrc.ca

IISD, International Institute for Sustainable Development, 161 Portage Avenue East, 6th Floor, Winnipeg, Manitoba, Canada R3B OY4. Phone 204-958-7700 www.iisd.ca

IITA, International Institute of Tropical Agriculture, IITA c/o Lamboune (UK) Limited, Carolyn House, 26 Dingle Road, Croydon CR9 3EE, UK. Phone (44) 020-8686-9031 www.cgiar.org/iita

Plants for a Future, The Field, Penpol, Lostwithiel, Cornwall, PL22 ONG, UK.
www.scs.leeds.ac.uk/pfaf/

Rodale Institute, 611 Siegfriedale Rd., Kuntztown, PA 19530-9320 USA
Phone 610-683-1413 www.rodaleinstitute.org

Center for New Crops and Plant Products, Purdue University, West Lafayette, IN 47907-1165, USA.
www.hort.purdue.edu

SEPASAL, Survey of Economic Plants for Arid and Semi-Arid Lands, Royal Botanic Gardens, Kew, Richmond, Surrey TW9 3AE, United Kingdom. Phone 440-20-8332-5772
www.rbgkew.org/ceb/sepasal/

World Neighbors, World Neighbors International Headquarters, 4127 NW 122 St., Oklahoma City, OK 73120, USA. Phone 800-242-6387 www.wn.org

World Resources Institute, 10 G Street NE, Suite 800, Washington, DC 20002, USA
Phone 202-729-7600 www.wri.org

Also review the HungerWeb Index of Brown University
www.brown.edu/Departments/World_Hunger_Program/hungerweb/list.html

Seed & Plant Sources for Exotic Vegetables & Fruits

The Banana Tree, Inc. 715 Northampton St., Easton PA, 18042, USA
Phone 610-253-9589 www.bananatree.com
Reliable source for seeds and plants.

Deep Diversity Seed, P.O. Box M, Corvallis, OR 97339-000M, USA
Catalog is $4.00. Only source for many exotic fruits & vegetables

ECHO (Educational Concerns for Hunger Organization), 17430 Durrance Rd., North Fort Myers, FL 33917-2239, USA. Phone 941-543-3246 www.echonet.org
Excellent organization, reliable source for small quantities of significant seeds.

Legendary Ethnobotanical Resources, 16245 SW 304 St., Homestead, FL 33033, USA
Phone 305-242-0877

Thompson & Morgan Seed Company,, P.O. Box 1308, Jackson, NJ 08527-0308, USA
Phone 800-274-7333 www.thompsom-morgan.com   Excellent source.

M. L. Farrar, PTY LTD, P.O. Box 1046 Bomaderry, NSW 2541, Australia
Phone 61-44-21-7966

Richters, Goodwood, Ontario, LOC 1AO Canada. Phone 1-905-640-6677.
Email: inquiry@richters.com   Source for uncommon herbs and spices.

Logee's Greenhouses LTD, 141 North St., Danielson, CT 06239-1939, USA
Phone 888-330-8038 www.logees.com

The Glasshouse Works, P.O. Box 97, Church Street, Stewart, OH 45778-0097, USA
Phone 740-662-2142 www.glasshouseworks.com   Super source for truly unusual plants.

Seeds of Change, P.O. Box 15700, Santa Fe, NM 87506, USA
Phone 888-762-7333 www.seedsofchange.com

Tropiflora, 3530 Tallevest Road, Sarasota, FL 34247, USA
Phone 941-351-2267 www.tropiflora.com

J. L. Hudson Seedsman, Star Route 2, Box 337, La Honda, CA 94020, USA
Great resource for heirloom and global seeds.

Bountiful Gardens Seeds, 18001 Shafer Ranch Road, Willits, CA 95490, USA
Catalog costs $2.00

Oregon Exotic Nursery, 1065 Messinger Road, Grants Pass, OR 97527, USA
Phone 541-846-7578 www.exoticfruit.com   Catalog costs $4.00

World Wide Exotic Seed Co., 307 "C" Friendswood Dr., PO Box 1488, Friendswood, TX 77549-1488, USA. Phone 281-648-7445

AgroForester Tropical Seeds, PO Box 428, Holualoa, HI 96725, USA
Phone 808-324-4427   Non-profit research center. Great source for tropical tree seeds.

Exotica Rare Fruit Nursery, PO Box 160, Vista, CA, 92085, USA
Phone 760-724-9093   SASE for catalog

Native Seeds SEARCH, 526 N. 4th Ave., Tuscon, AZ 85705, USA
$2.00 for catalog. A non-profit organization dedicated to preservation of Native American food plants and native species.

Evergreen Y. H. Enterprises, PO Box 17538, Anaheim, CA 92817, USA
Phone 714-637-5769 www.evergreenseeds.com   A great resource for Oriental vegetables.

www.globalgardening.info

The Global Garden of Tomorrow

The river swells with the contribution of the small streams
Bateke proverb

Many of us have the mistaken idea that science is the enemy and that human survival somehow depends on our retreat into some romantic past that never was. Science fiction books and movies have portrayed extreme consequences of cloning, genetic engineering, synthetic food production, and the excesses of greed and power lust. Others view science as a god that will, given sufficient faith and effort, answer all human needs. Science is only a way of looking at the world around us that has cured diseases, increased life spans, improved productivity, made us wiser about ourselves and our universe. Scientists have always been a part of the human experience as some of us asked why and how, then proceeded to observe and analyze. As our global wisdom increases, as each question is answered, new questions are born. Science is only the art of observation in the quest for understanding. What is done with the understanding is the domain of other human endeavors such as religion, economics and politics. It all becomes a part of the ever changing panorama of the way we live called 'culture.' Science is neither god nor demon, it is only a tool ever more finely polished by the humanity using it.

Because of the work being done every day by scientists all over the world, there are exciting possibilities for us all. We fear bio-engineering, cloning and genetically altered plants. True, there may be some dangers, some as yet unknown problems with these explorations. The same could be said of the invention of the plow and DDT. But the other side of this issue can be the development of grains that are resistant to insects or disease, can tolerate drought, or produce a more nutritious harvest. We already have the golden rice developed by Ingo Potrykus and Peter Beyer that has the potential to save the lives of children and adults all over the world because it contains more beta-carotene. This is a result of genetic engineering that plugged genes from a daffodil and bacteria into the DNA of a rice embryo. These are agricultural issues that may save lives. Of course we have the potential to make this hybrid seed available only to the wealthy agro industry and not the family farmer, or the backyard gardener. As Jimmy Carter said, "Responsible biotechnology is not the enemy, starvation is."

Will we continue to gain in our understanding of the soil and the way it functions as a living organism? We may well discover opportunities to partner with these life forces in ways never thought of before. We must discover the means to truly recycle, rebuild and restore. Our future, and the future of the planet, depends on controlling our lust to possess and the thoughtless destruction of our resources in pursuit of short sighted and short term goals. Perhaps the future will see synthetic foods produced in vats like the pharmaceutical companies that today produce synthetic versions of the chemicals, compounds and even hormones found in nature. What will these aspects of 'synthetic evolution' have on the balance, the intricate web of life of which we are only a part?

We can continue the decline in the number of species and varieties cultivated, as we utilize only the newest and the best for commercial harvest. Or we can explore new and newly rediscovered resources and traditional foods. We can perpetuate species, heirloom and open pollinated varieties and local favorites as we expand the biodiversity of our global garden. We can explore our native crops, wherever we live. The eastern half of the United States can rediscover the American ground nut, *Apios americana*, and gardeners in the great plains can grow the prairie turnip, *Psoralea esculenta*, and the ground plum, *Astragalus crassicarpus*. The North American gardener can grow and enjoy the delightfully flavored Jerusalem artichoke, *Helianthus tuberosus*. This is not a retreat from the future; indeed, it is yesterday becoming, as it inevitably does, tomorrow. Through science, practiced in laboratories and backyards by all those of us with curiosity and a desire for a brighter tomorrow, we may be able to discover improved varieties, new techniques and better ways to harvest, preserve and consume the bounty of the global garden.

We have a serious and valid concern about invasive species being imported to our shores. The Southern United States has been assaulted by kudzu, Florida by Australian pine, melalucca and the water hyacinth, the American Southwest by the tamarisk, and loosestrife poses a threat over much of the temperate regions of the United States. Cactus ran rampant in Australia. Most of these weeds in the global garden came to their new locales by design. But, before we condemn all plant importation and exploration and retreat into an impossible isolation of species, let's look at some of the other foreign imports. The potato, corn and beans permitted the European nations the opportunity to flourish that made these simple foods far more significant than all the gold hauled from the new world to the old. Thousands of lives are being saved in Africa because cassava and sweet potatoes were added to their menu. Without the experimentation and cultivation of exotic foods from far away lands, we wouldn't have the European vegetables like cabbage and beets, or fruits like apples and pears. Florida's agriculture would be somewhat limited without the citrus industry that originated in the Orient and came to these shores with the Spanish. Pineapples never would have found their way to Hawaii from the Caribbean on their own. The list could go on for pages and include tomatoes and peanuts from South America, watermelon and millet from Africa, or bok choy and chrysanthemums from the Orient. It is the diversity of our gardens, the diversity of our lives, that enriches our existence. Still, we must proceed with caution when it comes to importing and growing unknown or untested exotic plants, fruits and vegetables. The potential for disaster is present, as is the potential for great good. We must be responsible global gardeners. It could be argued that the human animal is the ultimate weed, the most dangerous of the invasive nonindigenous species.

The world's populations continue to fill the cities. It is estimated that over 50% of the earth's population will live in an urban setting by 2005. More land becomes degraded through unwise and shortsighted waste of resources. There must be concern for our place in the ecosystem and an increasing level of 'green understanding.' We aren't spectators viewing nature from a glass enclosed shelter as if the diverse life on this planet was some sort of theme park put here for our entertainment. We are a part of nature, one organism in the ecosystem, one cell in the global organism. It always has been and always will be thus. Ours is not an edict of dominion, a license for thoughtless and wanton destruction of life, ours is a gift of responsibility, a stewardship and partnership with the life systems that make this global garden home.

Without effort, no harvest will be abundant.
Burundian proverb

We will have to focus on intensive growing techniques and begin to cultivate the most productive vegetables. In the global village and the surrounding countrysides sustainable gardening and agriculture will become far more common. This is best described as 'living in harmony with the land.' It is possible to grow the food and nurture the land, create a balance between harvest and replenishment. We can replant forests, renew the soil and heal the mother earth if we are willing to exercise compassion, understanding and wisdom rather than an irrational pursuit of greed.

We all have the ability to embark on a journey of discovery that begins in our own backyards. We can explore exotic ecosystems, share with other cultures, be a part of a tomorrow filled with cooperation, compassion, inquiry and understanding. The future depends on us and our ability to, or willingness to, think in terms of what legacy we can leave our great-grandchildren and the generations beyond. The decision is ours. The future is in our hands. We can end hunger, we can defeat poverty, and we can provide a future filled with hope and beauty for everyone. Together we can cultivate peace in the Global Garden.

The authors invite your thoughts, comments, ideas, suggestions, notes on your experiences. It is our hope that this book will spark communication and conversations all over the world. Through the wonder of the Internet, we can be in almost instant contact, share ideas at the moment of their inception, respond immediately to both problems and solutions. Please, let us today join in the dialogue toward universal understanding, mutual respect and true peace.

Thank you for becoming a part of this book and the quest for an end to hunger.

Hank Bruce & Tomi Jill Folk
hankbruce@mail2.LCIA.com

Epilogue

The Possible Dream

An idea worth sharing originated as a response to the horror of the terrorist attacks that occurred on Sept. 11, 2001 With the firm conviction that dreams are more powerful than fear, love more powerful than hate, and peace more powerful than war, a family sitting around a table in Daytona Beach, Florida chose this unique and dynamic way to respond to acts of war and hatred. Michelle Jewett, Veronica Crider, Virginia Pasciuto, Elizabeth Peak and Patty Pasciuto developed the following response that communities all over the United States, and the world, can use to answer acts of violence. They are the founders of a non-profit organization, Celestial Therapeutic and Ornamental Gardens, based in Florida and dedicated to the use of gardening as a healing tool.

"By planting a Community Garden of Peace we can all join together, regardless of age, ability, faith, color or national origin," Michelle explained.

This doesn't have to be a garden acres in size, or millions of dollars in cost, but it does have to be a people's garden that celebrates the diversity of each community, the creative spirit of all humanity and the universal dream of peace. The first of what they hope will be a network of gardens covering the world with this tangible expression of the possible dream, peace within ourselves, within our communities and throughout the world, will be located in Jacksonville, Florida.

Every community in the world is invited to join them in this quest for a future filled with peace. The following is a brief outline of their vision.

- The size will depend on the community, available resources and the resolve of the citizens. It can be a corner of a park, or it can be a reclaimed abandoned shopping center. It can be a part of a school, a business, a community center, a public housing site, a hospital grounds, a senior center, or the gift of a private citizen. Anyplace that is open to everyone regardless of their background, heritage, abilities, education or faith can become a declaration of hope by becoming the site for this community's Garden of Peace.

- The objective is not to create a memorial, not to focus on the horror of death and destruction. Rather, this is a garden designed as a place where peace and compassion, hope and understanding can grow, flower and bear fruit. Perhaps we can all symbolically turn into compost fear, anger, sorrow, hatred and confusion. From this soil we can grow the colors of the rainbow and the joy of our human diversity.

www.globalgardening.info

- This is a people's garden, to be planted and nurtured by everyone, just as peace is something that each of us must cultivate within our hearts. For this reason they ask that individuals and groups within each community bring a plant, flower or shrub that has meaning to them or is significant to their heritage. These will be planted randomly throughout the garden so that the place of origin, the nationality of the plant is lost in the community of all the plants. The result will be beds of foliage and color, a joyful confetti of life that reflects the potential joyful blending of humanity that makes each community so beautiful. As we continue toward a truly global village, each community, everywhere has both a unique heritage and a diverse future to be celebrated in harmony. This is a real treasure possessed by each and every neighborhood.

- They suggested that the walkways be paved with bricks on which have been inscribed the word PEACE in all the languages of the world. How rich a world with streets paved of peace.

- Our children are our hope for tomorrow. This family suggested that children use the innate creative talents that reside within their hearts and souls to design special tiles to be used on raised beds within the garden. These tiles would be a reflection of each child's concept, each child's artistic expression, of what peace looks like. Schools everywhere could make this a classroom project. Special education classes, children of all ages could be a part of the creation of this garden by expressing their thoughts and dreams.

- Artists and art students at local colleges and universities could be encouraged to create sculptures that depict peace and hope. These works of art could be placed around and within the peace garden.

The Community Peace Garden should be open to everyone at all times, without admission charges or memberships required. It was suggested that individuals as well as organizations such as schools, diverse faiths, civic groups and businesses all be a part of the coming together of community to care for and nurture this garden on a regular basis. Peace, like a garden, requires tending and effort from us all if it is to grow and be fruitful.

By combining the artistic and creative arts with the living plants of the garden, we symbolically unite the spirit of peace with the physical expression of harmony and discovery that is possible within our human diversity. They suggest that the community peace gardens be gathering places for the music of humanity, a place where the drum, flute, guitar and trumpet of many peoples can be heard, where all people can feel the freedom to sing and dance their traditions from yesterday into tomorrow. Perhaps some of these gardens could be used for the production of food and a feast of peace could be celebrated with the harvest. In this way each heritage can share the flavor of their culture and discover the flavors of others.

Their goal is to bring each community together, not only to design the garden but to nurture and constantly renew it. Peace must be nourished within each of us, but the dream must be shared with all of us. As individuals and communities we can grow peace and hope.

The gardens that result from these community efforts will not be formal beds of single plants in rigid rows of uniform color. They will be a glorious patchwork quilt of faith in the future as they reflect the diversity of humanity and the strength of the human spirit. Let us come together in the spirit of peace and the universal vision of a tomorrow safe for our children and grandchildren.

It is important that each community's peace garden reflects the diversity of that community. For that reason they will make available outlines and guidelines for the creation of these gardens anywhere in the world, but encourage the community to come together to work out the details. In 1932, on the border between the United States and Canada the International Peace Garden was created. This has been an inspiration and a constant symbol that peace can endure, that people can join together and declare peace evermore. For more information about Community Peace Gardens view their web site **www.ctogardens.org**

Moringa (from left to right): the tree, leaf, fruit and seeds

The global garden produces a wide variety of fruits & vegetables and a wealth of leaf crops from annual plants, trees, shrubs and vines.

Leaves of moringa, "the miracle tree"

Traditional fruits and vegetables of the American garden

www.globalgardening.info

Leaves are a part of the global diet.

The African baobab is a versatile tree with edible leaves and flowers and fruit.

Okinawa spinach is a tasty, easy to grow vegetable that's also an attractive plant for the landscape

South America is the source of many of the root crops that feed the world today. They gave us the white (Irish) potato and the sweet potato, but that was only the beginning.

Cassava roots are the staple food of over 500 million people, and the leaves can also be cooked as a nutritious potherb

There is a treasure of less known Andean tubers waiting to feed the world, including oca, maca and ulluco.

North America gave the global village the sunchoke (Jerusalem artichoke), an easily grown and flavorful crop for temperate regions.

The sunchoke is an attractive perennial relative of the common sunflower.

Sunchoke tubers have the delightful flavor of the European globe artichoke.

Beans are an important food and protein source throughout the global village. They are also important as soil building plants.

The butterfly pea is valued as an ornamental, but it is also a food resource

The scarlet runner bean is a vigorous vining plant with edible beans and flowers

The lablab (hyacinth) bean is the ultimate multi-purpose and continuous harvest vegetable.

*The young purple beans are used like green beans or limas.
The dried beans can be stored for a long time and cooked as needed.*

The lablab produces edible flowers, beans, leaves and tubers continuously.

The wetlands of the world also provide a wealth of nutritious food.

The cattail is known throughout the temperate regions and is one of the most multi-purpose food sources we have. It yields more nutrition per acre than potatoes.

Taro tubers are a staple part of the tropical diet.

www.globalgardening.info

While generally considered an ornamental landscape feature, these aquatic plants can be cultivated as a food source.

Waterlilies are found in great variety throughout temperate and tropical regions of the world. They are a valuable food source for many cultures.

The Chinese water lotus is a multi-purpose vegetable with edible buds, flowers, stems, seeds and roots.

Two plant families are widely known and used throughout the global village. The gourds, squash and melons provide more than food, while the tomato family has kin with a variety of flavors including peppers, eggplant and more.

Gourds are extremely valuable, providing food, tools and musical instruments as well as a universal medium for artistic expression.

Gbome is an African perennial eggplant with edible fruit and leaves that can be cooked as a potherb

Large and small flowering plants can also be a source of food.

The globe artichoke, a thistle, has been a traditional delicacy and ritual food since the days of the Roman Empire.
We dine on the flower buds of this dramatic six foot tall plant.

The ice plant is a low growing, salt and drought tolerant plant with edible leaves that are great in a salad.

The Abundant Harvest Garden is a growing system that can provide a family's produce needs in limited space, with minimal water.

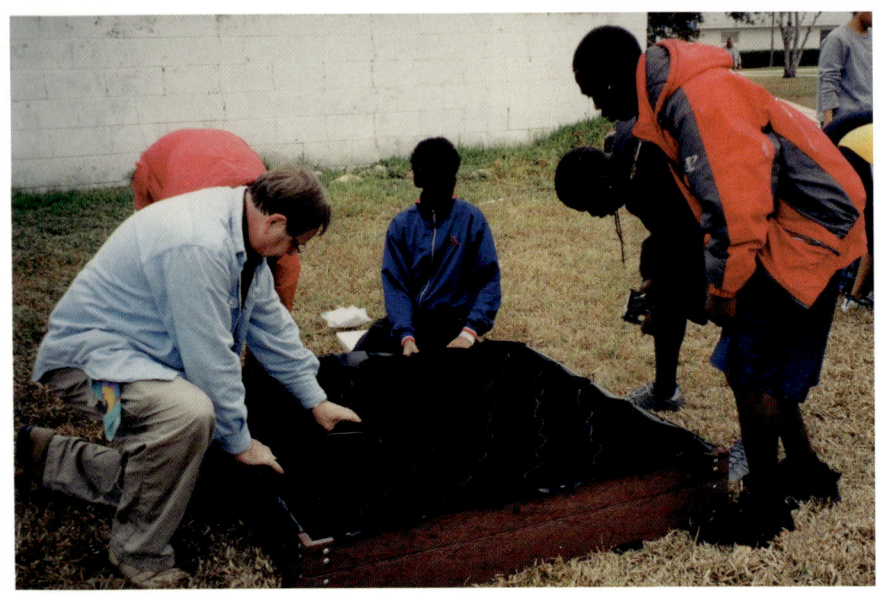

Hank Bruce assisting some youths in the assembly of a micro-intensive Abundant Harvest Garden.

Jessica Sullivan, a professional horticultural therapist, and friends eight weeks later, as the continuous harvest is well underway.

www.globalgardening.info

Index

A
A. Cordifolia 131
A. tricolor 41
Acanthosicyos horridus 179
Achira 112
Achocha 165
Acorus calamus 200
Adansonia digitata 85
African horned cucumber 166
African potato 124
African scarlet eggplant 153
African spinach 40
Ailanthus flavescens 92
Algerian Salad 65
Alisma plantago-aquatica 206
Alpine dock 70
Alternathera sissoo 41
Amaranth gangeticus 41
Amaranthus viridis 44
American basswood 96
American groundnut 104
angled luffa 177
Anredera tuberosa 131
Apios Americana 104
Apium bulbocastenum 132
Apium prostratum 209
Aponogeton distachyus 194
Arracacha 113
Arracacia xanthorrhiza 113
Arrowhead 193
Arthropdium milleflorum 131
Asclepias 186
Asclepias incarnata 188
Asclepias syriaca 188
Asclepias tuberosa 187
Astragalus crassicarpus 107
Atriplex canescens 211
Atriplex halimus 217
Atriplex hortensis 46
Atrocarpus altilis 87
Australian bush banana 189
Australian Celery 209
Australian grasstree 83

B
B. Variegata 100
Bambara groundnut 105
Bamboo 84
Baobab 85
Basella alba 44
Basella rubra 44
Bauhinia purpurea 100
Beach bean 144
Bellflower 71
Benincasa hispida 184
Bitter melon 167
Bitter potato 114
Bok choy 55
Bottle gourd 169
Brasenia schreberi 207
Brassica juncea 59, 64
Brassica oleracea var. Alboglabra 56
Brassica oleraceae 68
Brassica rapa 58
Brassica rapa var. Chinensis 62
Brassica rapa var. Komatsuna 58
Brassica rapa var. Nipposinica 61
Brassica rapa var. Pekinensis 60
Brassica rapa var. pekinensis 61
Brassica rapa var. pervidis 58
Brazilian spinach 41
Breadfruit 87
Breadroot Scruf Pea 106
Buffalo gourd 170
Bunium bulbocastanum 132
Butterbur 65
Butterfly pea 145
Butterfly weed 187

C
C. Deliciosus 190
C. Ensiformis 149
C. Parviflorus 124
Cajanus cajan 147
Cakile maritima 219
Camassia quamash 132
Campanula versicolor 71
Canary scolymus 76
Canavalia gladiata 149
Canavalia maritima 144
Canna edulis 112
Cannibal's tomato 154
Cape asparagus 194
Carob 90
Carpobrotus edulis 190
Casa banana 171
Cassava 125
Cattails 194
Cedrella sinensis 92
Celosia argentea 40
Ceratonia siliqua 90
Chaya 91
Chayote 172
Chenopodiaceae 39
Chenopodium album 79
Chenopodium bonus-henricus 77

Chenopodium capitatum 48
Chenopodium giganteum 49
Chickpea 145
Chicory 71
Chinese artichoke 55
Chinese cedar 92
Chinese kale 56
Chinese spinach 41
Chinese water lotus 196
Chinese water spinach 42
Chryptotaenia japonica 60
Chrysanthemum coronarium 56
Chufa 128
Cicer arietinum 145
Cichorium intybus 71
Citrullus lanatus 174
Clammy ground cherry 156
Clitoria ternatea 145
Cnidoscolus chayamansa 91
Coccinia grandis 176
Cocona 156
Coconut 93
Cocos nucifera 93
Coleus tuberosus 124
Colocasia esculenta 135
Colocynthoides 174
Common milkweed 188
Common reed 198
Corchorus olitrius 68
Cordeauxia edulis 152
Corn salad 72
Crambe maritima 216
Crithmum maritimum 212
Cuban Spinach 43
Cucumis metuliferus 166
Cucurbita ficifolia 175
Cucurbita foetidissima 170
Cucuzzi 173
Currant tomato 157
Cyclanthera pedata 165
Cyperus esculantus sativus 128
Cyphomandra betacea 162

D

D. batata 141
Dandelion 73
Day lily 129
Dioscorea esculenta 141
Dittander 75
Dolochios lablab 146
Duck spinach 44

E

Earth pea 106
Egusi 174
 ˙yptian peafruit eggplant 158

Eleocharis dulcis 201
Eryngium maritimum 215
European common linden 96
Eutrema wasabi 201

F

Fedia cornucopiae 65
Figleaf gourd 175
Fluted gourd 176
French Scorzonera 81

G

Garland chrysanthemum 56
Garlic cress 75
Gboma 158
Glasswort 210
Globe Artichoke 76
Golden samphire 211
Good King Henry 77
Gray sage brush 211
Ground plum 107
Gundelia tournefortii 78
Gynostemma pentaphyllum 183
Gynura crepiodes 47

H

Halimione portulacoides 218
Helianthus tuberosus 134
Hemerocallis lilio-asphodelus 129
Hon-tsai-tai 58
Hottentot fig 190
Houttuynia 198
Houttuynia cordata 198
Hyacinth bean 146

I

Ice plant 190
Indian Lettuce 67
Indian potato 130
Inula crithemoides 211
Ipomea batatas 140
Ipomoea aquatica 42
Iron cross oxalis 130
Ivy gourd 176
Ixeris dentata 199

J

Jack bean 149
Jaltomata procumbens 159
Jaltomate 159
Jeheb nut 152
Jicama 108
Jute 68

www.globalgardening.info

K

Kangaroo apple 160
Kankar 78
Katuk 95
Komatsuna 58
Kostelectzkya virginica 218

L

L. Cylindrica 179
L. Sativus 150
L. Tigrinum 137
Lablab bean 146
Lactuca indica 67
Lagenaria siceraria 169
Lagenaria Siceraria 'Longissima' 173
Laksa plant 59
Lamb's quarters 79
Lathyrus tuberosa 106
Leichhadtia australis 189
Lepidium latifolium 75
Lepidium meyenii 114
Lilium lancifolium 137
lime tree 96
Linden 96
Luffa acutangula 177
Luffa aegyptiaca 179
Luffa gourd 177, 179
Lupinus albus 150
Lycium chinense 163
Lycopersicon pimpinellifolium 157

M

M. scapigera 138
M. stenopetala 98
Maca 114
Madeira vine 131
Malabar chestnut 97
Malabar spinach 44
Manihot esculenta 125
Marama bean 109
Martynia proboscidea louisianica 185
Mashwa 116
Mauka 117
Mesembryanthemum crystallinum 190
Mibuna 59
Michihili 60
Milkweeds 186
Mirabilis expansa 117
Mitsuba 60
Mizuna 61
Momordica charantia 167
Montia perfoliata 43
Moringa 98
Moringa oleifera 98
Mountain spinach 46

N

Napa 61
Naranjilla 161
Narra melon 179
Nasturtium officinale 203
Nelumbo nucifera 196
New Zealand spinach 46
Nymphaea odorata 205

O

Oca 118
Okinawa spinach 47
Orchid Tree 100
Orogenia linerifolia 130
Oxalis deppei 130
Oxalis tuberosa 118
Oyster nut 181

P

P. Communis 198
P. Erosus 108
Pachira aquatica 97
Pachyrhyzus tuberosus 108
Pak-choi 62
Pale vanilla lily 131
Peltaria alliacea 75
Pepino 161
Perideridia gairdneri 139
Perilla 62
Perilla frutescens 62
Persicaria hydropiper 59
Petasites japonicus 65
Phaseolus coccineus 149
Phaseolus vulgaris 148
Phragmites australis 198
Phyllostachys dulcis 84
Physalis heterophylla 156
Pigeon pea 147
Pignut 132
Plectranthus esculentus 124
Pok Choy 62
Pok choy 55
Polygonum hydropiper 59
Polymnia sonchifolia 122
Popping beans 13, 148
Potato 119
Psophocarpus tetragnalobus 110
Psoralea esculenta 106

Q

Quamash 132

R

Red bone vine 181
Reichardia picroides 81
Rock samphire 212
Rumex alpinus 70

S

S. Seiboldii 55
Sagittaria latifolia 193
Salicornia europaea 210
Salsify 81
Salsola kali 213
Saltwort 213
Sauropus androgynous 96
Scarlet runner bean 149
Sea blite 214
Sea holly 215
Sea Orach 217
Sea purslane 218
Sea rocket 219
Seakale 216
Seashore Mallow 218
Sechium edule 172
Sesbania grandiflora 101
Sicana odorifera 171
Sium sisarum 133
Skirret 133
smooth luffa 179
Snake gourd 181
Solanum aethiopicum 153
Solanum aviculare 160
Solanum macrocarpon 158
Solanum muricatum 161
Solanum quiteonse 161
Solanum sessiliflorum 156
Solanum torvum 158
Solanum tuberosum 119
Solanum uporo 154
Solanum x curtilobum 114
Solanum x juzepczukii 114
spinach 39
Spinach oleraceae 39
Stachys affinis 55
Strawberry spinach 48
Streptopus amplexifolius 191
Suaeda maritima 214
Sunchoke 134
Surinam spinach 49
Swamp milkweed 188
Sweet coltsfoot 65
Sweet flag 200
Sweet Hottentot-fig 190
Sweet potato 140
Sweet tea vine 183
Sword Bean 149

T

Talinum triangulare 49
Tamarillo 162
Taraxacum officinale 73
Taro 135

Tasoi 63
tatsoi 63
Telfairia occidentalis 176
Telfairia pedata 181
Tetragonia tetragonoides 46
Thladiantha dubia 181
Tiger lily 137
Tilia americana 96
Tilia europacea 96
Toona sinensis 92
Tragopogon porrifolius 81
Trapa natans 203
Tree kale 68
Tree spinach 49
Tricosanthes cucumerina 181
Tropaeolum tuberosum 116
Tylosema esculentum 109
Typha latifolia 194

U

Ulluco 120
Ullucus tuberosus 120
Unicorn Plant 185

V

Valerianella locusta 72
Voandzeia subterranea 105

W

Wasabi 201
Wasabia japonica 201
Water Caltrop 203
Water chestnut 201
Water cress 203
Water lily 205
Water plantain 206
Water shield 207
Watermelon berry 191
Wax gourd 184
West Indian Pea Tree 101
White lupine 150
Winged bean 110
Wolfberry 163
Won bok 61

X

Xanthorrhoea australis 83

Y

Yacon 122
Yam daisy 138
Yampa 139
Yams 141
Yu choy 64

Chenopodium capitatum 48
Chenopodium giganteum 49
Chickpea 145
Chicory 71
Chinese artichoke 55
Chinese cedar 92
Chinese kale 56
Chinese spinach 41
Chinese water lotus 196
Chinese water spinach 42
Chryptotaenia japonica 60
Chrysanthemum coronarium 56
Chufa 128
Cicer arietinum 145
Cichorium intybus 71
Citrullus lanatus 174
Clammy ground cherry 156
Clitoria ternatea 145
Cnidoscolus chayamansa 91
Coccinia grandis 176
Cocona 156
Coconut 93
Cocos nucifera 93
Coleus tuberosus 124
Colocasia esculenta 135
Colocynthoides 174
Common milkweed 188
Common reed 198
Corchorus olitrius 68
Cordeauxia edulis 152
Corn salad 72
Crambe maritima 216
Crithmum maritimum 212
Cuban Spinach 43
Cucumis metuliferus 166
Cucurbita ficifolia 175
Cucurbita foetidissima 170
Cucuzzi 173
Currant tomato 157
Cyclanthera pedata 165
Cyperus esculantus sativus 128
Cyphomandra betacea 162

D

D. batata 141
Dandelion 73
Day lily 129
Dioscorea esculenta 141
Dittander 75
Dolochios lablab 146
Duck spinach 44

E

Earth pea 106
Egusi 174
Egyptian peafruit eggplant 158

Eleocharis dulcis 201
Eryngium maritimum 215
European common linden 96
Eutrema wasabi 201

F

Fedia cornucopiae 65
Figleaf gourd 175
Fluted gourd 176
French Scorzonera 81

G

Garland chrysanthemum 56
Garlic cress 75
Gboma 158
Glasswort 210
Globe Artichoke 76
Golden samphire 211
Good King Henry 77
Gray sage brush 211
Ground plum 107
Gundelia tournefortii 78
Gynostemma pentaphyllum 183
Gynura crepiodes 47

H

Halimione portulacoides 218
Helianthus tuberosus 134
Hemerocallis lilio-asphodelus 129
Hon-tsai-tai 58
Hottentot fig 190
Houttuynia 198
Houttuynia cordata 198
Hyacinth bean 146

I

Ice plant 190
Indian Lettuce 67
Indian potato 130
Inula crithemoides 211
Ipomea batatas 140
Ipomoea aquatica 42
Iron cross oxalis 130
Ivy gourd 176
Ixeris dentata 199

J

Jack bean 149
Jaltomata procumbens 159
Jaltomate 159
Jeheb nut 152
Jicama 108
Jute 68

Index

A
A. Cordifolia 131
A. tricolor 41
Acanthosicyos horridus 179
Achira 112
Achocha 165
Acorus calamus 200
Adansonia digitata 85
African horned cucumber 166
African potato 124
African scarlet eggplant 153
African spinach 40
Ailanthus flavescens 92
Algerian Salad 65
Alisma plantago-aquatica 206
Alpine dock 70
Alternathera sissoo 41
Amaranth gangeticus 41
Amaranthus viridis 44
American basswood 96
American groundnut 104
angled luffa 177
Anredera tuberosa 131
Apios Americana 104
Apium bulbocastenum 132
Apium prostratum 209
Aponogeton distachyus 194
Arracacha 113
Arracacia xanthorrhiza 113
Arrowhead 193
Arthropdium milleflorum 131
Asclepias 186
Asclepias incarnata 188
Asclepias syriaca 188
Asclepias tuberosa 187
Astragalus crassicarpus 107
Atriplex canescens 211
Atriplex halimus 217
Atriplex hortensis 46
Atrocarpus altilis 87
Australian bush banana 189
Australian Celery 209
Australian grasstree 83

B
B. Variegata 100
Bambara groundnut 105
Bamboo 84
Baobab 85
Basella alba 44
Basella rubra 44
Bauhinia purpurea 100
Beach bean 144

Bellflower 71
Benincasa hispida 184
Bitter melon 167
Bitter potato 114
Bok choy 55
Bottle gourd 169
Brasenia schreberi 207
Brassica juncea 59, 64
Brassica oleracea var. Alboglabra 56
Brassica oleraceae 68
Brassica rapa 58
Brassica rapa var. Chinensis 62
Brassica rapa var. Komatsuna 58
Brassica rapa var. Nipposinica 61
Brassica rapa var. Pekinensis 60
Brassica rapa var. pekinensis 61
Brassica rapa var. pervidis 58
Brazilian spinach 41
Breadfruit 87
Breadroot Scruf Pea 106
Buffalo gourd 170
Bunium bulbocastanum 132
Butterbur 65
Butterfly pea 145
Butterfly weed 187

C
C. Deliciosus 190
C. Ensiformis 149
C. Parviflorus 124
Cajanus cajan 147
Cakile maritima 219
Camassia quamash 132
Campanula versicolor 71
Canary scolymus 76
Canavalia gladiata 149
Canavalia maritima 144
Canna edulis 112
Cannibal's tomato 154
Cape asparagus 194
Carob 90
Carpobrotus edulis 190
Casa banana 171
Cassava 125
Cattails 194
Cedrella sinensis 92
Celosia argentea 40
Ceratonia siliqua 90
Chaya 91
Chayote 172
Chenopodiaceae 39
Chenopodium album 79
Chenopodium bonus-henricus 77

www.globalgardening.info

The Abundant Harvest Garden is a growing system that can provide a family's produce needs in limited space, with minimal water.

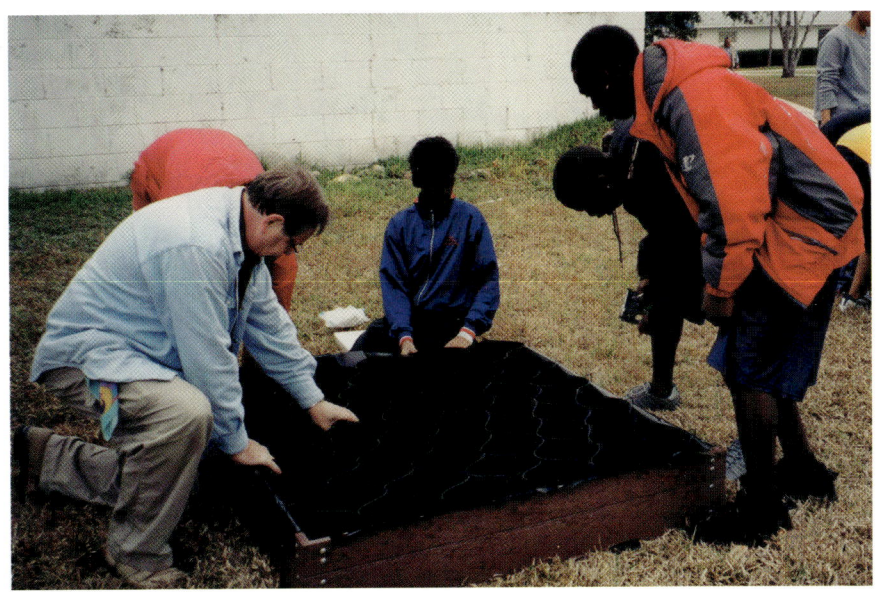

Hank Bruce assisting some youths in the assembly of a micro-intensive Abundant Harvest Garden.

Jessica Sullivan, a professional horticultural therapist, and friends eight weeks later, as the continuous harvest is well underway.

Common weeds and unusual plants can be a food source beyond our traditional vegetables.

The common milkweed is a versatile native American plant overlooked as a food, but the flowerbuds, young shoots and seedpods are edible.

The narenjilla produces imposing two foot leaves with spines, but it also produces a sweet flavored tomato like fruit that makes a great cold drink.

www.globalgardening.info